Always Home

Always Home

A Daughter's Recipes & Stories

Fanny Singer

FOREWORD BY ALICE WATERS
Photographs by Brigitte Lacombe

 Alfred A. Knopf | New York | 2020

THIS IS A BORZOI BOOK PUBLISHED BY ALFRED A. KNOPF

Copyright © 2020 by Fanny Singer
Foreword copyright © 2020 by Alice Waters
Photography copyright © 2018 by Brigitte Lacombe

All rights reserved. Published in the United States by Alfred A. Knopf,
a division of Penguin Random House LLC, New York, and in Canada
by Penguin Random House Canada Limited, Toronto.

www.aaknopf.com

Knopf, Borzoi Books, and the colophon
are registered trademarks of Penguin Random House LLC.

Images on pages 73, 80, and 295 are courtesy of the author's personal collection.

Library of Congress Cataloging-in-Publication Data
Names: Singer, Fanny, [date] author.
Title: Always home : a daughter's recipes & stories / Fanny Singer ;
foreword by Alice Waters ; photographs by Brigitte Lacombe.
Description: New York : Alfred A. Knopf, 2020.
Identifiers: LCCN 2019022766 (print) | LCCN 2019022767 (ebook) |
ISBN 9781524732516 (hardcover) | ISBN 9781524732523 (ebook)
Subjects: LCSH: Cooking. | LCGFT: Cookbooks.
Classification: LCC TX714 .S58545 2020 (print) | LCC TX714 (ebook) |
DDC 641.5—dc23
LC record available at https://lccn.loc.gov/2019022766
LC ebook record available at https://lccn.loc.gov/2019022767

Some of the recipes in this book include raw eggs, meat, or fish. When these foods are consumed raw, there is always the risk that bacteria, which is killed by proper cooking, may be present. For this reason, when serving these foods raw, always buy certified salmonella-free eggs and the freshest meat and fish available from a reliable grocer, storing them in the refrigerator until they are served. Because of the health risks associated with the consumption of bacteria that can be present in raw eggs, meat, and fish, these foods should not be consumed by infants, small children, pregnant women, the elderly, or any persons who may be immunocompromised. The author and publisher expressly disclaim responsibility for any adverse effects that may result from the use or application of the recipes and information contained in this book.

Jacket photographs by Brigitte Lacombe
Jacket design by Jenny Carrow

Manufactured in Germany

First Edition

For my mother

Contents

List of Recipes

Foreword

Alice Waters

It is very rare to have the opportunity to write the introduction to your own daughter's memoir. And it's perhaps especially unusual for me to be writing this because I'm so present here in the pages of this book. But you can also look at it another way: Who knows Fanny better than I do? And for that matter, who knows me better than she does?

Fanny has always been a keen and compassionate observer of human nature, but also of the natural world. So much of what she writes about here are the small moments of profundity that can be so hard to capture and that she is able to convey with such nuance and heart: the hallucinatory color of the new green growth on our back-yard redwood tree; the "amber-colored smell" of fruit cooking down in a pot on the stove; the "yeasty, fat smell of pizza dough rising" in the kitchen of Chez Panisse; the way the Provençal heat and drone of the cicadas create "a meeting of sound and heat so total that your skin wasn't enough of a barrier to keep things clear and separate." Fanny has a potent language of the senses—an uncanny, almost synesthetic talent for describing the shapes, sounds, smells, textures around her—that puts you vividly in the moment.

She also has a terrific sense of humor. Just when you're awash in atmosphere, Fanny can always catch you off guard with a joke. Often at my expense! No one can make me laugh the way Fanny does, and her finely tuned eye for the ridiculous keeps all of us—keeps *me*—grounded and in check.

I also love the recipes that are assembled in these pages. They're the defining dishes of Fanny's childhood and young adulthood, but they're all of my very favorite dishes too—the ones we come back to time and time again, collected through the years from the many dear and talented cooks that have come into our lives. I am so happy that the recipes are gathered together here, like old friends. It was also Fanny's idea to bring the extraordinary photographer Brigitte Lacombe into this book. Brigitte's images add a beautiful dimension to these stories and recipes, and that inspired marriage of art and writing is quintessentially Fanny.

This is Fanny's story, distinctly and utterly her own. And it's a story about our family, and our larger Chez Panisse family, *La Famille Panisse*. But I think it's also a story about the universal power of real food—how it knits us together, and how deeply our lives and relationships can be enriched by the ways in which we nourish ourselves. In the end, what Fanny has produced is an intimate, funny, and evocative book about food and love. I have no objectivity at all, of course—but it is the truth.

Always Home

Preface

A memoir, if that's the right word for this body of text, is an unusual undertaking for someone in her mid-thirties. But then, the word *memoir* isn't quite the right fit anyway; it suggests something far more comprehensive and, perhaps, chronological, than what follows. This is a collection of stories and remembrances, some less or more fleshed out, some more or less narrative, but no matter their subject or length, their protagonist, their reason for being, is my mother.

My mother has been "famous" for as long as I can remember, though I measured fame not by the visibility of her face in the media or her recognizability on a given city street—or even by the very occasional request for an autograph when we were traveling—so much as by her capacity to instantly materialize a table for four at the best, most overbooked restaurants. By all accounts, she was in fact not that well known, and certainly not outside the innermost circle of the food world. This has of course changed in the last twenty-odd years: she's since been the subject of a biography, a MasterClass, hundreds of articles, and several television shows; and the recipient of more honorary doctorates and awards than I can count, including a National Endowment for the Humanities medal bestowed by President Obama (she was the first chef to receive the honor), as well as copious awards (which far outnumber the trophies I amassed over a lengthy soccer career), a couple of knighthoods (France, Italy), and so forth. She is still not someone who gets mobbed out in the open or ever snapped by professional paparazzi, but she is loved by many across the globe.

No matter the country, however, one thing that distinguishes her notoriety is that she is admired, above all else, for her altruism. Which is to say, she is adored not as an actor might be, for a tour de force in which she plays a character, but for being emphatically, truly herself. And with such a degree of determination that even her moral inflexibility has become one of the defining features of her fame. This must be the best type of celebrity to have attained: invisibility to all but those who worship you for your actions (and the occasional detractor who feels compelled to join the small chorus of contrarians).

Still, I didn't think to write this book because my mother is famous. Rather I wanted to write it in spite of her fame. Even though there is considerable parity between her public and private personas, there still is a part of her more private self—which is to say, her family self—that makes the picture bigger, that amplifies the image. I don't have an expository story to tell, but I have had the experience of being the only person on this planet who is her child. At the end of a lunch recently, an older colleague turned to me and said, "You might well be the only person with a famous parent I've ever heard of who isn't completely fucked up."

The fact that I am close to my mother is self-evident. Even as I begin this opening, I write from a sofa in a room in her house that I still largely think of as mine and that has—no matter how many years I have lived in other states and countries—a closet containing more of my shoes and clothes than any apartment I've called home since I left California in 2001. That I decided to call this book *Always Home* refers both to the very literal place (the Berkeley home in which I was born and raised) but also to the fact that, no matter where I am in the world, if I am with my mother, it *feels* like home. As you will learn from the preponderance of accounts of her redecorating rental houses, or festooning temporary places with flowers and switching out lightbulbs for ones with lower, more flattering wattages, or just burning rosemary, she has a knack for making all places feel familiar.

In many ways, the learned set of tools and behaviors from a childhood with her has shaped my independent life after the image of the one I knew as a child. I arrange flowers as if my mother were standing at my back. I know when she would object to a certain color or bloom, or if something smells too fragrant to keep in the kitchen, and I omit it (or sometimes, in an act of rebellion, decide to keep it). Likewise, without thinking, I start a chicken stock when I've been away from home for a long stretch and, with comparable absence of reflection, light a branch of rosemary or bay to scent the house. I always find a connection to my mother—whether or not I think of it in such explicit terms—in the slow meandering of the smoke. These are not just self-conscious acts designed to engender a sense of closeness to her—I've never felt myself to be overdependent on her—but rather because these behaviors, these adaptations, always enhance my life, as they do for the many people who have learned from her, either at her restaurant or as her friends.

When I was studying in England, I learned the term *nostos* from a boyfriend who was a classicist. *Nostos* is a word from ancient Greek assigned to a theme deployed in ancient literature to refer to the experience of returning home after an epic journey. Homer's *Odyssey* is of course the most famous of these narratives. But it is not just the moment of physical return that characterizes nostos; rather, it is the feeling of home that Odysseus carries with him throughout. Home is, you could say, the very kernel of Odysseus's sense of self. Without trying to sound too grandiose, I have always felt this, even before I had a Hellenic expression to attach to it. My experience of nostos, though absent any particularly heroic journey, is nonetheless in the Homeric vein: the feeling of home—and by extension, my mother's proximity—is at once a kind of spiritual compass and a salve.

This is not to say that I haven't felt the need to go out in search of myself, a self I knew might not materialize so long as I remained in my mother's penumbra. I have often described her as having a gravitational force field, which is itself a product of a range of qualities: charisma, conviction, a touch of narcissism. She believes she knows what's best for everyone she loves, and she's not afraid to air her convictions, though they are often blind to context, even brazenly underresearched. She's usually right, but it doesn't give the object of her opinions much room to breathe. If I hadn't left for the better part of seventeen years (with a largely unbroken decade of living in England), I don't think I could have come home again. Certainly I wouldn't have been able to see this complicated woman, upon whom I depend for so much of my sense of self, with all the love and empathy that a book such as this requires.

You may notice that my father, Stephen Singer, is largely absent from this account, though he was in fact not at all absent from my youth—he and my mother were together until just after my thirteenth birthday. But while my mother was the dominating, oxygen-consuming force of my childhood, my father has been a critical guide and influence in more recent years. I certainly wouldn't have considered going to graduate school or have had the courage to live at such a distance, if not for his insatiable intellectual appetite. Still, this is not a book about my dad, nor is it really a book about my life. Rather, it's a paean to the woman who was captivated by me from the very moment I emerged from her womb, and who, despite reaching the greatest conceivable heights in her career, has slipped me a note on every one of my birthdays inscribed with "You are the best thing that has ever happened to me in my life."

Bob (A Footnote)

Because this book is nonlinear and non-narrative, occasionally people of enormous personal importance emerge with little or no introduction. One of these is Bob Carrau. While the general paucity of context around most characters feels appropriate to this format, I cannot in good conscience bring Bob into the story without some proper explanation. Bob is, after all, my third parent. He's the person who made our family into a madcap nineties sitcom, in which two young men raise a child with a zany older lady (although my mom, given her love of French cinema, probably perceived it as something closer to *Jules et Jim*). Bob also traveled with us almost everywhere we went, whether near or far, and even lived for periods in the cottage in our backyard. He babysat me uncomplainingly; he made art with me for hours at a time (teaching me that "art" could in fact be anything); he helped me become a writer. Most amazingly, perhaps, he managed to remain a fixture in our family despite its post-divorce permutations. He and my mom are now beyond close—on top of being one of my mother's dearest confidants, Bob has been her indispensable collaborator on most of her book projects and speeches for the better part of twenty-five years.

When Bob and my dad met in a film class at UC Berkeley around 1980, the two struck up an unusually close friendship—my dad the slightly older student (he'd already completed a BFA at the San Francisco Art Institute) with a precocious flair for criticism and art theory. They'd spend long hours looking at art, smoking dope, and talking about music, painting, and *wine* (that most critical of conversational lubricants, of which many fine bottles were consecutively opened by my wine-obsessed father). When my mom came on the scene, Bob wasn't so much supplanted as folded more deeply into the fray, and when I was born, he was transformed into a de facto third guardian. My mom would head off to the restaurant, leaving Bob and my dad to watch me together. They'd sometimes get stoned, listen to Talking Heads and Brian Eno records, and spend hours in the back garden as I toddled around. All of this is caught on tape because Bob was, among other things, constantly filming. Having seen Andy Warhol's genre-breaking films in school, some of which stretched on for slack, anti-climactic hours (*Empire*, for instance, which consists of eight hours and five minutes of slow-motion footage of an unchanging view of the Empire State Building), Bob decided to make a series called *Following Fanny*. Filmed on a *gargantuan* brand-new state-of-the-art eighties-era camcorder, the films comprise hours of footage of a very small me, rambling around according to whim. Even though these documents are largely absent any exciting action, or really any action whatsoever, they are proof of the degree to which this unorthodox trio was paying attention and watching and, moreover, making sure that my young life was very rich and full and just a little bit unconventional.

CHAPTER 1

Beauty as a Language of Care

My mom speaks a language of beauty that I think very few are fluent in. In fact, only my mom can use the word *beauty* without its sounding cliché to me (although I am a jaded member of the art community, where the word *beauty* is often frowned upon). When musing on my mom's particular contributions to civic life in Berkeley, a philanthropist and longtime supporter of her Edible Schoolyard Project suggested to me that above all she ought to be credited for emphasizing the importance of beauty in one's life. I think it's true that beauty is generally now considered to be superfluous, something merely cosmetic, but the way my mom thinks about it—which is to say *practices* it, really—places it at the core of a set of values she's evolved into a kind of pedagogy. The first Edible Schoolyard (at the Martin Luther King Jr. Middle School in Berkeley), which I sometimes think of as my mother's second child, was in a sense conceived out of beauty, or a perceived absence thereof. When the school's principal called out my mom for publicly maligning its quasi-derelict appearance (she had said something offhand to a reporter for a local paper), conversations began that resulted in the ripping up of an acre of asphalt.

Within a year, the Edible Schoolyard Project had begun to take shape. A once litter-strewn stretch of pitch had been replaced with a nutrient-generating cover crop of alfalfa, fava, and clover. Soon thereafter, a truly magical garden (a friend's five-year-old son recently told him that it was his "favorite place in the whole world") began to take shape, and its tending by students was woven into the curriculum (soil sampling in biology, threshing ancient grains in history, and so forth). At the far end of the garden is a Kitchen Classroom, a structure containing a culinary facility in which students are, on a weekly basis, instructed in the basics of making and sharing delicious food, under the tutelage of one of the most empathic and gifted teachers around, the aptly named Esther Cook.

In the early days, because of overflow, there was a temporary classroom—in one of those deeply dispiriting trailer things usually reserved for use by construction site managers—that was placed on the school grounds in close proximity to the Kitchen Classroom building. My mom, her tolerance for the industrial taupe of the prefab kitchen building having worn thin, dipped, I believe, into her personal accounts to have the structure repainted aubergine. The crew charged with this task mistook the nearby classroom trailer for a related building and, in error, repainted it too. The next week, my mom received a handwritten card from the sixth graders whose class she had inadvertently beautified, thanking her for making their space feel special— thanking her for caring about them. I was always struck by the poignancy of that story, because it demonstrates that those things I often perceive as my mom's utter folly (example: she also repaints our recycling and garbage bin brown every few years because she finds the underlying powder blue offensive) translate to a language of care. It's not really about beauty in the end, but about care. If food is plated carefully, it will almost always be beautiful. If a child is surrounded by lush color, by growing places, by the variegated plumage of the chickens that run wild across her schoolyard, that child, I would wager, feels and registers that care on a profound, if subconscious level.

It would be a bit tautological to suggest that beauty and care were things I grew up with and felt—beauty was the total fabric of my existence. I always think it's important, however, to stress that my mom's fixation on beauty never approached preciousness. The reason this whole system functioned was the general lack of sentiment attached to any given object. Yes, an antique bowl from France might be loved, but it would also be used and brazenly put in the dishwasher and cracked and glued and finally broken beyond repair, but that was the only way to live with things—why buy them otherwise? One would think this almost cavalier attitude could not live alongside the impulse to acquire nice objects—our house is full to *bursting* with culinary treasures, flea market finds, linens, books—but for my mom, atmosphere (which is about so much more than appearance) extends well beyond the organization of belongings. I am wary of overemphasizing the degree to which she is intolerant of poorly conceived spaces— especially ones in which a reception or meal or some other variety of convivial activity is meant to take place—as it can make her seem disproportionately blinkered, even insensitive to the widely held belief that hers is an unachievably romantic existence. Yes, she will arrive at the governor of California's mansion in Sacramento for the inaugural event she's catering and immediately insist on starting a fire in the disused, presumed-decorative fireplace—for grilling the bread for bruschetta, of course! Despite the initial eye rolling, sweating, and concerned protestations from the staff, my mother prevails—and the first guests arrive to the smell of woodsmoke and grilling bread, an elemental perfume. The grilled bread, the handmade mozzarella, still warm from the brine, the splash of green olive oil, together with the aroma of the room, make the place feel like no other well-heeled political event out there.

All of this amounts to an attitude toward living born of sensitivity to one's surroundings, dedicated to care, to the slow, meaningful collection of objects—not to money or privilege. She built her sensibility over decades of travel, of work, of friendship. The long-ago generosity of a stranger in Turkey when she was twenty—a young goatherd who

left a bowl of fresh milk outside her tent—has everything to do with how she extends herself, or elaborates her sense of atmosphere, into a public milieu meant to be experienced and enjoyed beyond herself. To become a restaurateur (or "restauratrice," as my mother has always put it, proud to be a woman occupying a traditionally male role), you have to want to share something of yourself with others; it might be among the most generous, most intimate professions out there. And Chez Panisse was built by a group of friends in what was originally a house, so, I think, a feeling of intimacy—of visiting someone's home—is especially redolent still.

My mom basically never stops creating atmosphere, whether her focus is a room of her own, a room in the restaurant, or a room in the home of an unsuspecting Airbnb host. No one, and I mean *no one*, gets to work as swiftly as my mom when there's a space—which is to say, most spaces—in "need" of a few alterations. If she has recently landed in a rental property in which she plans to remain for even the briefest of stays, she assumes the mien of a five-star general on a mission. She shifts heavy things she would normally ask me to move, she delegates if there's anyone to delegate to, she finds a room—preferably a capacious closet—into which undesirables can be ruthlessly deposited. Vase shaped like a flying pig? Decorative indoor weather-vane sculpture? Cutting boards shaped like the things meant to be cut upon them? Into the closet. A scribbled map is drawn to remind herself, and any other witnesses, where these items must be returned prior to departure. Inevitably, the pig vase meets its (un)timely demise in the back-and-forth. We are almost never returned a security deposit.

But sometimes it's not a question of the pig vase, it's just a matter of lighting, of a bulb that needs to be replaced with something of a lower wattage or perhaps just a lamp that needs a little dimming or a leaf of paper wrapped around it to dull the glare. Yet other times, just the slightest of interventions is required: a burning branch of rosemary, waved through room after room like a smudge stick to chase out the demons. If I ever smell the scent of burning rosemary anywhere outside of Berkeley, I feel myself lose equilibrium for a moment—it's as if my mom has just trailed through the room, expunging the ghosts through the introduction of her own.

CHAPTER 2

In the Mornings

In the morning, our house was never quiet. There were the usual sounds of a house coming to life: hot water rushing into the basin of a bathtub, a kettle's faint squeal as its contents approach a boil, floorboards sighing beneath the weight of human feet. But there were other sounds too—those of my mother stacking logs and snapping grapevine kindling, crumpling newspaper and striking matches to build a fire in the kitchen hearth. In my memory there was a fire in the kitchen fireplace every day, although this was most certainly not the case. Still, the way in which she tended to the ritual of fire-building and then to cooking over the fire's carefully calibrated heat is something that I will forever associate with her, and with being in the kitchen with her in the mornings before school.

The kitchen in my mother's Berkeley home is more or less one big rectangular room; a butcher block commands much of the floor space in the kitchen half, while a sleek oval slate table is positioned centrally in the dining area, running parallel to the indoor fireplace. When my parents initially renovated the house in 1982, their major intervention was joining these two rooms. But building a massive brick hearth, including a pizza and bread oven and an open fireplace built at hip height to facilitate grilling (but also fitted with a rotisserie), was no small undertaking either. It remains the most used and most loved—not to mention iconic—feature of the house.

My mother would always make herself a bowl of something warm and faintly caffeinated to sip on to ease her morning ministrations. When I was little, it was a bowl of especially milky café au lait, the preferred French coffee beverage that inspired the opening of Café Fanny in 1984, just down the road. The chief purpose of the café, a collaboration with my uncle Jim, was to purvey bowls of café au lait, but also my grandmother's granola (before granola became mainstream) and, somewhat incongruently, buckwheat crepes. These days, ever since her cholesterol was deemed a touch too elevated, my mom exclusively drinks an earthy fermented Chinese black tea called pu-erh, but from a bowl, as ever—mugs are not welcome in my mother's cupboards. Even though I live in a pragmatic world of mugs—tea stays hotter for longer!—I love sitting with my mom in the morning with our bowls, watching the tea leaves expand and slowly settle into the inky liquid bottom.

When I was a child, my perch was a little stool at the narrow end of the butcher block. From that seat I could observe whatever was transpiring lunchwise or just watch my mother as she negotiated our family's morning rituals. Breakfast in our house was either something of an event—an egg cooked in the fireplace in an iron spoon designed after a seventeenth-century French antique—or just, I suspect, like everyone else's. The cereal I ate most as a kid was Cream of Wheat, not even a salubrious organic hippie version made of freshly milled wheat berries from plants sprinkled with purified mountain dew. Nope, it was just the sanitized stuff whose butter-yellow box featured the cartoon likeness of the betoqued and eternally beaming Barbadian chef Frank L. White. Why my mom gave this stuff a pass, while jettisoning other nonorganic foods, is beyond me, but I suspect it triggered comforting feelings of nostalgia. It was my dad, however, who was deputized to make this part of breakfast, and I was very particular about its preparation. It was important, for example, that the cereal be cooked in milk, but not from the beginning because then the milk gets too cooked and tastes gross, like overcooked milk, and gets that creepy epidermal film on top. It had to be started in water, with milk only added slowly along the way. Meanwhile, I required my dad to read *The Wind in the Willows* aloud while not burning the porridge. I was a merciless porridge critic and had very strict requirements involving consistency, temperature, and administration of milk: an utterly exasperating customer.

My favorite breakfast when I was little, however, was the three-minute egg. If I was lucky, it would be a perfectly soft-boiled blue Araucana egg, with a marigold-hued liquid center into which I would delight in plunging buttered toast "soldiers." This was one of the few dishes for which some ancient nubbin of butter was retrieved from the freezer (its natural habitat in a home where olive oil was king). Still, there was nothing better than butter, that bit of salt and fat mingling with the sourness of the levain toast from Acme, whose crisped edges were exceptionally hard to eat without incurring mouthwide lacerations. My mom had some voodoo magic sixth sense for when the egg would be just right, which surely couldn't have been only three minutes, but we still called it that. Maybe eggs were just smaller in the 1980s.

Speaking of the eighties, I have to say that I don't really remember a time before taste, which is really to say that I don't recall there being a world that wasn't permeated by flavor. Flavor was the prism through which most things were seen or dissected or understood, even criticized. And it must have been like that from the beginning, because my mother never fed me anything she wouldn't have eaten herself, and, in fact, for the most part, what I consumed very early on was just her food, passed through a mouli. But she would also ask me—once I was old enough to give words to my experience—what I thought about the thing she had just deposited on my plate. I was invited to tell her that something was too salty or too bitter, and to cultivate a sense of autonomy in my likes and dislikes. I think being asked to dissect my feelings about a given food into its constituent parts paradoxically had the effect of making me like almost everything. And being encouraged to make a vocabulary—however simple early on—to explain this gave me a keener sense of what made food taste good. My mom always said she was blessed to have gotten a kid who would eat just about anything, and it's true that I rarely balked at trying something a bit unusual or new. And I did just always really like vegetables. Whether it was the weight of her former-Montessori-teacher attention and focus, or my having inherited a good part of my palate from her and my wine expert of a father, I learned early on to trust my tongue, and my nose, implicitly.

Blue Egg with
Soldiers

IN ENGLAND, where I lived for more than ten years from the age of twenty-two, no one keeps eggs in the refrigerator, nor will you find them chilled in any supermarket. This is owing to the fact that eggs in the United Kingdom (and in many other countries) are not washed the way they are in the States and therefore retain a natural protective barrier that allows them to be kept at room temperature. It took me a while to acclimate to looking for the eggs in the vicinity of the detergent instead of next to the milk, but, when it comes to cooking, it's almost always preferable to have an egg ready at room temperature, rather than cold. Have you ever seen a recipe that calls for an ice-cold egg? They don't exist! Many, many recipes, however, call for an egg to be at room temp, even warm—they perform better, whisk up fluffier, cook faster, and emulsify more seamlessly when they haven't recently been removed from the fridge. My theory as to why my mom always called it a "three-minute egg"? The eggs may indeed have been smaller back in the eighties—they often came hand-delivered by my mom's friend Patty Curtan from her backyard clutch of hens—but they were also always kept in a bowl on the countertop, as much for the beauty of their various colors as for the culinary convenience. Between the size and the temperature, however, three minutes in a pot of gently boiling water seemed to do the trick: liquid golden center, just-firm whites. If your egg is larger or colder, leave it in for longer. I'm not a fundamentalist about soft-boiled egg preparation: as long as a yolk still yields to the prod of a buttered bread baton, I'm happy. Which is to say that the key to the perfect egg breakfast, beyond a generous (and repeatedly administered) sprinkle of salt and freshly ground pepper, is a helping of crispy toast fingers to plunge into your yolk. I have tried dousing these with olive oil, I have rubbed them with garlic—nothing quite compares to butter. Cut a slice of sourdough levain and then slice it into "soldiers," preferably before toasting (to ensure maximum crispness). Have a bit of melted or very soft butter on hand to paint them with and serve immediately alongside your egg with an ample sprinkling of salt and pepper.

CHAPTER 3

Maroon and Chartreuse

One of the questions I used to ask my mother repeatedly when I was small and possessed a proportionately limited imagination was "What's your favorite color?" To my mom's credit, she kept things interesting, always furnishing me with the same wonderfully erudite answer. "Maroon and chartreuse—it's a tie. I love them both. I love them together. I can't choose," she would trill from the front seat if she was driving—a favorite time to pepper her with banal inquiries—or from the kitchen if I was asking the well-worn question from another room (or perhaps from across the butcher block while she prepared something at the stove). Maroon and chartreuse: two lesser-known shades of the tried-and-true complementary pair of purple and yellow. On some level those two colors sum it up; they give a perfectly concise picture of the aesthetic universe my mom has crafted and insists on living in.

Of course this isn't to say that there weren't, or aren't, deviations from this theme, just that she knows what she likes and rigorously sticks to it. Throughout my youth, she largely allowed me to ornament my room however I liked, which is to say with things that hewed to that terrible powdery teenage palette of the nineties, not to mention the "wallpaper" made of dozens of conjoined Absolut Vodka ads, embellished here and there with portraits of a pubescent Leonardo

DiCaprio. And in general she accepted my fashion and furnishing choices without reprisal or rebuke. It helped, however, that from the time I was twelve, my room was upstairs and behind a door that led to the converted attic—and thus safely out of view. To this day, anything that I leave around downstairs (a computer cord, say, or a more offensive bright red puffer jacket) will be quietly deposited at the foot of the stairs and sealed behind the door. It's easy to imagine that this aesthetic climate was stifling or oppressive, but she wasn't obsessive-compulsive, she just had an eye for beauty and a taste for maroon.

And if you take a moment to think about it, it's not difficult to imagine why the color maroon might appeal. It is, after all, the color of the feathery-petaled 'Black Parrot' tulips that came up in the spring in our front garden, or of every rose that grew in the backyard, from the deeply perfumed 'Othello' to my favorite-named 'Reine des Violettes' to the head of 'Prospero,' whose petals are more densely imbricated than the scales of a fish. Just as copper could be said to be the only permissible metal in this particular world, maroon was the color of every soft furnishing in sight: sofas and daybeds, rugs, bath towels, pillows, the newly reupholstered mid-century chairs, the robe brought back from a long-ago trip to Morocco. I once bought a white and black woven alpaca blanket from a design store in London as a present— something I imagined my mom cocooning herself in as she lay rapt before the always-playing Turner Classic Movies channel. Before I could say, "Do you like it?" she had condemned it to the dye pot. The next time I clapped eyes on it, it was, well, maroon.

There's something about the warm depths of the hue, though, the way it recalls the dripping velvety darks of Dutch Renaissance floral still lifes (of which my mom always had a tattered postcard, or several, propped around). Those paintings were a font of inspiration for more than just palettes, being reified in all their improbable tangled architecture in the form of the floral arrangements crafted and installed by the grumpy but extraordinary floral artist Carrie Glenn. I don't think a more quietly visionary florist existed in the United States for at least most of Carrie's tenure at Chez Panisse (thirty years, give or take); her arrangements were so uncompromisingly exquisite that no one in his or her right mind would have consented to the cost of their weekly construction—other than, of course, my mother, who is not in her right mind when it comes to things like flowers or lettuce or olive oil or lighting, or even just the smell of a place. Whether my mother was always this way, or whether her priorities were forged at some critical moment before I was born, I can't say, but in my recollection of her, her doctrinairism was the dominant feature. Of course she's had enough financial security in her adulthood so as not to have to think twice about choosing the best olive oil, but her inflexibility didn't necessarily mean a more expensive price tag. Many of the improvements she insisted on could be made for nothing, or next to it: a foraged bundle of branches, salad grown in the backyard or window planter, and so forth. And anyway, if good olive oil is your most crippling vice, you're probably not headed for ruin any time soon. At least that's how I rationalize it—I seem to have inherited a congenital inflexibility regarding quality condiments and superior produce, even if it means several dinners a month of lentils or sardines on toast (it turns out good olive oil is all you need to make even the most frugal ingredients taste delicious). As for flowers—or leaves, really—I mostly purloin those from the overabundance of mangy greenery growing on the streets of London or Berkeley or wherever.

I did, however, learn to assemble arrangements from the best of the best. I was often drafted, along with my childhood friend Sarah, into Carrie's employ, especially when something unthinkably tedious had to be undertaken in the service of a particular visual effect. There was the time, for instance, when we spent several after-school afternoons stringing blushy little crab apples onto copper wire to make garlands to drape around the amber-colored mirrors of Chez Panisse's downstairs dining room for a harvest dinner. Our fingers were covered in tart juice and the must of apple skin; the fuzz from the underside of their leaves caught easily in our long, juicy hair. We had loads of cuts and punctures from negotiating the copper wire, but then, it had to be copper, of course, so that all the colors would meld together, even disappear, into the warmth of the wooded, copper-toned room. Carrie approached her work with a shrewdness and control that would seem inconsistent with the sense of wilderness her arrangements exuded, but she was a master of barely bridled chaos. She was painting, really, with flowers. And no one ever considered her anything less than an artist in the truest sense.

Flowers were for my mom not just a confection to be enjoyed at the restaurant, but a part of what made any room complete. Billowing leafy branches and a few stems of some decidedly unshowy flower seem to be permanently installed in a large green urn in the far corner of the kitchen, adjacent to what was formerly a picture window and which, in a more recent renovation, was turned into a pair of glass doors opening onto the garden. These arrangements, which bore only distant relation to Carrie's consummately assembled masterpieces, were nonetheless a critical part of the feeling of the room and the house more generally, as were the many little vases—tiny copper lusterware pitchers from England or assorted mini vintage copper metal vessels (the homeliest of which I made in a high school blacksmithing class)—that she perched on the sill above the kitchen sink. These would often contain a couple of choice sprigs: the one gorgeous bloom whose stem snapped in the arranging of something taller but couldn't be jettisoned; a few citrus blossoms from our gnarled and underproductive Meyer lemon tree or, when the season rolled around, an immaculate little violet bouquet.

I know that violets are not strictly maroon, but they are a related shade of dark purple, and, more important, they are the flower that I will forever associate with my mother. If I were ever to get a tattoo to memorialize her (in forty years when she retires from running Chez Panisse at the ripe old age of a hundred and ten!), it would be of a violet. We have always had them growing in our front garden—the back one too, but those were generally more overlooked—and their appearance preceded the full arrival of spring; they were the shy ground-hugging little harbingers of warmer days to come. If you neglected to pick them in that two-week window, they would disappear as quietly as they appeared, never making a fuss like the red and yellow tulips, which, exhausted by a few days of full bloom, would swoon and collapse like melodramatic love-vanquished teenagers. While the violets were flowering I'd pause on my way in from school to collect a handful for my mother, visiting whichever plants I hadn't culled from the previous day, or the ones that had yielded a few fresh blooms ("They *like* to be picked!" my mother would reassure me). I don't think she ever told me she wanted me to pick them for her or requested a bouquet outright, but it became an unspoken tradition: every day new stems were added to the little bouquet on the sill; every day wilted or shriveled stems were plucked from it.

I loved hunting for the tiny flowers, always cowering beneath their beautifully lobed dark green cordate leaves. My mom would have entered the house ten or so minutes earlier, leaving the door yawning, and would usually be in the kitchen pretending she had no idea why I'd tarried in the front yard, or perhaps even "hadn't noticed" that I had yet to occupy my after-school perch for snacks at the butcher block. I delighted in offering this tiny arrangement, hemmed in a ring of leaves, to my mom. And every time, even if I'd been violet-hunting on a near daily basis, my mom would act surprised and delighted to receive it. Nothing could have reaffirmed my dedication to this ritual like my mother's truly unfeigned glee at being presented with this unspeakably modest gift—I honestly do not know of another person capable of such wonder. To this day, no matter where I am in the world, a violet will call my mother into the garden, into the room. Whenever I used to pick a handful from my London garden, it was with her in mind, and with regret that an emailed photo would have had to be dispatched in lieu of the real thing.

When I was eight years old, my mom published the first of two children's books themed around my experiences in the restaurant. At the time—I was *eight*—I thought this was a grand idea! Me? Center of attention? Heroine of a picture book? Sold! When the book was released I did not need to be coerced into tagging along with my mom to book signings, radio appearances, and the like. I went along skipping. To this day, I've never signed anything with as much brio as I did those several hundred *Fanny at Chez Panisse* books, emblazoning them with the Madonna-esque single moniker "Fanny." Once I reached high school and the book was belatedly being turned into a musical with Broadway ambitions, I had developed a healthy set of misgivings, hinging on bald regret. When the production was unfavorably reviewed by the *San Francisco Chronicle* with the headline "Fanny Lacks Spice," I arrived on campus to discover that several copies of the article had been taped to my locker. When it comes to my mother's feelings about the whole thing, she largely seems untainted by remorse, but I suspect that if I'd really put my foot down at any point she would have relented. I think everyone involved in the *Fanny* book was relieved that the theatrical iteration wasn't going anywhere near Broadway; still, any uneasiness—my own, primarily—was never extreme, and certainly didn't hinder the possibility of a sequel (*Fanny in France* was published just a few years ago).

Despite any latent mortification, I can still say that one of the best things to come out of the whole ordeal were the reams of letters I received between the ages of eight and eleven from girls my age who had read the book. Of course, these were the days before the internet and also at the height of my French school's pedagogical practice of forcing us into correspondence with like-aged French children, so I was primed to be the pen pal of any "fan's" dreams. I wrote back to every epistle, including recipes and drawings; sent follow-up letters (in some instances remaining in contact with someone for years); and tried my best to seem as cool and blasé as the alter ego who'd graced the pages of my mom's book. The letter I remember best was written by a young reader who, as evidenced by the single page of very careful, large, and labored text, appeared also to be a new writer. It read: "Dear Fanny, Do you know how to make violet-flavored gum? Love, Georgia." I did not know then how to make violet-flavored gum and still don't, but I wrote back and included a recipe for candied violets, which to this day remind me not only of Georgia but also, of course, of my mother.

Candied Violets   CANDYING FLOWERS is not something I undertake very often, but when I do, I find it's always worth the not-very-significant effort. Making candied violets at Easter to rim the edge of a lemon curd tart would be one of those times: purple and yellow in their most mutually beneficial pairing, and something sure to enchant anyone who comes to your table. It's one of those incredibly whimsical things that makes an enormous impression, while being actually quite easy. Line a baking tray with a sheet of waxed paper or baking parchment. In a medium bowl, beat 2 egg whites with a whisk just until frothy. Place a cup of white, finely granulated sugar in a small bowl. Taking one violet at a time by the stem (be sure to use the edible common purple violet, which grows both cultivated and wild—if you have doubts, consult an expert!), dip it into the egg whites, covering all surfaces, then gingerly dip it into the sugar, being sure to coat the whole of the flower. Two egg whites should be enough for at least a couple of dozen candied flowers. Place the coated violets on the prepared baking sheets and use a toothpick, match, or the end of a small knife to coax each flower back into its original shape if the dredging process has caused it to collapse a bit. Fill in any uncoated patches with an additional sprinkle of sugar. Finally, use a pair of scissors to snip off the stems. Allow to dehydrate in a warm, dry area for 24 hours or more. Once these are completely dry, store in an airtight container and keep for up to two months.

.   .   .

Why chartreuse, then? Well, it's the hallucinatory color of spring, of the first pea tendrils that would wind themselves up the naked bamboo poles my mom staked in the earth in our backyard to make a child-sized tipi, a construction that always started to list precariously to one side once the full crop of sugar peas arrived midsummer. I delighted in sitting in there, snacking on peas until I'd ruined my appetite for dinner. Chartreuse is also a color that looks particularly good with maroon (as it were). For my mom, chartreuse was not just a word she loved to say, and that I loved to repeat back to her like a talking parrot, but also the color of things growing, of things awakening. She always calls me to tell me when the fresh tips have started to emerge at the ends of the branches of our towering, centuries-old redwood tree. That new green, the kind of green that comes up overnight after a much-needed rain, transforming a dull parched sward up in the sprawling regional park behind our house into a vibrant carpet. The green that makes going for a walk in the California hills feel like a visit to a mythical Green Kingdom. It is the color of the inside of a fava bean pod and the color of the chervil my mom loves to throw into a salad.

My mom used to talk about a group of monks in the French Alps who lived in a monastery called Grande Chartreuse. They were called Carthusians, and in lieu of conversation (they obey a strict rule against speaking) made and bottled Chartreuse, that vividly colored, slightly poisonous-looking liqueur infused with mountain herbs. In my mom's fantasy there was a restaurant at this monastery too—a place with a hearth so ancient and vast you could walk right into it and a garden that stretched across several hilly acres—but I can't imagine a Carthusian silently explaining a menu and taking a food order or mutely firing a steak. The closest I ever got to the bottled stuff was in crème Chantilly (to accompany, say, a perfect slice of apple galette in the downstairs restaurant), but the second it hit my tongue, I'd bristle and refuse it: too potent, too boozy. A very willing sampler of wine, I was, but only a reluctant consumer of desserts that had been in any way desecrated by some variety of heady liqueur.

When my mom first met Susie Tompkins Buell (the founder of Esprit, whose charitable foundation was the first to support my mother's Edible Schoolyard Project), I was about eight years old. This belated encounter between two Bay Area doyennes was, it transpired, a true meeting of maroon and chartreuse: a friendship destined to last. Susie possessed a devotion to the latter color that rivaled my mom's commitment to maroon. Enter one of Susie's perfectly curated interiors—I owe her almost as much as I owe my mother when it comes to the influences on my present aesthetic—and you were submerged in a world in which grassy, bottle-glassy shades of chartreuse were everywhere on display: collections of vases and pots made by studio potter Barbara Willis, half dipped in chartreuse glaze, generous enveloping chartreuse sofas festooned with pillows of every tint of light green, the most covetable assortment of glassware and French flea market bowls, and piles, platters, altars full of perfectly worn but still-jeweled green sea glass, scavenged from the local beach. The house, so full of green, was like the Emerald City of Oz made real and relocated to Bolinas, California. Fittingly, the lettuces my mother and Susie most adore are the bitter ones, the winter greens that take happily to vinaigrettes with strong garlic and anchovy and glugs of olive oil and lemon. Their favorite is the Castelfranco, an Italian varietal of radicchio whose head looks like a massive rose and whose pale chartreuse leaves are speckled, appropriately, with deep maroon.

CHAPTER 4

Peeling Fruit

One of the most distinctive things about my mother is her hands, though I would imagine that the hands of anyone's mother would seem distinctive to them. Those are the hands, after all, that soothe us throughout so much of our childhood, that change our diapers and swaddle us and hold us, and comb our hair, and apply unwanted sunscreen and antiseptic and Band-Aids, and put on our clothes and tie our shoelaces. But there is something about the way my mom uses hers—which is to say, with total conviction and without fear—that makes them seem so unordinary. Her hands are in fact quite small, her nails perpetually shorn (from a mix of anxious biting and crude clipping and the occasional cooking accident, like the time she took off the very end of a finger trying to shell a green walnut to make a liqueur called nocino).

What other people often notice about her hands is her battery of rings: the stacks of unshowy stone-studded Victorian bands that grace nearly every finger. Having a modest treasury on her fingers doesn't, however, prevent her from plunging her hands into whatever she pleases: a salad that requires tossing, shrimp that needs shelling, a near-scalding broth whose bones have to be removed *immediately*. Needless to say, none of her rings are perfectly intact—there's always a stone missing here, an irreparable ding there, a scratch, a tiny pearl that will never, *ever* be replaced. But there is also something in the strength of her fingers—whether congenital or from years of kitchen work—that I find especially unusual. In this, her hands are a sort of mirror of her determination. Don't let appearances deceive you: she can pick up the largest cast-iron pan without a wince, carry a preposterously large suitcase that she'll pretend is too heavy for her if I, her trusty porter, am anywhere in sight. When I was little and straight from the bath, I'd kneel before her wherever she was seated (usually the living room sofa) and proffer my dripping head to her towel-cloaked lap. She'd gather up the towel on either side of my head and fold it over the back and rub furiously, the intensity of the pressure of her fingertips against my skull at once reassuring and electrifying.

And yet I would register some horror too at how brazenly she'd thrust her hands into something, and how unvexed she seemed by whatever residue it left behind. She also, more often than not, would at some point during a meal jettison her silverware and delve in with her fingers. I think it wasn't so much out of a lack of concern for etiquette, as it was a primal impulse to be closer to the thing she was eating, to be more sensuously acquainted with it. Her fingers told her what the mind and mouth would take longer to compute: was a crust crunchy enough, was the fish cooked through, was the salad amply or underdressed? Given my model, I had little chance to develop particularly evolved table manners. I was freely permitted to consume most things with my hands, without fear of recrimination, both at home and at the restaurant. I don't think I was ever once told "Use your knife and fork!" A favorite finger food at Chez Panisse was what I called "inside-out sandwiches," in which I would wrap several large, dressed lettuce leaves around a crusty Acme levain crouton to pop into my mouth. Some patrons, regardless of whether or not they were aware that I was the proprietor's daughter, looked upon the scene in mild disgust. When we traveled to France, where even *pizza* is consumed with fork and knife, I was regarded as a feral child brought up by a pair of *Américains pitoyables* (pitiful Americans). Still, I can't shed the conditioning. On one of my first dates with a boyfriend, I plunged my hands into a salad to toss it. He told me he'd never seen anyone, least of all a potential partner, get so close to food in that way, be so physical with something edible, something that would imminently be shared. I took it as a compliment.

The general climate of finger-eating in our household also meant that, for example, not a single paper form brought home from school for my mom's compulsory signature authorizing, say, a field trip, would be returned to my school unmarred by oil stains or a swarm of greasy fingerprints. This isn't much of a surprise, really, given that I once apprehended my mother attempting to "dye" a pair of pants in a pot of olive oil after having splattered them in an oleaginous constellation the previous evening. The washing machine has never recovered. Anyway, olive oil was just one of the substances whose aroma my mother routinely carried with her—her hands often smelled like garlic or vinegar. I worried compulsively about bacteria before I even understood what bacteria were. She in turn could not comprehend how she had produced such a hygiene-obsessed child and blamed my babysitters for the transference of a hypochondria so alien to her. If, for example, I had requested a back scratch (though this was more like a light massage given the absence of nails), so too would I have requested a thorough hand wash. "Scrub in!" I'd yell, having learned that this was a thing doctors did before surgery. She always eye-rollingly consented to this ablution but did it, in my opinion, far too hastily. I could still smell a lingering hint of anchovy, the heady, persistent aroma of her homemade red wine vinegar, the onion that had earlier found its way into a risotto. But then as she moved her impossibly smooth palms—how, with all the use they got?—in a circle over an upset belly or sore back, spelling out full moons with each clockwise stroke, my uncontrollable anxiety over bacteria would dissipate, dissolving with each honeyed stroke, her palm somehow at once warm *and* marmoreally cool.

But if there is a portrait of my mother's hands that is most etched in my mind, it is the way she holds a piece of fruit as she deftly slips the skin from its flesh. Our dining table has always had a bowl placed at its center containing some variety of fruit—whatever was at its seasonal peak. This constituted dessert in our house; there was no other type, save for very special occasions and holidays, or rarely, and only more recently, some slightly stale too-bitter chocolate that everyone nibbles apathetically and never finishes. But I can hear the phrase ringing in my ears, almost incantatory: "Fan, can you get me a sharp knife and a small plate, please?" And it would raise me from my chair at the table—she and my father remained seated—and propel me across the room to the knife drawer, which I knew to approach with caution. There I would select a small wood-handled paring knife and, standing on my tippy-toes, pull a small plate down from the cabinet behind me. The fact that she trusted me to select and carry a dangerous object even when I was quite small made this daily ritual exciting, or at least memorable. I would bring these things to where she was sitting in front of the fire—always, always, that same warm seat—and she would feel around the fruit bowl as if blindly feeling around in the dark, selecting only the perfect pear or the finest apple or the sweetest fig. The finger-feel, the knowledge in her fingertips, strikes me as singular, though I know it is the gift of many chefs: determining the difference between lusciously yielding flesh and a fruit that is over the hill, pressing a finger into the inscrutable surface of a steak on a grill and discerning, in an instant, its doneness.

Anyway, the best specimen would be chosen, and then a period of readying it for the mouths of family or guests would ensue. The time it took her to perform this sacrament seemed eternal, but in a pleasant way. She did (and still does) many things very quickly, but here the moment would elongate as she methodically relieved a peach of its fuzzy sheath or shimmied a ripe pear from its bitter, gritty skin. If the quality of the selection was in any way in doubt, she would sample it before offering it away. Otherwise she would slice the thing into perfect crescents and, depending on the company, either directly offer these fruit-moons to our mouths (I, her primary beneficiary) or array them on a plate to be passed around.

There is something almost outlandishly generous about the act of offering away the best of something—we humans are so innately selfish—rather than keeping it for yourself. And yet it was always like that with her: whoever has the good fortune of sitting at her side at a meal will be offered something from her plate—but only if it's so delectable that it cannot be missed. She would allow herself only a piece of the second best peach, the subpar pear, the plum that needed another day, so that her company might taste the very best fruit. It was like that with everything, really: the perfect morsel of lobster claw slid from its pincer shell. Anything that took effort, that might be messy, but whose taste was a reward—she would do the dirty work and, turning to me, give it away. The best berry in the blackberry bramble? The one (and only) ripe cherry produced by our beleaguered cherry tree? The most perfect handful of raspberries from the patch that grows in our backyard? These were delights harvested or prepared especially for me. There was a knowingness in it, though: it was as if she were saying, "I've been here before. I've sipped the ambrosia. It's your turn now." I do wonder whether this is typical of motherhood or of the love that attends that role. I can't yet venture an opinion, but I suspect the impulse is more driving in my mom's case than in most.

THERE IS NO "RECIPE" to accompany these memories other than that a perfect piece of fruit is genuinely the best end of a meal, and so much more satisfying than anyone ever gives it credit for. It's why the fruit bowl at Chez Panisse is a fixture and the subject of a frequently cited encomium by the author Michael Pollan. If you've ordered it once and tasted whatever fruit was ready *right that second in that exact peak seasonal moment,* then I can assure you, you will remember those insanely perfumed Bronx grapes or caramel-like Barhi dates or succulent, bloody mulberries far more intensely than the—of course still very delicious—slice of fruit galette also on offer. Not only does Chez Panisse have a full-time "forager" on staff (someone whose express job it is to ferret out the best produce from the hundreds of farmers in California and nearby), but it has been forging relationships with producers for forty-plus years. "Howard's Miracles"—among the best plums I've ever tried—used to be delivered to the pastry department by ancient Howard himself, from his three backyard trees, until he passed away and the trees moved along with him. The restaurant would serve those three trees' worth of plums while they were at their best, and then no more plums, because menu consistency was less important than the quality of flavor. If there was an unprecedented windfall, priorities were established: the finest fruit was dispatched to the fruit bowl, blighted fruit to the galette, overripe fruit to the big French copper jam pots, where it would be converted to a preserve or a glaze to be painted over the tops of cakes or the edges of tarts, or drizzled over ice cream.

CAKES AND GALETTES and glazes happened at home too, occasionally, but the most salient moment both in the life of the fruit and in our family was when the fruit was ready to be eaten, and my mom would ask me to prepare the instruments for her to dismantle, with loving slowness, the perfect specimen. Get a very sharp paring knife (Opinel and Victorinox are good), and take a long time to peel and cut something. Arrange it on a plate, but not too carefully, and send it around the table. It is always the best, most memorable dessert.

CHAPTER 5

First Fragola

Mine was not a childhood in which sugar reigned supreme. Unsurprisingly, I was largely deprived of it for long enough to have an actual memory of when I first tasted ice cream. We were on vacation in Italy. It was my parents' honeymoon (they were married when I was two years old), and it was late summer, verging on fall. We were moving

through Siena on our way to a rustic house somewhere in the not-too-distant countryside. Gelato seemed like the only sensible way to fend off the lingering seasonal swelter. I was allowed to choose a flavor. There were so many, like a rainbow containing even the deepest nuances of prismatic color. This frozen stuff, which I don't think I understood would in fact be cold, was kept beneath a sloping carapace of glass and modeled into soft, surreal mountains of vivid color, flecked here and there with seeds or nuts or bits of chocolate like the spots on a Dalmatian. I had never seen anything like it. I pointed to strawberry. It was pink. Plus, I loved strawberries and I think I could understand, conceptually, that there was a relationship between that beloved fruit and the substance behind the glass unbound by any organic shape of origin. It was made with the strawberries of the late summer of 1985—let's imagine, quite plausibly, that they were some heirloom varietal, that they'd been grown on an organic farm somewhere in the nearby Tuscan hills, and that they had suffered little intervention other than their meeting with sugar, a touch of cream, and of course cold.

When I received the golden waffle cone in hand, with just a modest ball slotted into it, I knew intuitively to apply it to my mouth. The smell was seductive, but muted by the cold. The taste, on the other hand, was intoxicating. The sugar used in this gelato produced a flavor that was completely indistinct from that of the fruit it was meant to intensify. Which is to say, it was exactly the right amount of sugar—neither too much nor too little. It had a platonic taste of strawberry, of the ripest honeyed late-summer berries so perfectly distilled that the taste seemed almost audible—it could not be confined to the realm of the tongue. So much so that I forgot that my mouth was in fact the best place to receive this newfound manna: I began to use the cone like a melting frozen marker to draw over the whole of my face. I wanted to merge with this food, not just to eat it, but to *experience* it. My clothes, my hair—all were victims of the brief but unforgettable encounter. I don't remember anything else about that day, and indeed very little, if anything, about that trip to Italy, but I know that my memory of my communion with the Gods of Sugar and Ice Cream is firsthand and real, not merely something told to me, or photographed—it is etched onto my palate alongside the most indelible of my life's food memories. I don't think my parents took a photo, nor did they try to stop me from sullying every inch of my dress. They just looked on at what happens in the moment that marks the end of two years of living on the planet ignorant of ice cream. And even though my parents returned to the sugar-free regime and adhered to it with lamentable rigor, I think they were both pleased to watch me fleetingly lose my mind in flavor.

Strawberry Gelato

THIS RECIPE does, I'm afraid, require an ice-cream maker. I'm not typically a proponent of extraneous kitchen equipment, but I do think summer fruit gelatos and ice creams are reason enough to acquire something whose use is so specific. If you really can't imagine investing but would like to experience something similar by way of flavor, you can make the below recipe as a granita instead (simply pour the mixture into a large, shallow casserole dish and freeze for 1 hour before stirring with a fork, then freeze for 2 to 3 hours longer or until completely frozen, stirring every 30 minutes). To make the puree, begin by hulling 1 pound of the ripest strawberries you can find. Put 1 cup, or about ⅓ of the berries, into a small saucepan. Add 2 tablespoons of water, heat over medium-high heat until boiling, then lower the flame and cover the saucepan in order to capture any juices the strawberries let off. Cook for just a few minutes until the fruit becomes very fragrant. Remove from heat and allow to cool for about fifteen minutes. Put the cooked fruit and any collected syrup into a blender, along with ½ cup of sugar and ⅓ cup of whole milk. Puree until smooth and taste. It should scream of strawberries from the moment it hits the tongue. If the flavor rings hollow or feels faint, add more sugar, a teaspoonful at a time. At room temperature, it should be a touch sweeter than you like—freezing will dull the perception of sweetness. When it tastes good, refrigerate the mixture in the blender or a bowl for a half hour in order to hasten the gelato's freezing. When your ice-cream machine is ready, squeeze a few drops of lemon juice into the strawberry puree. Stir thoroughly and pour it into the spinning ice-cream canister, freezing the gelato according to instructions. Eat this with abandon the day it is made, though it will remain delicious for a few days.

CHAPTER 6

Smell

What most sticks out to me from an array of childhood impressions overwhelmingly has to do with color and smell, with the two often working in concert in a synesthetic blur. But many of these recollections are not just a melding of faculties, but the amalgamation of many instances, repeated—the layering, day after day, of a near-identical happening or event. The memory of my mother, for instance, coming home from a day of work at the restaurant and my running to hug her, burrowing my face into her clothes so that I could inhale the smells that had clung to the fabric, or taking her hand to smell the inner softer flesh of her forearm or any surface that might have held a scent of something grilled or macerated or fried. Though my mom claims there were instances in which my guesses were eerily accurate (like when she'd poked a squid to test for freshness but done none of the actual cleaning, yet I'd still intuited her proximity to the squid), there is not one isolated time I can remember performing this ritualistic greeting. Rather I see an army of silhouettes, all in my mother's shape, coming to the front door, for a moment just a black shadow limned in the yellow gold of afternoon light, before stepping into the cool dark of our front room. And then my embrace, and the sniffing and the guessing, and the little shred of loving praise meted out if I had smelled something keenly enough to divine the ingredient of the day.

My mom wears no perfume of any sort—no eau de toilette or

cologne. Most serious chefs don't, for all of the obvious reasons pertaining to olfactory interference. But there were smells—beyond the ones I could detect on her apron or clothes—that I associate with her still. So much so, in fact, that some of these smells are virtually indivisible from her form. One of these is the lotion she used for the first twenty-five years of my life, a hippie drugstore formulation—now discontinued—that boasted the ingredients collagen and almond oil before these things were made popular by contemporary superfood trends. The lotion itself was not particularly viscous; a dollop in the palm of her hand was like a fat iridescent pearl turned liquid. She would cover herself head to toe in this stuff, every morning after the bath, without fail, believing it—quite rightly, I can now attest—to be for the skin an unmatched, youth-preserving balm.

The bath, I feel, practically merits its own chapter—and certainly an immediate interlude—so critical is it to my mom's routine. We did not have a shower when I was growing up. We had a massive salvaged antique bathtub sunk into a tiled alcove that could fit all three of us— Dad, Mom, me—very comfortably. Most mornings we would bathe together—like the bohemians we were in reality not at all—and this habit of communal ablution persisted well enough into my childhood that I began to doubt its broader social acceptability. Anyway, all this to say that this was anti-shower territory, which makes sense in the scheme of things, considering my mom's disdain for things that are loud or violent or in the least bit efficient or innovative. I believe the experience for her is not one that hinges on cleanliness but rather on warmth (she is almost always cold, unless of course she is driving and wearing an outer layer and suddenly becomes "SO HOT! FAN, HELP ME GET THIS JACKET OFF RIGHT THIS INSTANT EVEN IF IT SPELLS SUDDEN DEATH BY COLLISON!"). What we could handily label *hot flashes* have been going on for so many decades I think they hardly qualify for that categorization—let's chalk it up instead to a capricious internal thermometer.

My vision of her, from the vantage of her bathtub, where I sometimes submerge myself in her barely soiled water directly after her
exit, or from the closed lid of the toilet if I've entered the room to chat
with her, is as the left-most figure in Titian's *Pastoral Concert* from
around 1509, which I first saw at the Louvre on a school trip when
I was ten. In fact, my mother's form has always recalled the bathing
or linen-draped figures of the High Renaissance, with their porcelain
skin and gentle-seeming edges. After the bath, which was very short
and unindulgent but compulsory, she would begin the application of
lotion, and the smell of that almond concoction would grow entire.
Even when I was younger and not particularly morbid I would think
about this lotion and how if my mom was to die suddenly and someone was to crack open a bottle of it, a whiff would flatten me, possibly
even cause me to be snuffed out along with her. I guess it's a blessing
the stuff has been discontinued.

But a milky almond scent is hardly the only one I associate with
my mom and our home. There are many others that stand out like the
brighter threads in a weaving: the smell of woodsmoke, of course—
that smell, almost gasoline-like, when the char of wood infuses
clothing—and of roses, wet ones, gathered in handfuls from the back
garden to array a sill, an aroma like if the feel of velvet had a scent;
of rosemary burning, or sage, that purgative smell necessary when a
room's atmosphere felt stale; of garlic warming but never burning on
the stove; of honey and beeswax as the tapers burned down to nubs
in their brass holders at the end of a long meal; of the leaves of lemon
verbena blanching in a stream of scalding water for tisane; of Meyer
lemons in the winter when bowlfuls fill the house.

The restaurant had associated but different smells: for one, the
smell of a rug walked on daily by hundreds of feet—a smell I com-
plained about tirelessly to my mom as a child, though Chez Panisse,
despite its wall-to-wall carpet in the downstairs dining room, is one of
the few restaurants that doesn't have that mildly industrial smell of so

many (that miasma of old cooking oil, grease worn deep into creases, or of an ambiguous unfreshness, sometimes even a perplexing smell of disuse). But Chez also smelled of fire, of the fire smoldering nightly in the downstairs hearth, and then of the delicacies cooked over it: of quail with its blackening skin, or a leg of lamb, grapevine branches glowing, becoming long and spindly embers; a woody, amber smell of old redwood in the upstairs booths and the smell of the oil used in the copper lamps set at each table; the yeasty, fat smell of pizza dough rising in a big plastic tub; the smell of the galette's burnt sugar crust as you walk past the display of desserts. There are so many others, of course, and there are the smells that might actually be tastes and vice versa, but suffice it to say it was a rich sensory world, and only rarely one that provoked olfactory dismay—even for a kid with a prodigious nose, one that caused my parents more grief and frustration than pride.

Fruit Galette

THE SMELL OF THIS GALETTE, no matter the contents, is one of the aromas I most associate with the restaurant. It's the smell of the caramelized sugar that lacquers the browned crust, but also of how that smell—which really *is* a taste—works in harmony with whatever fruit is most perfect, itself on the edge of becoming a jam. Ultimately, this symbiosis makes the galette so seductive and enduringly appealing, even though it's not particularly innovative. The simplicity and straightforwardness of this dessert, however, is largely why it's been on the menu nearly every night since the restaurant first opened.

THE DOUGH, sometimes called "crunch dough," was taught to the Chez Panisse staff by the culinary icon Jacques Pépin in the early days of the restaurant and is, even for those of us not gifted in the baking department, reliably easy to make. I like to think of this galette recipe and the restaurant's fruit bowl as two sides of the same coin: both are intended to highlight the peak fruit of the season. And though I love to have unadulterated fruit for dessert, eating the best fruit of a given season arranged on a thin buttery dough, baked until its juices bubble and the pastry browns, makes for an incredibly straightforward and pleasurable end to a meal.

MAKE THIS GALETTE IN TWO PHASES. First prepare the dough, and then after chilling for at minimum an hour, roll it out, assemble the fruit, and bake the galette. To make the dough, measure ¼ cup of ice-cold water and set aside. Mix together 1 cup all-purpose flour, ½ teaspoon salt, and, if you like, 1 teaspoon sugar. Cut 6 tablespoons of cold butter into small (approximately ¼ inch) cubes. Work the butter into the flour mixture, using either a pastry blender or your fingers, until the dough becomes a mixture of well-blended flour and butter, and larger, unincorporated pieces of butter. (It's this very irregularity that makes the baked crust flaky.) Working quickly so as not to warm the butter too much, pour ¾ of the water over the dough in a slow and steady stream, all the while tossing the dough with your hands or a fork. At this point, the dough will look like a raggedy mess, with some parts wetter and more formed than others. This is okay. The key is to be gentle as you form the dough into a semblance of a ball—overworking it leads to a tough crust. You're trying to add just enough water to make a cohesive dough that will not crumble when rolling it to a 14-inch disc. But add too much water, and the dough can become unworkably sticky. As soon as the majority of the dough begins to clump together, gently form it into a ball. Wrap the dough in plastic and compress it so the ball flattens into a disc. Refrigerate for at least an hour or overnight.

WHEN READY TO ROLL OUT, remove the dough from the refrigerator, and, if it's been chilling for several hours, let warm for about 20 minutes. The dough should be malleable but not soft. Lightly flour a large surface and sprinkle a dusting of flour on the dough itself. I like to begin the process by using a rolling pin to flatten the dough even more before rolling it out. Tap it repeatedly across its surface with the length of the rolling pin. When ready to roll, start from the center and apply even pressure with the rolling pin as you work toward the edges. Every so often, flip the dough over, and, if necessary, dust each side lightly with flour. Patch up any holes or tears with the uneven outer edges.

ONCE IT IS 14 INCHES IN DIAMETER and about ⅛ inch thick, transfer the dough to a baking sheet lined with parchment. The easiest, though by no means panic-free, way to do this is to fold the dough in half, or in quarters, and then quickly move it to the baking sheet. Unfold it, and as you do, brush off any excess flour with your hand or, even better, a clean pastry brush. Chill the dough for at least 30 minutes before baking—about the time it will take you to prepare the fruit—and preheat the oven to 400°F.

NEARLY ANY FRUIT can be a filling for a galette. The main considerations are the amount of sugar to add and the quantity of juice the fruit will give off. If you're using berries, rhubarb, or apricots—fruits that will cast off a good amount of liquid—consider starting with a base layer of crushed amaretti, or a mixture of 1 tablespoon flour, 1 tablespoon ground almonds, and 2 tablespoons sugar.

A GENERAL RULE OF THUMB for one galette is to prepare 1½ pounds of fruit. I think the less fussy the better, so skip peeling plums, pluots, or apples. If you're using fruit other than berries, cut the fruit into slices about ⅓ inch thick—a little thinner for apples, while apricots (my favorite!) can simply be halved. Arrange the fruit in overlapping concentric circles until you reach the final 2 inches of the pastry. Make an outer rim of pastry by folding the border of exposed dough up and over itself at regular intervals, crimping and pushing it up against the fruit, so that it forms a narrow rope-like rim that will contain a filling of fruit. Brush this rim with melted butter and sprinkle it generously with sugar.

BAKE IN THE LOWER THIRD OF THE OVEN for 45 to 50 minutes, or until the fruit is tender and the crust is well browned, its edges slightly caramelized. As soon as the galette is out of the oven, transfer it to a cooling rack using a large metal spatula. This will prevent the galette from steaming and becoming soggy. If you're inclined to embellish the galette, have jam on hand that is either made of the same fruit or complements the filling: heat it up enough to liquefy it and then brush a little onto the surface of the cooked fruit so it glistens. Cooking apple peels with water, sugar, and lemon zest can also make a very simple, delicately flavored glaze. If you're using an apple for the galette that has either a thick or a bitter skin that would be better removed, this is the perfect opportunity to use the skins. Serve the galette warm, with ice cream or whipped cream.

CHAPTER 7

Chicken Stock

My mom makes a chicken stock whenever she arrives somewhere new. It's the aromatherapy of my childhood, a smell intermingled with that of burning bay leaves or rosemary. Of course making a chicken stock is something that requires getting a chicken first, and procuring a chicken is more easily achieved in some corners of the world than others, and certainly not at all hours. But in my memory, she begins to make a chicken stock the second she steps foot in a place. Another recipe that resides in this unmoored limbo—the space between arriving somewhere and actually being settled there—is Coming Home Pasta (page 313). But whereas that pasta implies a return, the simmering of a chicken stock doesn't require being "home"—rather it's enlisted to produce the feeling of home wherever you might find yourself.

Which is why, if we were traveling to a remote part of Sicily, say, she would use her nonexistent Italian to acquire a head-still-attached, feathers-on chicken from a next-door-neighbor-cum-farmer, or insist on a pit stop at a good butcher before we'd even arrived at the rental house. (These days, conversations with unwitting Airbnb hosts prior to our arrival tend to address concerns regarding the best local farmers markets, proximity to farmers, the choicest bar in town for an aperitif, and so on—not the expected "What's the Wi-Fi password?") Often, when I was either in college or recently graduated and living in unlovely environs commensurate with that status, she would arrive at my apartment with a chicken already in her purse, which she'd reveal as if it were the white rabbit of the proverbial magic top hat (before immediately stuffing it into a pot to get a simmer going, regardless of whether we had dinner plans). While I appreciated this ambience-producing gesture, and myself often make a chicken stock whenever I move into a new place or stay with a friend for a lengthy stint, I will admit that I do not always find the scent of bouillon to be a welcome one. Especially if the kitchen in question was the tiny corner of a windowless railroad apartment's living room and the only way for the chicken fumes to exhaust was via *my bedroom*. The smell of stock and also of a chicken roasting at a high temperature in a kitchen without ample ventilation is what led to my coining (together with my French ex-boyfriend) the verb *to be pouleted* (pronounced *poolayed*). As in "I got pouleted last night, but man, it was the best chicken I've ever tasted!"

There are many reasons to make a chicken stock, especially if you've roasted a chicken and want to make something good from its remains. Having some stock on hand—which is to say, frozen in a container in the freezer—is considered one of the most important acts of pantry provisioning in our house. If you were to open our freezer, you would find little else besides. Sometimes when I'm home for a longer visit, there'll be a small bag of rimy, frostbitten berries lurking in there for my smoothies, but the primary freezer dwellers are a half-dozen bloated reused Ziploc bags full of stock. Each one has been labeled in my mother's insanely indecipherable hand (her handwriting is the mutant offspring of long-ago calligraphy training and a freewheeling Sharpie): "wild duck, *fantastic*, 12/23"; "turkey, 11/23, USE NOW 1/10"; "chicken, 9/15???"; etc.

Chicken stock is a cornerstone ingredient in many dishes: used to enrich mashed potatoes or moisten stuffing for the Thanksgiving turkey, or as a base for many, many sauces or soups, including my mother's deeply palliative Garlicky Noodle Soup (page 60), but I always consider it most indispensable to the making of risotto. As uppity as it may sound, I will not make a risotto if I don't have a good homemade stock. Yes, you can add enough ingredients to make the taste of the rice and its brothy emollient less important, but I was brought up on the belief that a delicious risotto could be made out of rice and stock alone—the better the stock, therefore, the tastier the outcome. In our house, risotto also tended to be looser and more liquid than most, at times more like a thick soup studded with al dente grains of rice than the dense glob of cheesy porridge served at most restaurants. Don't get me wrong, I actually have a soft spot for the stuff (a beetroot version of which inexplicably seems to feature on the menus of most middling pubs in England), but my dad's risotto really was something special and altogether different.

It was for "Dad's risotto"—one of the few dishes my dad cooked with total autonomy, or rather zero interference from my pestering mom—that the precious bones of any bird consumed at our table were harvested and transformed into a homemade brew. Often my mom would stay up late to make stock right after dinner. I would fall asleep to dreams steeped in the potent scent of chicken bubbling away. The smell was, of course, richly embroidered, because there was always so much more added to the pot: celery and onion and carrots and a whole head of garlic severed latitudinally and fresh bay leaves from our tree and juniper berries and black peppercorns and thyme and, especially, the pungent garden parsley, stalky and robust from growing through the winter. Dad's risotto was worth eating a chicken for earlier in the week, just to have an excuse to make stock, and, then possessed of said stock, to have an excuse to urge Dad to make "Dad's risotto." Of all the many times I remember clamoring for risotto, there is nonetheless one preparation that was by far the best I've ever tasted, and which my mom and I still wistfully recall.

This risotto was made six or seven years ago, for a lunch produced by an unlikely band of reunited players. Given that certain friendships were recalibrated, or reshuffled, in the wake of my parents' separation when I was thirteen, it's rare to have my mom, my dad, Bob (formerly my father's closest friend, now my mother's current one), Bob's partner, Tony, and also Sue, Bob's ex-girlfriend, gathered in one place. Bob and Sue were together for several of my younger years, which meant that Sue was often our "fifth wheel" on family vacations—or maybe I was the fifth? Anyway, she became so integral to the family unit that I think of her as nothing short of blood. Best described as the "fourth parent" in my ungainly crew of guardians, Sue, along with Jessica Rabbit, was the primary subject of most of my early drafting and penmanship exercises and the reason I spent certain very underage evenings "disguised" in one of Sue's oversize nineties blazers, sipping Shirley Temples at a string of San Francisco comedy clubs (she was a stand-up comedian for the first fifteen or so years of my life). Though Bob starting seeing Tony—with whom he's been ever since—around the time of my parents' split, Sue and Bob have remained spiritually inseparable. Tony, we all agree, is basically the best cook among us, and is the only person I know whose devotion to garlic and bitter greens rivals my own. These five adults are the people who make up the core of my family, unified too by their shared perception of me as "communal offspring." Though I will admit my young teenage self was initially shaken, if not outright traumatized, by the shifting allegiances, I was lucky enough to have been taught that "family" can be defined beyond the limits of genetics and can expand and morph in unexpected, often beautiful ways.

But back to the risotto. Not long before, my mom had been diagnosed with something serious but treatable and I'd come home from London to be there for the surgery and to hang around with her during its immediate aftermath. Of all the people I know in the world, my mom is the least capable of fasting, even of skipping a meal; a few hours without sustenance and she declares herself to be having a (completely medically unsubstantiated) "blood sugar crisis." The trip to the hospital required her to be put under general anesthesia, and this in turn mandated that she not consume solids for a twenty-four-hour window prior to admission. This was tantamount to spiritual and physical torment. For those twenty-four hours I heard no end of her intellectual objections to this medical prerequisite, which she felt "couldn't possibly be necessary." Needless to say, when she returned home following the procedure, she heeded none of the advice of her doctors and instantly prepared herself a steak frites. This did not go down well; in fact the interference from the sedative medication produced terrible stomach pains, extreme enough to warrant a return to the ER. Only once she had been in the hospital twice in one week did she approach the reintroduction of certain foods with a heightened sense of caution.

By this point, I had been home for a couple of months and was only a few days away from my return to London. We arranged to have my dad over to make lunch *en famille*—which, save for the welcome introduction of Tony, is more or less the shape of the family of my youth. Despite any historical friction, this particular meal came together in the most generous and symbiotic of ways. Each person contributed a piece, prepared something for the other to use, moving in what felt to be an almost perfectly choreographed manner. The best risotto we had all ever tasted emerged: studded with black truffles and wilted nettles, cooked to al dente perfection by my father using what was I think my mother's best ever stock (made with the meaty bones of a wild duck and a Thanksgiving goose), laden with slices of Tony's perfectly grilled chicken breast, the rice just holding together in its pearlescent liquid. A few hours before my flight, we sat together to drink a bottle of wine and eat this delicious stuff, feeling very thankful that everything was going to be all right.

Chicken Stock (and Roast Chicken)

MY ADVICE FIRST OFF is to buy the very best organic and free-range chicken you can afford. There really is a substantive difference in the flavor of the outcome here. Plus, I rarely buy whole chickens just for the sake of making a stock, unless I need a lot of stock for a big meal like Thanksgiving. Usually I'll roast the chicken first and eat that for dinner, reserving all the bones in the refrigerator until the next morning, when I'll have time to make the stock.

WHICH BRINGS US to the tried and true roasted chicken recipe. Once I learned to roast chicken at high temperatures, I never looked back. While it's one of the simplest things I make, it's also one of the dishes my friends request the most. Start by overgenerously salting a chicken (ideally the day before, but at least a few hours before you plan to cook it) and pulling out the fatty deposits from just inside the cavity. If it's been in the refrigerator, take it out and allow it to temper until ready to roast. Turn the oven up to 500°F, or as hot as it will go short of switching it to broil. Take two leeks, wash them, trim them of the woodier dark green parts and halve them lengthwise, then cut them into 2- to 4-inch pieces. Toss the leeks in a bit of olive oil and thyme—if you have it—and lay them down in a tight little bed in a roasting pan (preferably a cast-iron pan just large enough to accommodate your chicken). Shower your chicken in black pepper, fill its cavity with a halved lemon, a couple of unpeeled cloves of garlic, and some sprigs of thyme, and place it on top of your leeks. Over the course of the roasting, the leeks melt—almost confit—in the chicken juices and become the sweetest, most flavorful accompaniment. I first tried this by chance more than ten years ago, and I love the way the leeks taste so much that I rarely roast a chicken without them now.

PLACE YOUR CHICKEN ON A RACK in the center of the preheated oven. To seal the skin and lock in the moisture, keep the oven temperature at 500°F for at least 15 to 20 minutes, even if the oven is smoking a bit. This is, needless to say, how I have set off numerous fire alarms in my day—to the extent that this dish is referred to by some of my friends as Fire Alarm Chicken. There was even a time in college when, in the midst of preparing a birthday dinner for a friend, I couldn't get my smoke detector to shut off in time. Two New Haven firemen promptly arrived at my apartment looking for the blaze, wielding axes and hoses and other firefighting paraphernalia. Fortunately, they were also very good-natured and reset the alarm without reprisal—they even posed for a photo with the birthday cake, playfully hovering their axes just above it, as if about to slice it up. Anyway, turn the oven down to 400–450°F after the initial blast, cooking for a total of 45 to 60 minutes (45 for small chickens, up to 1½ hours for large ones). After the first 20 minutes, you can turn the chicken upside down for another 20 to brown the bottom before righting it again for the final stretch. If my bird is on the larger side, I'll do this, but I generally don't find this rotating to be essential. The chicken is ready when a sharp knife pierced down low into the thickest part of the upper thigh yields clear juices (if they look a bit bloody, keep the bird in) and the joints feel a little wobbly and loose when you take hold of the end of a leg and give it a shake. Let the bird rest for 10 to 20 minutes, carve it, and serve with the leeks.

IF I'M BUYING A CHICKEN primarily for stock, I'll do what my mother always does, which is to remove the breasts and season them to cook for another meal (such as the Herby Chicken Paillard Lunchbox Sandwich, page 68). Separating the flesh of the breast from the rib cage is not difficult if you have a sharp knife, but you can likewise ask your butcher to perform this small task for you. Place the bird (minus the breasts) in a large stockpot, cover with ample cold water, and set on the stove over high heat. While you wait for the water to come to a boil, ready your vegetables. Wash thoroughly and then roughly chop: an onion, skin on; a leek, white and green parts both; a couple of unpeeled carrots; two ribs of celery; and a small head of fennel.

WHEN THE WATER IS BOILING, use a ladle or spoon to skim off any foam that may have accumulated at the surface and discard. Add the vegetables and turn down the flame to a simmer. Add a head of garlic, shorn of just its outermost skin, cut crosswise as if along an invisible equator. Add a few bay leaves, a small bunch of parsley, a couple of sprigs of thyme, a small handful of peppercorns, a couple of pinches of dried fennel seeds, and a few allspice and dried juniper berries. (You can make a stock with just a chicken and an onion and some salt, so a lot of these additions are not strictly necessary, so much as a way to nuance the flavor. I'm a maximalist in this regard: a pungent stock will make for a more layered soup, a more deeply flavorful risotto.) Use a spoon to stir the aromatics in. Allow the stock to simmer for 2 hours or thereabouts, and for no more than 3 hours total (overcooking the bones will make the broth cloudy). After an hour it will begin to smell fragrant. Taste it at this juncture to determine its doneness; more cooking will intensify the flavor as it reduces. Turn off the flame when it's ready and allow to cool completely; then strain the liquid through a fine mesh sieve. Use immediately, store in the fridge for up to 4 days, or freeze for use in a future recipe (such as risotto).

My Mom's Garlicky Noodle Soup

TO MAKE A SIMPLE, deeply comforting chicken noodle soup like the one my mom—in truth, moms everywhere—always made for me when I was sick, you'll need little besides the chicken stock (page 57), a head of garlic, some dry pasta, and a bunch of parsley. My mom always repeated, like a mantra, that "garlic is as good as ten mothers," a phrase cemented in her consciousness, no doubt, by Les Blank's 1980 documentary of that same name, in which she and Chez Panisse featured heavily. Intended as an homage to this most indispensable allium, *Garlic Is as Good as Ten Mothers* displayed stretches of footage filmed at the restaurant during preparations for its annual Fête de l'Ail, celebrated on the fourteenth of July, Bastille Day. The garlicophilia, however, extends to our home, where meals are rarely undertaken without at least a half or full head of garlic coming into play. I start to feel slightly anxious when I have anything less than a basketful of firm, fresh heads of garlic in the kitchen—and in general, I tend to be more paranoid about running out of garlic than toilet paper.

TO MAKE THE SIMPLEST VERSION of this soup for 2 to 4 people, combine a cup or two of cooked noodles, a minced head of garlic, and a chopped bunch of parsley in a pot of simmering chicken stock, removing after a minute or two when the garlic is just blanched and the flavors have had a moment to marry. You can also, of course, embroider a bit. One option is to add poached chicken. In some chicken stock, simmer a chicken breast or thigh until completely cooked and the flesh is yielding, then shred the chicken and add the pieces to the pot with the cooked noodles, garlic, and herbs. You can also enrich it with an elaborated mirepoix (which you would make first): dice a peeled carrot, a rib of celery, an onion, a small peeled parsnip, a bit of a fennel bulb, and a couple of cloves of garlic and melt in olive oil in a heavy-bottomed pan over medium heat until fragrant and semitranslucent. Then add it to the stock along with the cooked noodles, the shredded chicken, the freshly minced garlic, and the parsley (maybe even some chopped dill too), warm everything together, and serve with a slice of Garlic Toast (page 71).

CHAPTER 8

Salad

I was trying to get away with talking about salad only elliptically: mentions here and there, embedded in the context of other more narratively substantive stories, but there came a point when I had to accept that salad deserves its own chapter. It is, after all, my mother's answer whenever someone asks her to name her favorite food. And whether by inheritance or influence, I've taken to responding to that question with an identical reply. It has also always been at the core of her appraisal of me as a child; whenever she was asked about her offspring's culinary predilections, she would say, with more than a measure of relief, "At least I got a kid who likes salad."

Salad is the one thing whose absence is most felt whenever we're traveling to "salad deserts" (Mexico, for instance, or Japan). We could be eating the best food on earth, but after four days without roughage, we emit a lot of moaning and begin discussing our unquenchable yen for a simple green salad as if the yearning were news of grave political import. *A simple green salad* is incidentally also the exact phrase my mother has uttered on hundreds of occasions, both at home and abroad, whenever she's trying to order something that is conspicuously absent from a given menu. "Do you perhaps have, you know, *a simple green salad*?" "I'm sorry, what do you want, ma'am?" "Oh, you know, maybe just a few leaves? Vinaigrette on the side?" This innocent-enough request is often met with bafflement (who goes to a restaurant to eat *salad*?), or, worse, with a plate of chopped iceberg littered with parched grated carrot and wan slices of out-of-season tomato. On a recent trip to Sicily, for instance, not even the finest establishments seemed to stock so much as a single head of lettuce, never mind that every stall at the adjacent vegetable market was brimming with a dozen varieties.

No amount of disappointment delivered at restaurants ever proved a deterrent, however; ordering a green salad, regardless of whether it was listed on the menu, became a kind of litmus test for a given establishment. But not because my mother was trying to catch out the cooks at said establishments—she really just *wanted a salad!* Still, if a restaurant can deliver a plate of crisp, beautiful leaves, dressed in the correct amount of balsamic-free dressing, that restaurant will very likely skyrocket in our family's estimation, even if every other dish proves unremarkable. Which, I think, is one of the reasons that Chez Panisse has always kept a green salad on the menu. Not only is it what my mother most craves to order when she visits other restaurants, it's also a very straightforward way for Chez to telegraph its central values. Even the humblest dish on the menu is special: a heap of leaves from Bob Cannard (arguably the best farmer in North America) dressed in a scant quantity of perfectly acid-balanced classic vinaigrette . . . and for only ten dollars! Whenever we eat downstairs, the chefs know to make an extra-large helping of the leaves that accompany the main dish on the prix fixe menu. A supplementary bowl of the beautiful tiny greens reserved for the downstairs restaurant arrives at our table like clockwork a few minutes after we've begun tucking into our quail. It's always our favorite part of the meal.

Even though the green salad is a mainstay of the upstairs café menu, the bulk of our salad-eating occurs at home, where readying lettuce for a meal is a highly ritualized undertaking. I think we *had* a salad spinner when I was younger, but it was treated with some degree of contempt and, in my memory, rarely used. Instead, my mother would place an enormous bowl—and next to it an enormous footed colander (collected at some flea market somewhere)—in the center of our even more enormous copper kitchen sink. To properly dislodge dirt from actually dirty lettuce, you can't just give it a rinse; it needs to soak in a bath or it will be gritty—and there is nothing worse than crunching into some sand when you're halfway through a plate of salad. If you have a (clean) kitchen sink, it's easiest to just plug it up and use it as the basin, but a large bowl works well too.

Once the lettuce has soaked for long enough (with the water having been renewed once, maybe twice, depending on its grubbiness), my mom will transfer it to the colander to drain. When enough water is cast off, the whole of the butcher block is covered with dish towels and a layer of lettuce scattered across them, followed by another layer of

dish towels on top. Each towel-lettuce "sandwich" is—in my favorite step of all—rolled up into a bundle, as if the lettuce were a filling of cinnamon and sugar in a roll of dough destined for morning buns. This salad baby, as I referred to it when I was small, is then tenderly transported to the refrigerator to await its cameo in the meal (always near the end). There, in that chilly cavity, the towels do the work of absorbing any remaining moisture, with the cool ensuring that the leaves arrive crisp and dry to the table. There is no greater enemy of vinaigrette than damp leaves, and this patience-requiring method is the best way to guarantee they are completely dry.

Though I engage in this practice at my mom's house and find it especially good for large meals necessitating that a ton of salad be washed, I'm not an obsessive traditionalist: I own and regularly use one of those din-generating OXO salad spinners. I've even been known to gift them to friends whose kitchens are, in my opinion, underequipped. I once brokered a "deal" with a friend at whose house I often cooked: I would buy us a pair of extremely pricey and coveted concert tickets if he would just buy a decent salad spinner. It was, I think, a win-win for him. When it comes to salad-spinner-free homes, the Brits are often the worst, but only because so much of their produce is delivered beneath a film of plastic. Whole grocery store aisles exist in which you can't pick something up to smell or feel it unhindered by an impermeable barrier of plastic. Sanitized, deoxygenated bags of lettuce are the norm, so the idea of dismantling a head of lettuce and discovering enough grit clinging to its innermost arteries to require a thorough wash (and dry) has become a foreign concept. And even if that bagged lettuce hasn't been prewashed, no one ever seems to think twice about just dumping it straight into a bowl. I left a trail of salad spinners (and salad-spinning converts) in every shared home I lived in in England.

I love salad so much that it's the thing that many friends most associate with my cooking, and also the thing that certain partners have come to gently resent. Because anyone who's eaten more than once at my table will tell you that I am unable to make the "correct" amount of salad—I *always* overshoot the mark. It's not uncommon for me to make as much as four times as much salad as might be required for a given number of guests, and because salad doesn't keep once it's dressed, what ensues is colloquially known among my friends as "Fanny's salad torture," in which I force additional helpings of salad onto all guests—self included—until a dish everyone initially enjoyed becomes a kind of agony. It's hard for me to not project my own lettuce lust onto others, but I will grant that not everyone grew up with a mother whose favorite food was *a simple green salad.*

CHAPTER 9

The Lunchbox

I would say it was around age ten or eleven, when I was about to enter middle school or just before, that my school lunch situation went from being more or less normal (peanut butter and banana sandwiches; celery and almond butter dotted with raisins—ants on a log) to what amounted to completely bonkers acts of culinary prowess. In retrospect, this may have had something to do with the fact that my parents were separating around then, but, from a child's perspective, it just seemed like my mom had gotten *really into* making lunch. My father moved fairly swiftly into a new romantic partnership; my mother committed herself fanatically to my lunchbox.

My brown paper bag was deposed. In its stead arrived a soft-cooler creature so aesthetically offensive that I'm frankly amazed she could tolerate the sight of it long enough to insert its prandial contents. It says a lot about my mom's obsession with keeping certain foods at cool temperatures that she admitted this insulated red synthetic sack into a kitchen otherwise visibly devoid of plastics, or for that matter any shiny metal or other material invented after the Industrial Revolution. I won't pretend I had just the one cooler bag from middle school through to my departure for college; I lost the damned thing every other week. It was so big! So ugly! And because it was weighted down with ice packs and Tupperware and actual silverware, it was as heavy

as the carry-on bag you'd take for a long weekend trip. I think pretty much the only things my mom purchased from the Longs Drugs down the street from Chez Panisse were those lunchboxes. I remember one evening when we pulled into the parking lot for a drive-by: she didn't even get out of the car; she just handed me a twenty and said, "Get three of them this time! I'm sick of driving over here."

For obvious reasons, reporters and other admirers of my mother have found the subject of the contents of my school lunchbox endlessly fascinating. And understandably. We're talking about the kid of the woman who has made it her life goal to feed a free school lunch to every child in America. Still, those lunches *were* genuinely remarkable—the product of a very dedicated bit of mothering by someone who takes her role as mom very seriously.

My lunches were not broken into courses so much as they were divided into multiple parts. There was a largish container that held a salad, a medium container for garlic bread (levain toast rubbed with olive oil and garlic), another for a seasonal fruit compote or macédoine, a very small jar with a vinaigrette because, of course, we were both aware of the perils of prematurely dressing the salad. If she wasn't sure I was going to be wild for the anchovy dressing she'd made the night before (I hated anchovies as a child and would eat them only in highly camouflaged form), she'd provide an alternative along with an explanatory note: "I know, I know, you hate anchovies, but try it! You might like it! But *just in case* you don't, there's some regular vinaigrette in there too. Love, M."

Anchovy Vinaigrette

POUND A LARGE CLOVE OF GARLIC with a big pinch of sea salt in a mortar and pestle or Japanese suribachi. Rinse and debone a salt- or oil-packed anchovy, and add a single fillet to the mortar (you can add a second fillet if you prefer the dressing on the more pungent side). Grind to a paste with the garlic and add a teaspoon of lemon juice and a teaspoon of champagne or white wine vinegar. Allow the ingredients to macerate in the bowl of the mortar for several minutes. Use a fork to whisk in a few glugs of extra virgin olive oil (about 2:1 oil to acid) and a generous showering of freshly ground pepper. For a more Caesar-inflected sauce, add a tablespoon of finely grated Parmesan. As long as the word *anchovy* doesn't come up in the description of this dressing, most children will happily eat it.

Herby Chicken Paillard Lunchbox Sandwich

THIS IS A VERSION of a sandwich my mother made for my lunch every other week—it was my favorite of the lunchbox items on rotation for a stretch in the late nineties. In high school I had to be at the North Berkeley BART station just before seven o'clock in the morning to make it to class in San Francisco by eight. I'm pretty sure she made this sandwich at least in part because the pounding out of the chicken breast required for a paillard would always rattle me from bed. If you do plan on making this for a lunchbox, you can make it the night before and keep it in the refrigerator overnight. Likewise with the aioli, since making it from scratch—even for the most expert and confident among us—is still a somewhat time-consuming and nerve-racking exercise. But even if you have doubts about making aioli yourself, I recommend making this sandwich just once with it—aioli makes everything it touches infinitely more delicious. If you fear the reward will be too brief, I promise there will be enough for leftover aioli (which will last for days in the fridge).

TO MAKE AIOLI, bring 1 egg up to room temperature. (If you're in a hurry, immerse it in warm water for 10 minutes or so.) Pound 2 garlic cloves with a pinch of salt in a mortar until smooth. Separate the egg and put the yolk in a medium-sized metal bowl, setting aside the white for another use. Add about half of the garlic to the yolk and mix well with a whisk. Fill a liquid measuring cup with 1 cup of good-quality olive oil, though it doesn't necessarily need to be extra virgin. Slowly dribble the oil into the yolk mixture, whisking constantly. Continue at a slow, drip-by-drip pace for the first ¼ cup of olive oil, whisking all the while, so that the yolk absorbs the oil, thickening and lightening in color. If it becomes too thick to whisk, thin the yolk mixture with a few drops of warm water. Continue to add oil until the entire cup has been incorporated, thinning with water as many times as necessary. Add a few drops of lemon juice or champagne vinegar and taste, adding more salt or garlic if you desire. If you're making this well ahead of using, cover and refrigerate.

ONE CHICKEN BREAST provides more than enough meat to prepare one large sandwich or two modest ones. Remove the skin, and, if there is a bone, use a sharp knife to remove that too. Place the chicken breast skin-side down. Remove the tenderloin—the small piece of meat attached to the breast. Set aside. Butterfly the breast by using a sharp knife to make an incision down the entire right length of the breast, halfway between the center line and the edge. The knife should enter at a slight angle, about 45 degrees, and stop about ⅓ inch short of the underside of the breast that's resting on the cutting board. Repeat this process on the left side, halfway between the center line and the edge. Open up the flaps that you've created. Prepared this way, the breast will flatten more evenly and easily.

COVER THE MEAT with baking parchment or plastic wrap and use a smooth mallet or any heavy flat object (like a small cast-iron pan) to pound the chicken until it's ¼ inch thick. Go at an easy pace and with moderate force in order to prevent the breast from tearing. When it feels even in thickness, remove the plastic or parchment and place the chicken on a plate. Season it with salt and pepper and set it aside while you prepare any combination of herbs you like. I favor brighter herbs for this—1 tablespoon finely chopped parsley and 1 teaspoon finely chopped marjoram make for a savory yet fresh flavor. In colder months, a little rosemary, together with the parsley, is a nice alternative. Dry the chicken with a paper towel if it has let off any moisture from the salt, and then rub it with the herbs on both sides.

WARM A SKILLET over medium heat for a few minutes. Sauté the chicken in a little oil, flipping after 2 to 3 minutes, and cooking on the second side for just as long, or until cooked through. Remove from heat until ready to assemble the sandwich.

TOAST 2 SLICES of rustic levain bread or focaccia-like "pizza bianca." Rub one side of each with a cut garlic clove and slather generously with aioli. Place the cooked chicken on one piece of toast, pile it with arugula that's dressed with a little lemon juice and a pinch of salt, and top with the other piece of toast.

IF YOU'RE MAKING THIS FOR A LUNCHBOX, make sure to let the garlic-rubbed toast and chicken cool entirely and refrain from dressing the arugula. In this manner, the integrity of the sandwich will be preserved until lunchtime. A simple rub of garlic and a drizzle of good olive oil on each side of the bread is a good alternative to aioli (and, in fact, is the only kind of "garlic bread" we ever serve in our house). And if you want to forgo the bread altogether, the chicken, with or without the aioli, makes a great meal on top of brightly dressed salad greens.

Garlic Toast

ANOTHER LUNCHBOX STAPLE was the very simple and, in our home, ubiquitous garlic toast that accompanied virtually every meal. It's the simplest thing to make, but it still seems to blow the minds of the uninitiated. It even garnered me popularity in the high school cafeteria, when, by all counts, it should have been doing the exact opposite. Everyone wanted in on my lunch. To make garlic toast, use whatever bread you like—we always default to a rye-heavy Acme pain au levain— and cut it into approximately ½-inch slices. Toast it until it's browned, then rub immediately and vigorously with a halved clove of garlic. Splash extra virgin olive oil generously over top and sprinkle with a touch of sea salt to finish.

Fruit Macédoine

SOME VERSION OF THIS MACEDOINE, or fruit salad, was likewise in heavy lunchbox rotation, but it is also a regular dessert at our table. People never think they want to eat a fruit salad after a meal until they try it, but they often find that it makes an incredibly satisfying, flavorful alternative to a heavier, sweeter, or richer finish. The most important feature of a good macédoine is, of course, the fruit. And fruit is always, always best when it's in its peak season. The most delicious concoctions are the summer ones, when soft fruit, and especially strawberries, are plentiful. In the winter, I make citrus macédoines by sectioning blood oranges, grapefruits, tangerines, pomelos. It's nice to always have a variety of colors (pink *and* white grapefruit, say, or both navel *and* blood oranges—one of each of the nicest-looking fruits at the market). Sometimes I cheat a bit and add passion fruit pulp (when *are* passion fruit in season, anyway?! It's a mystery!) to lubricate the mix. Likewise, a bit of lemon zest and juice encourage the fruit to sweat and the juices to meld. The liquid is key. It's what makes this dessert feel more special than a cup of dry cubed fruit.

IN BANDOL RECENTLY, when my mom and I were visiting Lulu Peyraud at Domaine Tempier in the South of France, I picked a basket of loquats (known as *néfliers* in France) from her tree. Lulu gave me a dirty look—she considers them a second-rate fruit and ate them only during the war when supplies were scarce. I persisted, however, with this idea of making a lemony loquat macédoine and carefully peeled, deseeded, and sliced their flesh into small crescents. I rarely add sugar of any kind, but when you're dealing with fruit of higher acidity levels, some sweetener is necessary. The loquats absolutely needed honey, as, occasionally, less sweet berries will, but the flavor of the honey you select—nothing too distinctive—can give a nice roundness to the fruit. Even Lulu approved.

A FEW TIPS: Strawberries, in particular, love a little lemon juice. They can also be steeped with a few bruised leaves of rose geranium or fresh lemon verbena (removed just before serving). If the strawberries are not especially flavorful, I'll buy an extra pint to cook down into a quick jam to mix into the sliced fresh ones. If they really need something to lift them, a tablespoon or two of high quality rose syrup is a lovely addition. Many people don't know that strawberries are in fact part of the rose family (Rosaceae), and I think this has something to do with why those two flavors pair so beautifully. If I'm serving a strawberry macédoine for dessert, I love to top it with a generous spoonful of soft, subtly sweet, rose-scented whipped cream. For a "high summer" variation, blanch ripe peaches to slip their skins off, slice into lovely crescents, and douse them in a bit of sweet white Beaumes-de-Venise, or toss them in lemon and drizzle with blackberry syrup.

∙ ∙ ∙

When my mom and dad went away for a week-long trip once, when I was about eleven, they left a single page of bulleted rules, some straightforward ("No television until homework is completed"), others a little more parochial ("Rented videos must be 'something of value'"), but the clincher was the lengthy section dedicated to pack-

RULES OF THE GAME

1. No phone between 9:30pm - 9:30am

2. Desk should always be in order & bed made everyday (check)

3. Homework done <u>before</u> the phone (Check)

4. Healthful snack in the afternoon except one day a week

5. Fanny must be home *exactly on time* - be sure you know where she is going & with whom -have phone numbers (no Telegraph Avenue)

6. No TV on weekdays & limit on weekends

7. Videos must be approved - get "something of value"at the video store

8. Respectful of adults and teachers always

9. Fanny to bed at 9:30 - 10:00pm and up at 7:00am on weekdays

FOOD

      PICANTE - use family card
      CHEZ PANISSE - call and reserve with the host in the cafe @
       4:30pm 548.5049
      BERKELEY NATURAL FOODS - (On Gilman)
       Strauss nonfat milk
       The best selection of oraganic fruits & vegetables
       Lowfat cottage cheese

BREAKFAST

      Nothing too sweet   Cream of wheat
      She likes: half a grapefruit   Poached egg on toast
      Rice & Shine   Orange juice
      Shredded wheat w/ bananas   Bananas in milk

LUNCH

salad	applesauce	garlic toast	vinaigrette
lettuces from Kona Kai	kiwi in orange juice	ham sandwich-	
carrots	wedges of orange	on toast	
radishes	lowfat cottage cheese	leftover pizza	
avocado		pizza from Chez	
cucumbers		tortilla chips	

ing my lunch. This thing was drafted and printed in the early days of the personal computer. We didn't have a computer; in fact, I wasn't even aware that my mom could type—until, that is, I was presented with this list of rules at my twenty-first birthday by the very woman to whom I had been entrusted a decade earlier. Despite the clean type-written format, there were actual diagrams to scale of Tupperware containers. Under each little container—rendered in surprisingly accurate perspective—potential contents were painstakingly detailed. Needless to say, had I been presented with such a list of instructions at the beginning of some period of babysitting tenure, I too would have held on to it, to gift to the child in question at some important coming-of-age moment, along with a note: "Your mother cared A LOT about your lunch."

I hated that cooler sack lunchbox, fitted with its chunky shoulder strap that made it look as if I were going on some sort of corporate camping trip, and I did regularly leave that thing on the bus or on the commuter train that I took to high school every day, but I *loved* those lunches. Far from resulting in my ostracization as "the nerdy kid with the briefcase-sized lunchbox packed by Mommy," I became quite popular at lunch hour. Friends would clamor for morsels of gar-lic bread or carrot curls plucked from my salad, or would beg for a strawberry when the first of the heady 'Mara des Bois' arrived in my lunch. Some days, if she'd happen to have ventured into the back gar-den for some herbs, my mom would harvest a few scented flowers, a Meyer lemon blossom, a few rosebuds, some lemon balm, which she'd twine together to make what she called a nosegay—a heavenly scented little bouquet that would make my plastic cooler not merely a container but a portal to a drenched spring garden or the shelves of a Parisian *parfumier*. These were not ordinary school lunches. Still, I don't feel them to be irreproducible. Given the desire, any lunchbox maker can transform a mundane midday meal into something deli-cious and transporting.

Lunchbox
Nosegay

IF YOU HAVE A BACK GARDEN or live near a flowering park or even just have a few pots on your sill, you can easily make a special little spirit-lifting bouquet for a friend, a child, or yourself, to tuck into a lunch sack. Nothing improves a day like having something beautifully scented to inhale every now and then. My understanding is that nosegays entered the scene during a time (circa the seventeenth century) when bathing was not common practice and the smells of the city were—in the absence of modern plumbing and general civic infrastructure—on the ranker end of the spectrum. A little sweet-smelling bouquet might therefore be pinned in the vicinity of the face to provide much-needed olfactory interference. Of course a nice rose'll do the trick, but I especially love the greener, earthier smells of things like marjoram, oregano, lovage, verbena, mint, rose geranium, and rosemary. And nothing smells better than citrus blossoms; if you can find a sprig of those, I promise you anyone sitting near you will want to join you for lunch.

CHAPTER 10

Pat's Pancakes

My mother's parents moved to Berkeley from Southern California in the late sixties, following their westward migration from New Jersey to Los Angeles (via Indiana) when my mom was in high school. By the time I belatedly arrived on the scene (I think they'd given up hope my mom would have a child until my father swooped in at the eleventh hour), they were of that age that some people attain as early as seventy and *re*tain for the balance of their lives. Which is to say, from seventy to ninety-one, my grandparents were that vague thing we call elderly. Still, they were rather spry and, despite not seeming to me to be exactly youthful, were actively involved in my early life. I spent enough time in their mid-century time capsule of a home in the Berkeley Hills to have felt completely at ease there, even fluent in its quirks. The loose brick, say, that would send you tumbling down a few stairs in the terraced back garden. The reassuring smell of the Noxema cold cream my grandmother would slather on her face nightly and remove with a damp washcloth. The nubbly, slightly scratchy texture of the seventies-era textile in which every furnishing in their household was upholstered. The sublime view of the silvery bay from the vast picture window in the living room on a white-hot afternoon. And the cirrus clouds over the distant Golden Gate Bridge, like tails of galloping horses whisked into articulated tangles that my grandmother made paintings of, their pale tangerine hues at sunset rendered in her lovely amateur watercolors.

Whenever I arrived there for a sleepover, I made an immediate pilgrimage to the upstairs hallway to pay homage at the shrine to retro femininity: four silver gelatin portraits of my mother and her three sisters, each snapped at their respective high school graduations. I was transfixed by their beauty; there was something otherworldly about their composure, but then also about their coifs and their clothing. My mother wore her hair in a blond beehive, a string of pearls ringing her neck, her perfect demi-smile, skin radiantly silver toned, surrounded by her beautiful sisters, all eternally eighteen years old.

On overnight occasions, my grandfather would make pancakes in the morning. My grandmother had been a longtime follower of health food trends, even back in the fifties when such things were viewed with suspicion and bacon and eggs were considered salubrious. She also kept a "victory garden" when my mom was little and endeavored to feed her family from it as much as possible. Still, like all housewives of her time, she was a victim of the postwar commodification of foodstuffs and was indoctrinated in a form of cooking that made ready use of the newly marketed culinary "conveniences." While my mother went from sampling French country cooking more or less straight to innovating proto farm-to-table fare (she could not abide the brown rice and lentil "hippie stews" of the ubiquitous sixties communes), my grandparents' conversion to an increasingly healthful diet in their older age took them by default to the sometimes wan bulk and health food aisles of those few grocers championing early versions of "organic."

Which brings us back to the pancakes. My grandfather's pancakes were no ordinary pancakes. These were superfood pancakes before *superfood* was a word in common currency. Chock-full of wheat germ and whole grain flours and maybe powdered skim milk and yogurt and definitely grated apple and mashed banana, they resembled absolutely nothing purveyed at my own house down the hill. I loved them. My grandfather and I would always make them together, meticulously measuring and then sifting all of the dry ingredients, carefully decanting the milk (could it have even been soy?) into the wet measuring cups. They were distinguished by the addition of banana, whose sugars would caramelize upon contact with the hot pan and redeem any amount of wheat germ or other criminally nutritious ingredients. The final step before cooking, which was my favorite, was to fold the beaten egg whites (frothed to glossy peaks with one of those old-fashioned eggbeaters I'm sure they'd had for more than forty years) carefully into the wet batter. This folding process required all of my focus and restraint, since I was—and remain—by nature a hasty and impatient cook. My grandfather, by contrast, was a picture of prudence—in cooking and in life. If I was folding too violently and risking the deflation of the carefully aerated whites, he would softly place his hand over my smaller one and guide the wooden spoon into gentler motions. This process meant that the batter would be striated with fluffed whites, which in turn guaranteed an utterly pillowy pancake. I don't know if my mom learned this trick of separating the eggs and beating the whites from her father, but she always insisted on it at home if she ever made pancakes, which was rarely, and only ever from a mix (but not Bisquick! It came from Bette's Oceanview Diner down on Fourth Street). To this day, I don't know why she didn't make them fully from scratch—I think maybe she was under the impression that they were more complicated to produce and required more "baking skills" than in fact they do. I really learned that you could make pancakes as easily as a bowl of cereal only when I was eighteen. A family friend gave me a recipe that called for nothing more than a cup of flour, a cup of milk, some baking soda, an egg (no whisking of whites required), and a pat of liquefied butter. The result was just as tasty as the labored pancakes of my youth. I've since become the pancake authority in our house, which is hardly that illustrious a title. It simply means that whenever I'm home, my mom requests some version of Fanny's Pancakes. They do not contain wheat germ.

Still, there was something legitimately special about my grandpa's pancakes, which I miss dearly. And not just because they were invariably served with tiny links of organic chicken-and-apple sausage on the side—a flavor so indelible I can conjure its taste just by writing the sentence. I would always take a little sausage in my fingers, wrap it in one of those golden-brown pancakes like an oversize duvet, pronounce it a "pig in a blanket," and pop it into my mouth. Absolutely no maple syrup allowed! This was a sugar-free household!

Pat's Pancakes

Breakfast
Sausage

THERE WAS NEVER even the slightest gesture toward homemade sausage-making in my grandparents' house—we only ever ate tiny little organic chicken-apple links that my grandmother kept in the freezer. It is, however, quite easy to make tasty sausage patties at home (and a lot harder to acquire and prep casings and make links). All you need, basically, is some variety of ground meat, preferably not super lean. My preference is for pork—it's by far the tastiest—though my grandparents would never have permitted it. Still, this recipe is more about capturing the spirit of those fondly recalled breakfasts, so I've made some allowances here. You can experiment with whatever you like, subbing easy-to-find ground turkey for pork, for instance. As for spices, a good amount of salt is key—additional seasonings are nice but not necessary. I like to use strong flavors like smoked paprika, ground coriander, fennel seed, black pepper, and chopped fresh rosemary or sage (though not all at once). Regardless of what spices I'm using, however, I always cook off about a tablespoon's worth of sausage mixture to taste and, if necessary, correct the seasoning before committing to the cooking of a whole batch of patties.

TO MAKE PORK-APPLE BREAKFAST SAUSAGE, start by heating a couple of tablespoons of oil in a large skillet over medium-low heat. Add a diced small yellow onion and cook, stirring, until it begins to soften and grow translucent. Add a small apple that's been peeled, cored, and cut into a tiny, uniform dice (I like Gala or Gravenstein for this recipe) and cook, stirring, for another few minutes until the apple also begins to yield and grow soft. If the onion is beginning to burn, add a tablespoon of water. Once the onion-apple mixture is very tender, transfer it to a large bowl and allow to cool completely. To this bowl, add 1 pound of ground organic pork, one very finely chopped small leaf of fresh sage, 1 tablespoon of maple syrup, ½ teaspoon of chopped fennel seeds, 1 scant teaspoon of sea salt, a tiny pinch of nutmeg, and a lot of freshly ground pepper. Using your hands, mix thoroughly for a minute or so until the meat begins to grow tacky and sticks to your fingers. Divide the sausage meat into 10 patties, about 2¼ inches in diameter. Place the patties on a plate and refrigerate for 30 minutes to an hour. When ready to cook, turn the heat to medium and generously coat your cast-iron skillet with olive oil. When the pan is hot but not smoking, add the patties, leaving some space between them. Cook the patties for about 3 to 4 minutes per side until they are browned and cooked through, turning down the heat if you suspect they might be burning. Drain briefly on a towel and serve with Pat's Pancakes!

.　.　.

When I was very small, maybe three or four, my grandfather was occasionally tapped to collect me at my preschool, an idyllic Montessori-esque place called Duck's Nest. After collection, he would take me back to my house, and if it was the correct season, my mom would prepare my favorite snack: a bowlful of freshly shelled lightly steamed peas, crowned with a tiny bit of salted butter. In retrospect, I think she had to outsource the school pickup because she was at home shelling peas. This might not be something that takes *forever*, but it certainly isn't a speedy task. Still, I remember this well because the peas were sublimely delicious, the sweet buttery green orbs each bursting as I ate through a bowl of them, always at an excruciatingly slow speed. In general, I'm not a slow eater—I love food and eat with gusto—but, in this instance, I was beyond measured. This is because my pea-eating was accompanied by my grandfather's reading me a story, and I wanted the peas to last exactly as long as the reading. Given that at this point in my life I could not myself read, I relied on the thickness of the selected book to dictate the pace at which I would consume this snack. Slim volumes: whole heaping spoonfuls of peas at a time. Weightier volumes: as few as two, maybe three peas per bite. Passages from *The Hobbit* required single-pea servings. Even though it does take a small eternity to shell enough peas for a big bowl of *just peas,* I do think it's worth the effort from time to time. There is a very distinct kind of pleasure in eating generous mouthfuls of something you know requires labor, especially when the product is as sweet and tender and delicious as fresh spring peas. Of course, it didn't occur to me at the time, but the memory has stayed with me for decades, and over years of reflecting on that moment, I've come to realize that it was just another way—however conscious or not—my mom telegraphed to me the extent of her love. Nothing seemed to disappoint my mother more, when we'd Skype during my British dinnertime, than for her to discover I was having a solo meal of frozen peas that I'd cooked with a bit of butter. They pale in comparison to the fresh peas of my youth, but I'm going to stand by frozen peas—they're not bad in a pinch.

When I was a touch older and could make it through books on my own, the diversionary activity of choice was Scrabble, a game the Waters clan has been obsessed with for so long I can't remember a family gathering in which several boards weren't spread around surrounded by quartets of intensely competitive players. When I was a child, the desire to win before I had a true grasp of strategy—or, for that matter, spelling—led to a fair amount of cheating on my part. At one point, at the age of seven, I had a full-fledged tantrum when my grandmother foiled my chance to put down the seven-letter word *pharaoh,* make my first bingo, and earn that coveted extra 50 points that comes with voiding your tile rack of all of your letters in one go. I've since eschewed the cheating, but the competitiveness remains, no doubt inherited from my mother, whose appetite for the game of Scrabble (she plays against the computer on her iPhone during any idle moment) is rivaled only by her desire to *win* at Scrabble. She is ruthlessly strategic, endlessly "inventive" when it comes to neologizing vocabulary (taunting me to look it up if I wish to challenge her), and, despite fifty-odd years of the game under her belt, refuses to memorize the full list of two-letter words (mainly, I think, to allow her to continue to at least *try* to play ones that don't exist). For your information, *ai is* in fact a word, but no, it's not an abbreviation for *arti-*

ficial intelligence; rather, it's defined by the Scrabble Dictionary as a three-toed sloth—go figure. If you're wondering what a vacation with my mother looks like, picture at least three hours of playing Scrabble, interrupted only by discussions relating to the preparation of lunch or dinner, and my mother behaving like a merciless shark, glass of rosé in hand. For this great tradition of cutthroat board gaming, we have my impossibly sweet maternal grandparents to thank; I'm certain they couldn't have anticipated the fallout, but I wouldn't have it any other way.

When my grandparents were put in charge of an after-school pickup—from about third grade onward—I would head to their house up in the hills with them. This would usually include an after-school snack and possibly even an evening meal, and sprouts would invariably be involved. Sprouts of all varieties were a mainstay of their kitchen—they worked themselves into almost everything I ate there. The two most memorable sprout-focused recipes (if they can even be called that) were a piece of sprouted (of course) whole wheat toast slathered in unsweetened almond butter and topped with that crunchy variety of sprout mix I think largely involves brazenly raw beans and lentils. The other was a *highly customized* pizza from a pizzeria in Berkeley called La Val's (a nostalgic Northside local opened in 1951). My grandparents would call in a takeout order for a "whole wheat vegetarian pizza, no cheese, no chili, no salt." Once we had fetched it and returned to the Campus Drive pad, we'd apply so many alfalfa sprouts to its surface as to erase any evidence of an underlying pie. I took a certain amount of pride in freighting my slice with an especially heavy load of sprouts, something like a 5:1 ratio of sprout to crust that required extra dexterity in the maneuvering from plate to mouth. Amazingly, the abundance of sprouts on offer at my grandparents' house did not ignite in me a hatred of the ingredient. In fact, about eight years ago, during a summer in New York City, I started making my own sprouts in a specialized jar with a perforated lid. I ate a version of my grandmother's after-school snack nearly every morning for breakfast.

Should you wish to sample this weirdly delicious hippie "bruschetta" (let's generously call it), I would strongly recommend you pick up one of those jars designed for sprouting and growing your own (they taste so much better than the variety that's been languishing in the refrigerated aisle of Whole Foods). Making sprouts is also—for someone like myself who lacks a green thumb—an exceptionally gratifying experience; they basically make themselves! You just soak whatever seeds or beans you like and rinse them daily in fresh water for three or five days. Then, as if by magic, they germinate and become edible. My favorite combination includes a measure of fenugreek seeds, because even if my colleagues at the Morgan Library that summer wanted to kill me for smelling like a spice aisle, fenugreek adds a rich, heady, and intensely savory edge to the mix. I also like to use adzuki beans, small green lentils, and mung beans. I prefer rye toast to my grandmother's presliced whole wheat, but any bread-like surface will do (even a robust cracker in a pinch), so long as you cover said surface in more almond butter than she would have, calorically speaking, approved of. Blanket with a liberal coating of sprouts—which can be satisfyingly pressed into the nut butter—and follow with a big sprinkle of sea salt and freshly ground black pepper. I promise, it's better than it sounds.

CHAPTER 11

Egg in the Spoon

One of the ways I could tell if my mom liked a boyfriend I'd brought home was how readily she volunteered to make said boyfriend an egg cooked in the fireplace. For sure, it was no insignificant undertaking to build a fire, coax the logs to a perfect smolder, construct a little "salamander" oven to distribute the heat from all sides, and then finally balance an egg in a long-handled spoon above the coals until the egg had puffed into a perfect, crisped, soufflé-like breakfast confection. But it wasn't just the specialness of the egg that indicated the measure of my mother's approval. It was also an opportunity, if she found my suitor particularly charming, for her to do a little coquettish, peacock-like performance. I can see her now, eyes slightly downcast as she serves the young man his lacy-around-the-edges egg atop a piece of garlic-rubbed toast—which always seemed to emerge from the toaster at precisely the correct moment to receive the egg. Oh, and never without a little side of leaves dressed in her homemade red wine vinegar, maybe with a slivered radish or two, a curl of radish leaf still attached.

I was born more than twelve years into the life of Chez Panisse, so I have only historical accounts to go on regarding what the restaurant was like in the early days, or, of even greater interest to me, what my mother was like as a younger woman. Problematically, where acuity of memory is concerned, many of the players in question were too drunk, high, or otherwise cerebrally altered—it was the seventies!—to have committed much in the way of non-hazy recollection to their mental hard drives. I was at lunch in Paris recently with my mother; my godmother, Martine; her husband, Claude; and their daughter, Camille. Martine and Claude lived in Berkeley in the early seventies while Claude undertook a postdoc in mathematics at UC Berkeley; his wife, Martine, an artist and exquisite home cook, was one of my mom's earliest collaborators (she co-wrote and illustrated *Chez Panisse Pasta, Pizza & Calzone*). During their time in Berkeley, Camille was born, very shortly before the opening of the restaurant in 1971. The dialogue over lunch went something like this:

MOM Were you both at dinner on the opening night?

MARTINE *Mais, bien sûr!* You don't remember, Alice?!?

MOM It was all a bit of a blur that night . . .

CLAUDE We *were* there?? *T'es sûr, Martine?*

MOM No, no, I remember, you were *definitely* there, Claude! Remember, we served duck *aux olives*!

CLAUDE Yes! Yes! That duck! Of course! How could I forget?

CAMILLE So, hold on, I must have been, what, a few months old when the restaurant opened? What did you do with me? Where was I?

[*Claude and Martine exchange a wide-eyed, confused regard.*]

MARTINE Hmmmmm . . .

CLAUDE *Mais, Martine, tu ne te souviens pas? Mais où était Camille?!*

MARTINE *Avec nous! Avec nous!*

CAMILLE You brought me to the opening of a restaurant?!?

MARTINE *Oui . . . je pense . . . non . . . oui!*

CAMILLE Okay, let me get this straight—you remember the f*&%&&

canard aux olives, but you don't remember if you had your newborn infant strapped to your body?!?

And so on . . .

In other words: I've learned not to rely on any of the eyewitness accounts. And anyway, even in the most ideal circumstances, memory is fallible and changeable, susceptible to the bronzing of the passage of time. And yet I remain fascinated by the person who started a restaurant at the quite tender age of twenty-seven with next-to-zero business acumen and transformed it into an institution. The same admixture of audacity and insecurity that defines her uneasily bifurcated self today was, I gather, also quite manifest in 1971. She has often been described as having gotten her way through an amalgam of charm, flirtation, and white-knuckled tenacity—when she serves that egg to a boyfriend, head bowed, the glint of her flinty iris just visible through her lashes, I see that inveterate flirt. But then, the egg is *perfectly* cooked, the toast just brown, the leaves a balance of acid, the plate a beautiful piece of Mexican pottery—it is the work of a consummate cook, but also a consummate host, someone who understands that the pleasures of the table extend far beyond the contents of a dish to the atmosphere of an interaction. The glance that says, "Fall in love with me, but really, fall in love with this egg."

In fairness, my mother often makes the Egg Fried in a Spoon in the Fireplace, as it's cumbersomely known, for me too—it's not presented just on the occasion of an encounter with a potential son-in-law. And, for this reason, it is a dish that I've found myself writing about on more than one occasion when asked to contribute a recipe that sums up my relationship with my mother. Perhaps it's the use of the hearth—the few square feet before which is the kitchen real estate I most associate with her—or the fact of the building of the fire, which takes a certain kind of skill and patience. Mostly, however, it's the way she moves when she's cooking something over an open flame. Of her many skills, her ability to perceive and anticipate the movements and moods of a fire I think impresses me most. Maybe it's because I very clearly did not inherit this bit of culinary DNA. I tend to err on the hockey-puck end of the "doneness" spectrum when grilling burgers, *just to be safe;* my grilled chicken is always *very grilled.* My mom, by contrast, seems to be having a supralinguistic level of communication with the flame or ESP with the lamb chop. She may set down a platter at dinnertime and claim she's grossly overdone the steaks, but I have personally never eaten anything she's overcooked (or undercooked, for that matter)—it's always just as it should be.

When I was a child, I think at least 70 percent of our meals involved something cooked over the fire. That must sound like an outlandish effort for a single home-cooked family meal, but consider the fact that the weather in Northern California almost always encourages the building of a fire in the evening—even in the summertime, only a few days refused to cool amply enough to dissuade my mother from lighting a fire in the hearth. And then once the fire is lit—because it is one of the major sources of heat in a house devoid of central heating—why not just throw on a few of those sweet, silvery spring onions, or a little piece of fish, or even just the garlic bread? The flavor of almost every ingredient is enhanced by the slightest lick of a flame.

What makes my mother's skill as a *grilleuse* (as she might call herself) so worthy of note is not just that she moves with a mix of balletic dexterity and surgical punctiliousness—a swift rearrangement of logs here, a handful of dry grapevine cuttings for a surge of flame there—but that she was able to recognize an innate ability in herself early on and fearlessly cultivate it. At a time, no less, when very few women chefs were to be found in major restaurant kitchens, and even fewer at the grill. My mother, standing fully erect, is *maybe* five-two and, even when she complains about having overindulged on a recent trip to Italy, weighs next to nothing. My nickname for her—or maybe it's her spirit animal—is Hummingbird: she's tiny, beautiful, even mesmerizing, preternaturally energetic and fast moving, and plunges into conversations, meals, or demonstrations with the single-mindedness of a hummingbird encountering a vivid nectar-filled bloom. Still, when it comes to hoisting a log onto the fire or manipulating the height of her wrist-breaking cast-iron Tuscan grill, you'd forget she's next to miniature.

Egg Fried in a Spoon in the Fireplace

MY MOM FIRST DECIDED TO TRY HER HAND at a fire-cooked egg after reading about it in *The Magic of Fire: Hearth Cooking: One Hundred Recipes for the Fireplace or Campfire*, William Rubel's 2004 compendium of hearth-based recipes. She begged her Sicilian blacksmith friend, Angelo Garro, to fashion her a spoon after an illustration of a seventeenth-century French implement featured in Rubel's pages. Angelo consented and later even furnished her with a double-cup version (in an endearing heart shape) so that she could cook two eggs at once. The egg spoon was such a beloved implement that I even started a small design company that, among other things, produces a new version made by a female blacksmith in the Bay Area. If you can find a blacksmith or have a handy friend who makes such things, it's worth trying to twist his or her arm into producing something suitable. I've also searched antique shops far and wide, and while it's not impossible to find a cast-iron spoon, their handles are often too short and their cups a little too deep. Still, I always keep an eye out.

IN PREPARATION, light a fire. Any type of fireplace will do: living room, potbellied stove, campfire, possibly even a barbecue grill, provided its basin is generous enough to allow for some maneuvering. Wash and dry a big handful of lettuce leaves. Then use a mandoline to shave a bit of fennel and radish finely to toss with them. In the summer, add a few halved cherry tomatoes. Make a vinaigrette by pounding a small clove of garlic with a pinch of sea salt, adding some good red wine vinegar, a squeeze of lemon juice, and a bit of freshly ground black pepper. Let the garlic-vinegar brew sit a few minutes to macerate; then whisk in some extra virgin olive oil to taste. Keep it on the bright, acidic side so that it will balance the richness of the egg.

CRACK YOUR EGG into a little bowl and season with a pinch of sea salt, some freshly ground black pepper, and a sprinkle of Marash pepper or cayenne. Arrange the logs and coals to create something like a little "salamander" oven (coals spread across the floor, with smoldering logs at either side and across the top, and a log in flames at the back) so that heat comes from all directions—this will encourage the egg to puff up. Dress your salad and put a slice of bread in the toaster or on the grill. When the toast is ready, rub it lightly with a clove of garlic and drizzle it with olive oil. Grease your shallow, long-handled iron spoon with olive oil and warm it briefly in the fire. Pour in the egg and return it very carefully to the "oven" for about 2 or 3 minutes, or until the egg puffs up a bit and browns along the edges. Use a spoon or knife to gently loosen the egg and slide it onto the toast and serve the dressed leaves alongside. We've recently discovered that an egg spoon can also be successfully used over a gas stove top; it behaves something like a small, hypermobile cast-iron pan. You don't get the same infusion of woodsmoke flavor, but the egg still puffs up and cooks in a way unique to the spoon, and this method is somewhat less daunting for those uninitiated in fire cooking.

CHAPTER 12

Chez Panisse

In 1983, the year I was born, Chez Panisse was so far beyond its infancy, it had, you could say, even passed into young adulthood. Still, despite the restaurant's relative independence, my mom spent the better part of every day there, even if she wasn't cooking nearly as much as she once had. In fact, she hadn't cooked on the line for years by that point, aside from the occasional coverage for someone out sick or on vacation. She nonetheless seemed to be endlessly busy. She would flit around the restaurant making sure everything was as it should be, talk to the chefs about the week's upcoming menus, swoop in to do tastings before the evening service, rearrange the vegetable or fruit displays to her liking, or polish a mark off the front of the copper facade of the walk-in refrigerator. Regardless of what it was that kept her preoccupied there, for me it meant potentially long hours spent under the loose supervision of the floor and kitchen staff (some members of which took to the task more enthusiastically than others).

Photographs taken in the early eighties suggest that my mom was undeterred by whatever hygiene and safety laws might have precluded a newborn infant from entering a commercial kitchen. As soon as I had stabilized after a drawn-out phase of postpartum colic, she started to bring me into the restaurant regularly. There she'd swaddle me in clean dish towels and put me in an enormous salad bowl, atop a mattress of . . . more dish towels. A pale grub dressed in hand-knit coveralls, face marked by a look of mild rebuke, I would remain while she tasted prospective dishes or discussed operations with the manager. I don't remember this, of course, but I feel like my disproportionate love of salad might have something to do with my early kitchen cribs. Though the beatific chef, Catherine Brandel, was a close contender, my favorite person at the restaurant when I was little was a man named Royal Thomas Guernsey the *Third*, whom everyone referred to simply as Tom. Tom was a lithe, handsome bearded man in his late thirties, with a fabulously charismatic smile—the kind that easily disarms even the most truculent diners. He had worked as a waiter in the early days of the restaurant and eventually rose to become my mom's most immediate and trusted partner (as head of the dining room, and later, as the president of the restaurant's board of directors).

Before I was born, my mom had briefly entertained the idea that Chez Panisse could, and indeed should, serve brunch. David Goines—my mother's erstwhile fiancé and the graphic artist responsible for the visual identities of at least half the businesses in Berkeley—even created a dedicated poster to announce the service. The words *Le Matin* were emblazoned across an image of a steaming coffeepot; below these was a promise of "café and croissant" to be offered between the hours of nine and eleven. During that period, which began *and* ended in 1976, Tom was charged with making omelettes on a little burner right in the middle of the dining room. Brunch was so popular that "the management" had to rather promptly shut it down—the business was still too shambolic at that point to accommodate any volume of visitors. People were lining up around the block for this special little *omelette aux fines herbes* crowned with a dollop of crème fraîche, and Tom had never otherwise spent a moment on the line. Though it was clear he was a gifted cook who with a smile as luminous as they come could whip out a fabulous egg dish in camping-like conditions, my mom was loath to lose her head of the house to the kitchen—brunch was swiftly canceled.

Whenever I was afoot, Tom would take time out of what he was doing to entertain me. He'd often swoop me out of my mother's arms to carry me back to visit Mary Jo Thoresen in the pastry section, knowing that she would have some variety of treat awaiting us. Tom was right: Mary Jo reserved one shelf in the freezer for a tray of raspberries. When Tom and I came by for a visit, she'd place a frozen berry on each of my small four-year-old fingers and use a ballpoint pen to draw tiny faces on each one. Together she and Tom would make a little narrative for all the finger gnomes that thankfully always culminated in my being permitted to decimate the population by eating, one by one, their frozen berry heads. Tom was also especially tolerant of under-the-table imaginary tea parties, which required not just a suspension of disbelief but also the curling over of his tall frame to enter the "teahouse." Ideally, teatime came directly after the first busser on duty had draped all the tables with their linens before service, so that the assembled guests could eat their invisible finger sandwiches unperturbed.

Occasionally, the daughter of Jean-Pierre Moullé, the chef downstairs, would join in. Maud, who was a year younger, became one of my closest friends growing up. It wasn't just that we attended the same French American school for a decade (to and from which we often carpooled); we shared something altogether more intimate. Maud's father worked at Chez Panisse for more than thirty years, on and off from the mid-seventies to 2012; in many ways, it was as much his restaurant as it was my mother's. Chez Panisse, however, never adhered to the French system of having just one chef, the rigorously hierarchical culture in which Jean-Pierre had trained. Rather, it had many, rotating on and off within a given week—two upstairs, two down. Sticking to that democratic structure was in a way my mother's concession to, or honoring of, the utopian vision of community propounded by so many of her hippie contemporaries. Nonetheless, at various points in Jean-Pierre's tenure, it became clear that the absence of full autonomy was wearing him down. A slightly mutinous impulse would bubble to the fore until he'd decide to leave . . . only, invariably and thankfully, to return. Things could descend into mayhem without him.

In any event, Jean-Pierre was a fixture, and, as a result, his two daughters had a relationship to the place that mirrored my own; a sense of ownership, not of the business or of the employees, but a feeling that *the place itself* belonged to us. But then, there were other kids besides me—and Maud and her sister, Elsa—who felt as profound a sense of connection there. Most people who have worked at Chez Panisse have stayed for years, if not decades. Whole lives have been articulated in the rhythms of the place. Whether it's Clare Bell-Fuller, who bartends only a night or two a week but has been doing so for more than thirty years, or Steve Crumley, the recently retired maître d' who graced the floor for the better part of my life, or Khalil Mujadedy, the preeminent fix-it man, who could repair or make anything, from the plumbing system of the whole restaurant to the copper lamps that grace its tables—there was never a sense that people wanted merely to pass through, or to move on and up. Whether you got there at the beginning, middle, or end of a career, Chez Panisse was a place to *arrive*. And, once you'd arrived, you rarely felt a pull to leave.

The staff parties held annually are in some way the apotheosis of this familial feeling. It's only on these occasions, after all, that it's possible to see the full expanse of the family, since of course not all employees are at work at the restaurant at the same time. One party I distinctly remember, convened up at Bob Cannard's farm in an extra-green pocket of Sonoma County. Bob has been the main farmer for Chez Panisse for close to forty years, having brokered a deal with my mom in the early eighties to sell everything he grew to the restaurant (some restaurants have their own farms now, and many call themselves "farm to table," but this arrangement was at the time unheard of, even revolutionary). He used to say that he was "monogamous; it was the restaurant who slept around," referring to the fact that Chez Panisse did in fact supplement their haul from Bob with produce from a variety of other local farms.

Bob's place, however, is not an ordinary farm, nor is he an ordinary farmer. He operates in a state of controlled chaos, in which the wilderness is allowed to coexist with, even infringe upon, his rows of crops. He doesn't believe in weeding. He doesn't fertilize. Nature is the presumed authority. When I was visiting once, I trailed behind him as we walked the edge of a vegetable plot, Bob holding his hand outstretched toward the vegetables as if to caress them as he passed. I swear I saw each frond of fennel gently shimmy beneath his fingers, even bow backward slightly in a show of delight. I would not be surprised if his plants did indeed sense in him something numinous—it's hard to imagine a steward more in tune with nature. In fact, the house he lived in for the better part of my life contained a window intentionally absent a pane. There was a bird, a swallow, who had built his nest among the beams of the living room ceiling, and this bird was treated not as a pest, but rather as a joint resident of that home, free to come and go as he pleased.

Needless to say, Bob's farm is a place in which the divisions between species are rendered intentionally porous, and it might be for that reason that everyone who visits feels so naturally at home there, as if arriving on that parcel of land allowed you to strip down to a more primordial state. Which is why the staff parties held there are always the best and most populous, taking on the flavor of a reunion. Former employees always join the ranks of current, and everyone brings their children, even the friends of children, to make up the largest extended family imaginable. Add to this a paella in a pan of at least six feet in diameter, cooked over a wood fire in Bob's garden, and enough hay bale seating to wind through half an acre of orchard. The afternoon would grow pregnant with pleasure, dwindling only after nightfall,

when all the children had eaten themselves to bloat on underripe fruit and passed out unconscious in the tall grass.

.   .   .

Rather appropriately, Chez Panisse was made out of a structure built as a single-family home in the 1930s. From the time of its purchase in 1971, it's been molded to accommodate a business—a family, really—that necessarily expanded over several decades of use. When the restaurant first opened its doors, the downstairs hearth—now the most prominent feature of the kitchen—had yet to be built. All the grilling for dinner service was performed over a steel drum in the back courtyard. This ad hoc outdoor grill station was adjacent to where the first pastry chef and co-owner of the restaurant, Lindsey Shere, conceived of confections in the gussied-up toolshed that predated a formal pastry department. The addition of an open kitchen upstairs in 1980—to execute a café menu distinct from the downstairs prix fixe—was followed by a series of auxiliary buildings, storage areas, a wine cave, staff changing rooms, and offices next door, both for the restaurant and the Edible Schoolyard Project. Chez Panisse spread out like a kind of medieval market town—in phases and as dictated by a growing family—and prevailed despite two significant fires, in 1982 and again in 2013. The fact that it's now on the cusp of a fiftieth birthday is at once incredible and completely obvious. There are too many invested "children" for it to fail.

My mother always romantically refers to the expansive body of employees as La Famille Panisse. Many couples have met there, have fallen in love and gotten married, have had children, and have still been there fifteen years later when their kids started a first shift as prep cooks in training. Elsa worked in the kitchen alongside her father; Maud became one of my mother's favorite hosts. Cal Peternell's elder two sons came through the kitchen, working their way through college summers alongside their father. Nico Monday, my mother's godson and the son of Sharon Jones, one of the first waitresses, cooked upstairs *and* down, met his wife, Amelia O'Reilly (then a garde-manger), and moved with her to Massachusetts to open two restaurants. Former chef Paul Bertolli's son was recently a busser downstairs, his graceful, elongated form and pacific demeanor an echo of his father's. This list could go on; there are so many of us. For an only child like me, it meant feeling myself a part of a massive extended family, with a hundred aunts and uncles, cousins, siblings, and grandparents to spoil and scold me in equal measure—a family on the whole more functional than most. I've always thought my mother should have had a dozen children; she's possessed of such a mothering nature, sometimes bordering on an archetype. But, for whatever reason—timing? ambition? lack of a suitable mate?—she didn't get around to having children until she was approaching an age at which it was already considered very difficult, if not impossible, to do so. I think the familial nature of the restaurant, and the constant acquisition of young surrogates and mentees, quelled the anxiety over the eventuality of childbearing, or at least provided ample distraction from any absence of family she might have felt before she met my father.

That said, my generation was the first to actually grow up at Chez Panisse. And I, like my contemporaries there, knew the place inside out. For starters, I had internalized its litany of smells: the astringency of the cedar that paneled the cloak closet, the ripe fruit that was stored on the shelves of an outdoor breezeway in the summertime, the faint smell of the ethanol lamps glowing on each table, the freshly vacuumed carpets of the downstairs dining room, the smell of a pizza blackening in the wood-fired oven. My knowledge of the place was like different layers of a map: overlaying the olfactory blueprints were the memorized oddities of the building's architecture. And I used this knowledge to flagrant advantage—like a thief equipped with the plans of a building, weeks before attempting a heist. I knew the best alcoves for games of hide-and-seek, performed with whomever, staff or staff's offspring, was willing to engage; how many of the steep back stairs could be cleared in a single leap (I'm amazed Nico and I are still alive and unconcussed in light of this activity); from which shelf in the walk-in refrigerator a selection of pastry delights could be looted undetected. I had a particular penchant for the barely sweet, gummy-textured rounds of uncooked galette dough. Why, I don't know, but I would open their plastic wrap, pinch off a buttery mouthful, eat it silently in the cold, pat the round back into shape, and reseal the wrapping. It never occurred to me that the pastry chefs might be scratching their heads about the slightly diminished galettes that showed up every now and again. If I wasn't in the downstairs walk-in getting up to no good, I might be found sidled up to the bar, ordering "a pint of foam, please, no liquid milk," from the lunchtime bartender. I hated the taste of coffee as a kid, but loved the sweet, densely creamy texture of the kind of foam that topped a cappuccino, and would often spoon it off my mother's when she wasn't looking. At Chez Panisse, if my mom was too distracted to pay attention to what I was doing, I knew I could request this "drink," and that, out of a sense of professional obligation, the poor bartender would prepare it for me, even though it took at least a quart of milk to yield that quantity of foam. The less outrageous request was for a Chez Snapple, a drink frequently ordered by the cooks on the line on summer days: black iced tea mixed with apple cider and a squeeze of lemon, poured over ice.

Another sure attraction was the delivery of a great big crate from the Chino Farm, one of the few farms my mom consented to buy from that wasn't located in Northern California. The Chino Farm, situated just outside of San Diego, traces its history to the early 1920s, when Junzo Chino emigrated from a small Japanese fishing village and settled in Los Angeles. Junzo and his wife, Hatsuya Noda, worked in a farming community there before moving south, where they rented

land in a rural expanse near Del Mar. After a period of forced intern-
ment in Arizona during World War II, the family returned to the area
and purchased fifty-six acres of farmland. It was on that land that they
raised their nine children and established the now-venerated Chino
Farm. They were the first to grow certain rare and heirloom varietals
of vegetables in the United States, and my mom was the first chef
of any notoriety—in the early seventies!—to truffle them out. Their
friendship has persisted unbroken ever since (and has included her
near-annual visit to the farm—sometimes with me in tow—to par-
take in their traditional Mochi Festival, which marks the beginning
of the Japanese New Year). My mom once described the Chinos as
having tended their land with "an inexhaustible aesthetic curiosity,"
and I think it's fair to say that their attention to beauty was at least
as responsible for my mother's being seduced by their work as the
exceptional flavor of their produce. Of course, when I was a kid, being
present for the opening of the delivery box from the Chinos was akin
to watching a treasure chest be prized open. Before anyone else was
doing it, the Chinos were growing a rainbow of carrots (red, white,
pale orange, yellow, and purple); white, violet, and pale green eggplants; unusual tomatoes before "heirloom" was a thing; and dozens
of other vegetables and fruits from seeds sourced around the world.
It was as if they trafficked in an alchemical type of agriculture. What
they grow is still some of the most beautiful produce I've ever seen or
tasted.

Of course, the collective *favorite* place of all the restaurant urchins
was the pizza station in the upstairs café, with its oak wood-burning
oven and endlessly obliging *pizzaiolo*. Michele Perrella, who worked at
Chez in the same capacity for more than two decades, was in the most
wonderful way possible almost a caricature of an Italian cook. Over
more than twenty years, very little changed about his appearance—he
wore the same tidy mustache and the same visored white cap, and
his creaseless skin remained completely smooth, with the exception

of a proliferation of wrinkles fanning out from the corners of his eyes whenever he smilingly greeted us. He also spoke in heavily accented English, as if he'd landed in California mere minutes before his shift.

For the under-ten set, visiting Michele at his station during dinner service was the highlight of a meal at Chez Panisse. And despite the constant thrum of diners flowing in and out, not to mention the persistent automated buzz of a countertop printer spewing orders, Michele would always find a moment for me to join him. There the two of us would stand awash in the heat of the oven, as intense and unexpected as the feeling of stepping off an air-conditioned plane into a hot, arid climate. Sometimes Michele would hoist me up by the armpits to look at the progress of the pizzas but also to "get a suntan," so that I could go back to my *"mamma"* and tell her I'd taken a trip to Hawaii. When I was still too small to see over the counter, he'd invert a large plastic tub—the sort used for dough—and hold my hand to help me climb up. We'd turn the dough out of another bucket to let it spread out over the flour-dusted counter. First I'd help him cut the big swollen mass into the smaller blobs we'd gently massage into balls for individual pizzas. The smell of the yeast exhausting from the doughy form was intoxicating. That smell, he would patiently explain, is what allowed the dough to grow from a paste to the fluffy elastic stuff I could stretch between my hands. Once the balls of dough had been allowed to rest and rise again to nearly double on their oiled sheet pans (this usually required the amount of time it took to eat a course or two back at my table), I returned to my roost to make a pizza . . . but "ONE extra-small pizzetta ONLY," my mom would mouth from our booth across the way, referring to the smaller of the two sizes featured on the menu.

I'd use my fingers to begin stippling the dough, gently pressing it outward, mimicking the motions I'd learned from Michele. Finally I was allowed to pick it up and stretch it between my hands. We scarcely employed the rolling pin—I was less interested in perfecting a restaurant-grade pizza than in making a series of custom shapes:

a bottle of olive oil, say, which I'd thematically decorate with black olives, or a swimming fish, whose scales were fashioned of gypsy pepper ribbons. Regardless of the shape of the pizza or its topping, Michele would show me how to brush garlic-infused oil evenly over the dough and how to carefully lay down ingredients so that the flame would touch each judiciously. As the fire did its swift work, he'd hold me up again to watch the transformation, our faces glowing hot before the spectacle.

Pizza Dough   THIS RECIPE is essentially the one made daily at Chez Panisse, although this version will make enough dough for only two pizzas (the one used in the kitchen at the restaurant will make enough for an evening's worth of service). If you need dough for more, it's very easily doubled or tripled. One of the secrets to making really delicious pizzas is the garlic oil mentioned above; whatever pizza topping you decide on, it will make the final product that much more delicious and savory. To make the garlic oil, very finely mince a clove or two of garlic, place it in a bowl, and add a couple of big glugs of extra virgin olive oil to completely cover it. It should be liquid enough to easily brush or spoon onto a pizza when the time comes.

FIRST YOU'LL NEED TO MAKE THE SPONGE by dissolving 2 teaspoons of dry yeast in ½ cup of lukewarm water and then adding a combination of ¼ cup of unbleached white flour and ¼ cup of rye flour. Allow the sponge to sit until it becomes quite bubbly, about 30 minutes. In another bowl, mix together 3¼ cups of unbleached white flour and 1 teaspoon of salt. Stir this into the sponge, along with ¼ cup of cold water and ¼ cup of olive oil. Turn the dough out onto a floured board and knead until it is soft and elastic, about 5 minutes.

PUT THE DOUGH in a large bowl, cover, and let rise in a warm place until doubled in size, about 2 hours. For a more complexly flavored and supple dough, you can let it rise overnight in the refrigerator. (If you do this, though, remove the dough from the refrigerator two hours before shaping, as the cold arrests the rising process.) When doubled in size, gently remove the dough from the bowl and divide it in two, forming each piece into a smooth ball. Wrap each one loosely in plastic and let rest at room temperature for an hour or so. Flatten each ball into a disc about 5 to 6 inches in diameter, flour lightly, cover with a dish towel, and let rest for another 15 minutes.

PREHEAT THE OVEN TO 500°F, and gently stretch one of the disks into a 10-inch round. Place on a floured peel or an inverted baking sheet. Brush the dough with the garlic olive oil, sprinkle with salt, and, leaving a ½-inch border uncovered, top with your choice of ingredients. When I'm making pizza at home, I like to keep the toppings simple: for example, a tomato sauce (made by puréeing and reducing on the stove top a couple of handfuls of very ripe summer tomatoes) with just a scattering of fresh mozzarella, and basil leaves sprinkled over the top when it's just out of the oven. That said, homemade pizza should always be a free-for-all in my opinion. I often just prepare loads of different vegetables (onions, summer squash, peppers, cherry tomatoes, and so forth, all cut very thinly or quite small), some cheeses, and the *very essential* garlic oil, and let people apply their own combinations. When the pizza is ready to go into the oven, slide it onto a baking stone (or keep it on the inverted baking sheet) and bake for 10 minutes, or until the crust is browned.

•   •   •

Throughout my childhood, our family would eat upstairs at Chez Panisse at least once or twice a week. Even though my mom wasn't cooking that much by that point, she felt it was essential that she be there to taste the dinner menu and proffer real-time feedback. It also delighted diners, both regular and new, to see her fluttering around the dining room. We normally sat in one of the booths upstairs, across from the line, so that my mom could keep the chefs and servers in her peripheral vision. She preferred an orientation that would allow her to maximally observe the climate of the room, and would never allow herself to get fenced into a position from which she couldn't easily spring to action. My dad and I reflexively ceded the outer seat because she would reliably get up from the table close to twenty times per meal. We sometimes joked that we were in fact eating just the two of us, and that the host had made an error in bringing a third table setting. To pass the time between her visitations, I'd get a glass full of colored crayons and begin to plaster the white paper table cover with a warren of drawings, sometimes getting my dad to play my favorite game of Squiggle (introduced to me by Mary Jo), in which one player would draw a loopy abstract line that the other had to transform into some type of figurative sketch. Roller coasters, snakes, and trains were forbidden. My father would accuse me—as all dads everywhere seem to do—of "having some bread with my butter." At the end of the meal I would obsessively "help" the busser more effectively decrumb the table, picking up every single glass or bottle so as to make what few glutenous flecks remained available for removal.

Inevitably, I reached an age when I could contribute more to the restaurant than I was doing by pointing out stray morsels of bread to the waitstaff. It was time to get a job! And where else other than Chez Panisse? These were generally short stints—a summer here, a winter holiday there—and I was mostly behind the scenes doing prep work and "running," only graduating to the floor (as a lowly busser, mind you) once I stopped looking criminally underage. I started my first shift when I was fourteen, the summer after ninth grade. I was placed, to begin with, under the command of the cooks overseeing the salad station, helping to ready the various sauces and ingredients needed for both lunch and dinner services. I had it in my mind that I would be plating salads, though I'd had exceptionally limited practice doing this type of thing, even at home, where my mom largely took control of preparations. On the contrary—and quite rightly given my age and inexperience—I was assigned far simpler tasks, such as the daily cleaning of a container of salt-packed anchovies. This was not a small container, mind you, but something of rather industrial proportions. Until this turn at Chez, I hadn't even been aware that anchovies came in such enormous vessels, or that the restaurant was—unbeknownst to me—hiding vast quantities of my least favorite food in multiple dishes and vinaigrettes each day.

It seemed it was my karmic lot to be charged with the intimate handling of these stinky little fish, which required first soaking, in a large metal bowl filled with water, and then degutting and boning. The final step was to array the fillets in a dish and cover them with olive oil. The experience of submerging my hands again and again in the increasingly murky and innard-filled water—followed by a maniacal Lady Macbethian effort to scrub my hands free of the odor—is unfortunately one of the things I most keenly remember from my time in the kitchens of Chez. Which is not to say that I didn't acquire the bulk of my culinary skills from having worked there. I was the daughter of the "boss," yes, but I felt that the generous and patient tuition extended to me was actually very standard. Mona Talbott, who went on to helm the Rome Sustainable Food Project at the American Academy (my mother's third child, after the Edible Schoolyard Project), I vividly remember, once paused what she was doing in the middle of a lunchtime rush to calmly instruct me in how to properly cut paper-thin slices of smoked salmon. At its core, it is a teaching kitchen, and indeed, *stagiaires*, as they're known, are a constant feature: people young and old, of all shades of experience, who come to work in the kitchen for a few days, sometimes a few months, to hone their skills. I remember when one young intern, who'd labored in a slew of kitchens in New York City, marveled to me that "at Chez Panisse, everyone is so nice! You can leave your knives out, and no one steals them!"

There was one instance, however, where neither the equanimity of the cooks nor the fact of my parentage could insulate me from reprisal.

As part of my initial gig, back in the summer of 1995, I was meant to cycle through all the departments: salad, sauté and grill, wood oven, and pastry, helping with whatever prep or cooking would render service as frictionless as possible. When I arrived in the pastry department, it was fairly assumed that I could read a recipe and execute on the concrete measurements listed therein. I was, after all, a literate young adult who had had at least some exposure to both cooking and mathematics. This, however, proved a grave failure of judgment, for in my first week I managed to both omit the molasses from a gingerbread cake *and* double—DOUBLE!—the quantity of eggs required for a custard. You would have thought, as I cracked open a fiftieth egg, that it might have occurred to me that I'd veered off course. But no, my extra-caloric error was discovered only *after* we'd baked up dozens of inedible puddings. I often make reference to my lack of baking skills; I truly believe it to be, in my case, a congenital deficiency. I've even, at times, managed to disable consummate bakers working in my vicinity, as if by some invisible nefarious force. Anyway, I was discharged from my pastry duties and sent back to salad. Salad is, after all, where my Chez Panisse story began, all those many years ago.

Simple Chez
Salad Dressing

THIS IS BASICALLY the dressing I make at home, though I'm flexible about which types of acid I incorporate, often replacing the Banyuls vinegar that Chez uses with a bit of sherry or apple cider vinegar or lemon juice. Start by placing a clove of garlic and ½ teaspoon of sea salt in a Japanese-style mortar (suribachi) or marble mortar and use your pestle to grind it to a translucent paste. Cover the garlic with 1 tablespoon of red wine vinegar and 1½ tablespoons of Banyuls vinegar and allow it to sit for at least ten minutes so that the acid has time to mellow the heat of the allium. Whisk in a scant ½ teaspoon of Dijon mustard and then add 6 tablespoons of extra virgin olive oil, beating vigorously to emulsify. Add a grind of black pepper at the end and taste, adjusting for acid balance and salt—I like mine on the acidic side, so tend to err on the more vinegary end of the spectrum. Use this to dress enough salad for six.

CHAPTER 13

Domaine Tempier

The heat is the thing I remember the most about summers at Domaine Tempier—the dry, crackling heat of Provence. A heat so unrelenting it would turn the sap liquid in the trunks of the pines that blanket the coast, those iconic umbrella-like silhouettes whose canopies throw vast puddles of warm shade at their feet. I loved that heady smell, though it usually meant spending most days with indelible smears of black sap across browned arms or thighs, later dusted in the fine powdery earth of the vineyard to render them as jagged, sinister scars. That heat was inseparable from the thrum of the cicadas, the constant, maddening soundtrack of a summer spent in the South of France. There was something about the meeting of sound and heat—both so total that your skin wasn't enough of a barrier to keep things clear and separate: the heat became the heat of your blood; the sound, the music of your organs. As a child, I felt like there was no end to my body, just the pure sensation of moving through the world without friction: a membraneless being plunged back into the warmth and welcome of amniotic fluid. Berkeley, with its summer fog and perennially chilly temperatures, rarely let you forget your human form.

From the time I was a newborn, a thing more belly and cheeks than limbs, I've regularly visited Domaine Tempier in Bandol. Domaine Tempier is a winery of some renown, thanks to decades of produc-

ing some of the more distinctive wines in the region, not to mention my mom's indefatigable advocacy of their rosé (and by advocacy, read daily imbibing)—she's featured it for the better part of forty years on the Chez Panisse wine list. For me, however, Domaine Tempier has mainly been a kind of second home, and the home belonging to Lucien and Lulu Peyraud. These were people I understood to be a third set of grandparents, though the exact lineage wasn't made clear to me until I was old enough to understand that we lacked the blood ties that would have validated that conviction. (Still, I believe I'm the only one of their "grandchildren," by blood or otherwise, who has a Domaine Tempier label tattoo. Acquired at the age of eighteen, this permanent sign of familial commitment sits in the middle of my lower back, and was used in college to get occasional discounts at the one New Haven wine shop that sold bottles of the vaunted stuff. Lulu keeps a photo of this tattoo, a zoomed-in shot featuring a modest sliver of bum, in her office in fairly prominent view.)

Every summer my family would head to Bandol, staying either with Lulu and Lucien at the Domaine or in a rental house nearby. We'd remain for close to a month, settling into the leisurely rhythms of the South: swimming multiple times a day in the Mediterranean; shopping for food in the markets; cooking, always cooking, no matter how oppressive the temperature; and napping with a kind of intentionality I've never known elsewhere.

Lulu and Lucien had, even when I was a child and many more generations were yet to be born, a seemingly endless family. Born in 1917 in Marseille, Lulu, the third child in her family, remembers being the only one of her siblings to express interest in her father's vineyard estate in the then-*very*-rural Bandol. At eighteen she married Lucien and they moved to the nineteenth-century villa at Domaine Tempier and began to make the Mourvèdre varietal wines that not only set them apart but eventually earned the region the dedicated *appellation d'origine contrôlée* of Bandol. Despite the punishing austerity of the wartime years, they had eight children (eight children! an unfathomable number to an only child), just one of whom, Philippe, didn't survive early infancy. By the time I came along, Lulu and Lucien were swimming in grandchildren, and many of them were my age, or close enough to it—it was heaven for me. I had siblings, if only for one month out of the year.

My mom's first trip to France in her twenties, during her junior year at UC Berkeley in 1964, is by now a well-documented maiden voyage, not least of all by her. She speaks of that time as being the beginning of a new consciousness, a "coming to her senses," as she often calls it. She was first exposed to a culture in which food had yet to be industrialized: everything was very direct, but also very specialized. A man would raise a small herd, butcher the meat, and bring it to market, and was just one in a long line of farmer-butchers—producers who knew their trade as innately as if it had been passed down in their DNA. She traveled around the countryside eating in village restaurants, glorified farmhouse kitchens serving dishes made from whatever they had in their potagerie: a little roasted hen, a salad strewn with herbs, a rata-touille. She always told me that most of her time was spent lolling on the grassy verges of country roads in cider-induced stupor ("I had no idea it was *alcoholic*!" she'd exclaim).

Perhaps because I so want it to be the case, I've always imagined that my mother met Lulu on that first trip to France, when she was a girl, or still young enough to have been—in my fictionalized version of events—adopted by Lulu. Even though my mother had a mother— a wonderful, kind woman I knew mainly in her senescence—Lulu sim-ply *is* my mother's mother, or at least in that most important of ways: a mother of the spirit. My mom and Lulu actually met later, after she had already started Chez Panisse and some wise soul suggested they might have a thing or two in common. It was still, however, well before my birth, so by the time I came onto the scene, Lulu was already the same towering (though exceptionally physically diminutive) figure in our own family that she was, and remains at age a hundred and two, in her own. I was born a few months after one of Lulu's own grand-daughters, whose mother, reportedly, had wanted to name her Fanny. My mother's devotion to Marcel Pagnol—the famed 1930s-era Pro-vençal writer and director from whose considerable oeuvre my mom had already plucked the name Panisse—was so complete that it was taken for granted that I would be called either Fanny or Marius, the lovers and leads of the trilogy *Fanny, Marius,* and *César*. Perhaps an apocryphal tale, but at some point I was told that Lulu had forbidden her own daughter from naming *her* daughter Fanny, because *"Ce nom appartient déjà à Alice!"* Veronique chose Manon instead, another Pagnol protagonist, and, as if predestined, we were inseparable as children.

Having grown up in a country in which *fanny* was an elementary shorthand for one's behind (which is to say nothing of the graver ridicule I encountered upon moving to England), I can hardly express the mix of relief and pride I felt visiting Provence with the name Fanny. Not only was it not considered a source of embarrassment, it was an outright badge of honor! To be named for a Pagnol character! What could be better than that? Well, I discovered, to have a best friend named for yet another. Manon and I were adored—adored not just by Lulu, who would lavish us with especial grandmotherly affection, but also by every shopkeeper, barman, lifeguard, and other business owner in the parts of Bandol we were allowed to navigate unchaperoned.

One afternoon, when Manon and I were about eight years old, we were permitted to go out on our most daring solo adventure: a trip to the island of Bendor, a rocky outcropping with a coastline of less than a mile. A quarter mile out from the main public beach in Bandol, Bendor is home to a hotel, a handful of restaurants, and a couple of other tourist attractions. It was bought in 1950 by industrialist Paul Ricard, the founder of a French company that produced the anise-scented liqueur Pastis; he converted Bendor only somewhat successfully into a resort. It is reached by frequent ferries leaving from the port. Because it was not too far from where Manon's mother operated a beachfront café (a place I identified with endless quantities of Orangina and little sips from Lulu's glass of Pastis), our parents decided we could make the trip alone. The ten-minute ferry ride felt eternal, in that way that time elongates when you're young and without a watch or other device to regulate the minutes. It was a voyage from which we emerged covered in salt spat up from the water as we stood at the bow like explorers. We'd brought our bikes along with us so we could trace the perimeter of the island, crisscross its interior. Manon had been to Bendor many times with her father and older brother, so she led the way. I trailed behind watching her orange and magenta candy-striped dress flutter. I don't remember much about our little jaunt other than a sense of freedom more profound than I'd perhaps ever felt, sailing on our bikes to the farthest point on the island. But, of course, just at that moment of feeling some kind of proto-adult autonomy, I rode over a sharp rock or shard of glass and got a flat tire. The sense of freedom transformed swiftly into the terror of being not just without a parent but *across an ocean* from a parent, and without much in the way of life skills to manage the problem at hand. My bike was heavy. Its now very flat tire created a viscous resistance as I tried to drag the thing back toward civilization. Manon seemed convinced that someone would come to our rescue. I was filled with doubt; at the time of puncture, we were quite alone at the edge of the island, two young girls beneath a stand of silent pines. Finally, after what felt like several hours of dragging the bike, but couldn't have been more than twenty minutes, a café appeared on the horizon.

The proprietor—a man of maybe fifty with a big belly and a mustache and a swath of white apron tied directly around his widest point—immediately identified us as beleaguered little urchins and asked us to relay our troubles. Before, however, we could launch into our travails with the punctured tire and our fears of missing the ferry we'd promised our parents, hands over hearts, we'd sail back on, he asked us our names. "Manon et Fanny!" we chirped. I'll never forget what transpired next: the vision of a man, a very large man, overwhelmed by the sheer nostalgia provoked by our names, a regional history so poignant that finding it reified in the form of two small girls was enough to strike a deep, invisible blow. He staggered backward, as if a great weight had been thrust into his arms. "Manon et Fanny?!" he shouted back at us, the question soaked through with incredulity. "*C'est pas possible! Les filles de Pagnol! C'est pas possible! Comment ça se fait!?*" He looked around the open-air room, only sparsely populated by what were no doubt foreign tourists unfamiliar with the Pagnol corpus, but nonetheless locking each person into his gaze, as tears, actual tears, began to form in the corners of his eyes. "*Mais c'est pas possible . . . les petites filles de Pagnol . . . Où est Marius, Fanny? Et tes sources, petite Manon?*" When at last he recovered from the shock, he offered us a citron pressé and called his son, a mechanic, to hustle over to repair our lame bicycle. We were the last passengers to board the promised ferry, but we did make it in time.

Citron Pressé THIS PARTICULARLY FRENCH VERSION of lemonade was the only beverage resembling soda that I was allowed on an even intermittent basis when I was a kid (notable exceptions were: Coke when deathly ill with the flu, 7UP at Chinese restaurants, Shirley Temples at bar mitzvahs, and Orangina, sometimes, when in France). When you order a citron pressé at a café in France, you get a tall, slender glass half full of pure freshly squeezed lemon juice. On the side comes a small carafe of tap water and a bowl of white sugar, along with a long-handled spoon for stirring. I liked to drink mine minimally diluted, with enough sugar to render it just potable, like a super-sour, super-flavorful, liquid lemon candy.

THIS VERSION OF THE DRINK is a touch more involved, but nuances the flavor by using the rind too. Make a lemon-infused simple syrup by putting a cup of sugar and the peel of one lemon in a saucepan with a cup of water. Bring to a boil and allow to roll for 5 minutes. Remove from the heat and cool completely. To serve, put 1 tablespoon of lemon syrup in a glass with a few ice cubes. Squeeze in the juice of a lemon and stir in cold water or sparkling water to taste. Sweeten with more syrup if you like. What you don't use straightaway can be retained in an airtight jar in the refrigerator for up to a month. There is no better lemon drink than this, no more potent an experience of that citrus flavor, and certainly nothing more refreshing on a hot summer day.

·　·　·

In the summer, you couldn't keep fruit for more than a day—its gleam began to fade the second you got it home from the market. The threat

of an unseemly bruise, a spreading yellow-brown contusion, was always looming. And yet my mom could not resist displaying platters of fruit around our rental house, arraying it as an invitation to the elements: "I dare you to spoil my fruit!" They always dared. More mornings than not, I'd wake up to the smell, wafting into my upstairs bedroom, of fruit cooking in a pot on the stove. Whatever plum had blossomed with rot overnight would—the damaged section excised—meet the raspberries flattened by the heat and maybe a peach whose ripeness could not be externally gauged but whose feel wasn't encouraging. Pits and all, a splash of water, never any sugar. This smell, of fruit cooking down quickly, entering a different state, is an amber-colored smell—a smell not of freshness but of warmth and concentration, of sugars beginning to caramelize. I love fresh strawberries, but there are few smells more intoxicating than the smell of strawberries cooking.

Jam-making was not my mother's forte. In general, anything requiring patience or exacting methodology or just any measuring whatsoever was bound to be foiled by her hummingbird attention span. Sadly—or fortuitously?—I am exactly the same: I cook with high heat, very fast, always with intense amounts of flavor and zero measuring. I have a total absence of interest in actually following recipes (though I like to look at them) and generally exhibit brazen ignorance of their wisdom when it comes to baking. This version of "jam" that my mom made in the morning to coax everyone from his or her bed is really just a cooked fruit compote; it doesn't require pectin or the correct proportion of sugar or a jam muslin or a sterilized jar. It was almost always eaten directly from the pot with a spoon, but sometimes it made it to the table to be ladled over yogurt, with the pits having to be fished out of your bowl. Very infrequently, some small amount would remain for an afternoon tartine: a crust of bread toasted, buttered, and primed to receive this loose, fragrant concoction.

A lot of our cooking in the South lacked the structure of our meals back home—perhaps because it was vacation, and that meant that you could wander into the kitchen at any time and fix something to eat. This doesn't mean that a great deal of thought wasn't given to meals and their preparation, just that if we weren't dining over at Lulu's or up at Richard Olney's, we were making simple things: a grilled fish, a couple of cheeses, some green beans blanched and dusted with chopped hazelnuts and ribbons of roasted red pepper. Lulu's was always more of a production, because, despite the humbleness of the ingredients and their traditional Provençal preparations, she adhered to a certain degree of formality that had defined the meals of her youth. We often sat in the main dining room rather than around the long table in her kitchen. A little wooden cart used to circulate the plates of food to be served, as well as the condiments and occasionally silverware or glassware, has since become a kind of walker for Lulu. For someone who has recovered from a broken hip and a broken shoulder, Lulu remains even now, as a centenarian, disinclined to use any mobility aides. The cart—long a fixture of the villa's dining room—is a perfect surrogate for a more aesthetically objectionable device.

The meals I remember best at Lulu's were either the very large ones (when Lucien was still alive) or the very small ones. The front garden of the villa dissolves at its boundary into the vineyard, facing the valley that, at its far side, rises up again into the medieval town of La Cadière-d'Azur. But dividing the garden from the front of the villa, whose proud, upright facade is unembellished save for the storm shutters and magnificent wooden door, is a brick-laid patio, a terrace shielded in part by a dripping grapevine arbor. And it was beneath this grape cover that we often had meals in the summer, when the heat of the day was still preferable to the sepulchral cool of the inner quarters. No matter the time of year, Lulu would make a fish soup. Sometimes this was an enormous bouillabaisse, cooked with no shortage of ceremony in a copper cauldron over an outdoor fire of gnarled old vines. Sometimes this was a more humble affair. One of the most comforting and beloved things in her repertoire is a very simple version, of which the following is an approximation. What will really make it taste like something out of Lulu's kitchen is the addition of rouille, a very Provençal condiment that enriches an aioli with bread crumbs and the poached liver of a meatier fish like monkfish.

Simple Fish Soup

START BY FILLETING YOUR FISH (or by asking your fishmonger to do it for you—either way, you need to retain the bones and cleaned head). I prefer a firm-fleshed whitefish that will hold together for this recipe: something like rockfish, snapper, halibut, or lingcod. Make a stock with the bones and well-rinsed head: place them in a medium stainless steel pot, cover with water, and add a cup of dry white wine; set on medium-high heat. Bring to a boil, skimming off the white foam from the top of the stock as it appears.

WHILE YOU ARE WAITING for the liquid to come to a boil, ready the vegetables: a chopped small leek, a few chopped ribs of celery, a thinly sliced carrot, two halved cloves of garlic, a sliced white onion, a thinly sliced small bulb of fennel, a teaspoon of black peppercorns, a bay leaf or two, a few sprigs of thyme, and some flat-leaf Italian parsley. Reserve a small amount of your carrot, leek, and fennel to add to the stock after straining, but put the rest of the ingredients into the pot with the bones and head. Add a bit more water if the vegetables aren't covered by the liquid. Once the stock has come to a boil, allow it to simmer gently for 20 minutes. Remove the stock from the heat, and let it steep for 10 minutes before passing it through a fine-mesh strainer into another medium-sized stainless steel pot (or rinse and clean out the original one to reuse it). Taste the stock and season it lightly with sea salt, if necessary—it should be tasty. I add a splash of very good olive oil at this juncture. Put the pot of strained stock back on the stove and bring to a gentle simmer. Add the reserved carrot, leek, and fennel and allow to cook until tender but not mushy (about 10 minutes). Then poach your fillets in the stock until they are just cooked through, about 7 minutes. Sweet ripe tomatoes, peeled, seeded, and broken up in your hands, are something Lulu frequently added in the summer months. If using, add them to the stock along with the fillets. When the fish is cooked, ladle equal portions of fish, stock, and vegetables into individual bowls. Garnish with Lulu's rouille (below), or a big dollop of garlicky aioli (page 69) and a dusting of coarsely chopped parsley, and serve with Garlic Toast (page 71).

Lulu's Rouille

START BY DISSOLVING ¼ teaspoon of saffron powder in a few tablespoons of hot fish soup. Poach one fish liver—Lulu uses the liver of a monkfish—in a simmering pan of fish broth, until it has firmed up but is still pink. Put a cup of fresh bread crumbs (without crusts) into a bowl, and, with a fork, mash them with the dissolved saffron, adding a bit more fish stock, if necessary, to make a loose paste. In a mortar, pound two dried cayenne peppers to a powder with a wooden pestle (or use powdered cayenne). Add a large pinch of coarse salt and three garlic cloves and pound to a paste. Add the poached monkfish liver, and continue pounding until you have a consistent, thick, smooth paste. Add an egg yolk and the saffron-bread paste and stir it briskly with a pestle until the mixture is uniform. Finally, mount it as you would a mayonnaise, whisking vigorously, while adding about two cups of olive oil in a thin, slow trickle.

CHAPTER 14

The Mistral

This morning I woke up to the wind. California in the winter can sometimes feel like the South of France, especially when the weather's been withholding rain and there's little moisture hanging in the air. The mistral, a strong northwesterly wind that blows from the south coast of France into the Gulf of Lion—a wide embayment in the northern Mediterranean—is a wind I came to know well as a child. I think it was Lulu who first told me about the mistral when I was small, and, the way she spoke about it, I understood it almost to be the spirit of an old familiar, long since passed but still intent on returning from time to time to cause a ruckus. Lying in my bedroom in the attic of the Domaine in the afternoon, when everyone had retreated for a postprandial nap, I would listen to the clattering of the louvered shutters against the window frame and watch the prismatic dance of sunlight on my chest and bedspread, feeling myself to be in the company of a ghost.

There is something about a wind like that that will shape whole days, that will give body to the out-of-doors and make the atmosphere hum in a state of anticipation as if charged through with electricity. I loved the mistral, whisking the smoke up from faraway agricultural fires and transporting its burnt-grass scent to the stoop of the Domaine, bringing up seagull feathers from the beach, making the cypress trees creak and whistle in a kind of arthritic ecstasy. I was also a little afraid of it, when for days and days it wouldn't relent, and the fishermen couldn't go out to sea, and the wildlife would go quiet, and if it had been a very dry year, the viticulturists would fret about a single spark setting off a devastating blaze. Nothing could be heard over the wind: not the cicadas with their dry-winged drone, not the crash of waves, not even the sound of cars on the nearby autoroute. (The latter, paved in overclose proximity to the perimeter of the Domaine in 1974, continues to wound my mother's aesthetic sensibility, though her complaints have petered out of late.) There is almost a color to the mistral, as if it could texture the air and pick up sunlight, but it was never the warm sun color of summer—rather a slant, cooler shade, the color of winter from a faraway sea come in to chill the South.

We'd be forced indoors for meals when the mistral struck, and there wouldn't be a fish in sight. There was in fact something of a de facto mistral menu: things that didn't depend on a placid, hospitable sea. I could tell too that even though Lulu felt a kind of a kinship with that wind—a shared mischievous spirit, perhaps—she'd begin to feel restless if it persisted too long, robbing her of her daily swim in the sea or stroll along the strand at Sanary-sur-Mer, and, most frustratingly, preventing her from cooking fish, her favorite thing to prepare. Which is why when I think of windy days, I think of the cool dark of the indoors—the heavy wooden blinds closed to prevent the wind from slamming them or, worse, rattling a window hard enough to shatter it. Lulu would light a fire in the kitchen hearth and we'd listen to the wind sing in the chimney, sucking up vine smoke with a ferocious draw and sometimes puffing it back into the room like a capricious child regurgitating something unappetizing.

These fishless days might call for a *gigot d'agneau à la ficelle,* a favorite preparation of a leg of lamb in which the haunch is suspended before a fire by a long taut string wound tightly round its ankle. Once the leg was strung up like this from a horizontal bar installed a little ways into the chimney, Lulu would wind it up and then let it unwind.

It would whirl fast at first, like the hypnotic dance of a dervish, and then move slowly as inertia worked to reduce its movement to a melancholic twirl. When gravity had pulled it to a near stop, Lulu would pass by and wind it up again, brushing it intermittently with a rosemary branch dipped into the rendered fat collecting in a dish at the mouth of the hearth. This varnish of liquid fat would give it the luster of reflected fire, so it glowed yellow as if gilded in gold leaf. I could watch this twirling and untwirling for hours, which is more or less the length of time it takes to cook, as the fire needs to be hot but not scorching, with the warmth penetrating and browning the meat only very slowly. It is a dish for the patient. But it is also a dish for the kitchen spectators. And certainly it's a good thing to make if you'd like to keep your children out of your hair for an unbroken stretch of time. This thoroughly unmechanized method of rotisserie cooking remains one of the magical things in Lulu's repertoire and, in the simple elegance of its engineering, could keep me captive in her kitchen all morning. This also meant, of course, that I could be recruited to perform small kitchen tasks, like peeling garlic cloves or plucking the little leaves from the stalks of wild flowering savory or de-pitting those shriveled dry-cured black olives found in so many Provençal dishes so that she could make a rustic tapenade.

A gigot like this was usually prepared in the morning to be ready for lunch, which was always the largest and most ceremonious meal of the day. Quite rightly, I think, one was expected not to eat in excess straight before bed, but lunch was an altogether different story. The rambling meals at long tables cobbled together to stretch nearly the length of the front patio were always lunches, never dinners. Likewise the more formal meals taken in the dining room with all the proper china and silverware—these were lunches too. And even though Lulu is not one to stand on ceremony, she has, especially in her more advanced years, come to appreciate the civility of the more dignified dining room and the ritual of extracting the nice china and flatware that has been in the family for generations. Having crested a hundred, she is anything but sentimental—in fact, she regularly squirrels away a little dish or other memento from her house in our luggage—but she does love to engage in the rituals of the table. Her convivial, generous approach is something my mom learned from her, and I in turn from the two of them, and my kitchen and table are a kind of extension of Lulu's—or at least aspirationally so—to the extent that I've even acquired, dish by dish, a set of antique porcelain scallop-shell-shaped dishes like the ones she has at Domaine Tempier. And, in her tradition, I've never, no matter what I felt I had provisioned for, turned down a possible extra guest. There is always room for one more at Lulu's table, which I think is a reasonable adaptation that comes from having a family of more than thirty grandchildren and great-grandchildren. It's a lesson that carried naturally over to my mother's table. We have a saying in our house: our table is ever expanding and always open; any friend, child, or partner is always welcome to tag along.

Gigot d'Agneau à la Ficelle

THIS PREPARATION is not for the faint of heart, nor is it for homes lacking an indoor hearth of some description. Still, if you either have a kitchen hearth or are willing to cook something very savory and aromatic in your living room fireplace, it's worth trying at least once. It will, however, also require a spirit of adventure *and* some rigging. Somewhere beneath the mantel, you'll need to install a horizontal metal bar or hook high up enough to suspend an entire dangling leg of lamb about five inches from the floor of the hearth. It will also require a fire to be lit well in advance, so that a strong, enduring core of heat is built up, to which logs will regularly need to be added. Richard Olney, who included this preparation in the pages of his book *Lulu's Provençal Table*, rightly describes it as "the most primitive and most satisfying method of roasting a leg of lamb."

PLACE A 6-POUND LEG OF LAMB (with pelvic bone removed, but the leg bone and ankle intact) into a large dish. Rub the surfaces of the lamb with a

couple of glugs of good olive oil, 8 crushed, peeled cloves of garlic, a couple of tablespoons of fine sea salt, and torn herbs—several bay leaves and a couple of sprigs each of thyme, savory, and parsley. Cover and refrigerate overnight.

BUILD AND LIGHT A FIRE, and feed it continuously. Remove the lamb from the refrigerator to temper (this should be done at least 3 hours before cooking). Make a basting mixture by combining several glugs of olive oil with salt, pepper, the juice of a lemon, and a big pinch of powdered cayenne. Discard the garlic from the surface of the lamb, and add any residual oil from its pan to the basting liquid. Tie one end of a strong piece of kitchen twine to the shank bone, and tie the other end to the aforementioned bar or hook so that the leg hangs right in front of the center of the fire. Arrange your logs so as to bring the core toward the leg, feeding the fire at an angle from both sides in order to move the hottest embers to the center, behind the meat. Place a pan below the lamb to catch the drippings. Give the heel a firm twist and inertia will do its work—it will wind itself up in one direction and then down again in the other, requiring only very occasionally that you additionally twist it. Don't be afraid to give it a little encouragement from time to time.

AFTER ABOUT 15 MINUTES, start to baste the meat regularly. Dip a long, sturdy rosemary branch into the basting mixture and brush the whole of the leg as it continues to rotate. Keep the fire hot. After about an hour and a half, stop adding fresh wood and allow the flames to die down. It should take somewhere in the neighborhood of two hours total to cook the lamb, with an instant-read thermometer registering the internal temperature at around 130°F. Remove the leg from the hearth and place it on a large serving platter to rest, covered with a sheet of aluminum foil, for 15 minutes. Discard the drippings. Carve the leg at the table, ladling any juices over each serving.

•   •   •

Another classic "mistral dish" was Lulu's Soupe au Pistou. It was a natural corollary to her gigot, since she would throw the lamb bones into a stockpot after the meal to make a rich stock from the remains. This savory liquid formed the base for her soup. A rustic concoction, it was one of my favorite things in her repertoire, laced, as it reliably was, with her ragged, hand-pounded basil pesto. The contents of the soup are, as far as I can tell, completely subject to change and seasonal availability, but it is at its core a hearty vegetable soup. Lulu's summer version always contained a sautéed mirepoix (diced onions, celery, carrot, and a bit of minced garlic) that she'd lubricate with her stock once the vegetables had grown translucent and a bit caramelized. Into this, she would add cubed zucchini or other fresh summer squash, trimmed green beans cut into small segments, and some variety of freshly shucked shell beans—maybe some white flageolets or borlotti—which she'd have cooked separately ahead of time until they were tender and buttery. Once the flavors of these things had been allowed to marry in the broth for ten or so minutes—it was important the zucchini not become overcooked—she'd add a few small tomatoes slipped of their skins, tearing them apart slightly in her hands as she did so. What was non-negotiable was the basil sauce—what tasted to be almost equal parts basil and garlic—a heady garnish she'd loosen with a liberal pour of olive oil and embellish with a little grated Parmesan, if she had any on hand. A winter version substitutes cubed butternut squash for the zucchini and cooked dried beans for the fresh ones, and omits the green beans altogether. My mom sometimes adds cooked farro to make it a bit more substantial in colder months. If you can't find basil, a pounded parsley-oregano pesto makes a delicious alternative (just don't forget the garlic!). Still, it's for the memory of the smell of basil wafting out of Lulu's mortar like an intoxicating perfume that I make this soup—a reminder of her sitting in the deep cool of her kitchen as the mistral harassed the region, whisking things into disarray.

CHAPTER 15

Les Petites Mouettes

Even though the Domaine contained a villa of sizable proportions, we rarely stayed there during our longer summer stints. I think my mom liked the thought of being able to return Lulu's hospitality, since we were always being invited for meals. But she also relished having her own kitchen, a place she could roam freely, preparing something whenever the mood struck, rather than feel herself to be constrained by the rhythms of a given host's appetites. The rental house I remember most was called Les Petites Mouettes and was situated more or less right on the water a few minutes out of the center of the town of Bandol. There are few beaches in that part of the Côte d'Azur; rather the earth seems to jut out of the water at precipitous verticals, or, from an elevated vantage, to drop off suddenly into the sea. The sublimely beautiful stretch of coastline called the Calanques, a protected region a little ways west of Bandol, has a quality similar to the more famous White Cliffs of Dover but is made of that dark gray volcanic rock native to the Mediterranean.

Our house that one summer wasn't exactly on a cliff, but the "path" down to the water was more a scramble over a sheer stack of foot-cutting boulders than a pleasant meander to the shore. Once at the bottom, you could enter the water only by hurling yourself from the rocks—there was no gentler way to achieve submersion. This is why

my mother—whose ideal ocean temperature is pegged to Hawaii's waters on a midsummer day—rarely elected to swim. It was nonetheless in the protected cradle of the small bay on which Les Petites Mouettes was situated that Lulu's son François would take whatever kids were hanging around to dive for sea urchins. Which is to say, *he* would dive for urchins while we clustered on the rocks closest to the water, excitedly awaiting his reemergence. When he surfaced, his hands would be full of spiny violet-colored creatures whose formidable armor did nothing to deter the intrepid forager. I can't remember if François whipped a jackknife from his impossibly minuscule Speedo, but I wouldn't have been surprised if the blade he used was obsidian gleaned from the ocean's floor. In any event, he opened a few of these echinoderms right there on the rocks for us to sample. I may have had sea urchin before this point, since it was not a completely foreign ingredient in California (where urchins are harvested in Mendocino and Santa Barbara), but this was certainly my most memorable experience of eating one. François extended the thorn-rimmed cup and we kids dared to gingerly fish our little hands into their hearts to extract the quivering marigold-colored flesh, the salt of the sea the only condiment. I was a precocious lover of oysters and fish roe, so this was no great challenge to my palate, but I remember being struck by how it managed to taste at once like land and sea, both of butter *and* of fish, but also of something almost fruity, like the flesh of a slightly overripe peach. My mother was always overjoyed with the haul. On those nights she would make spaghetti, whisking the urchin with butter to make a sauce, just a scant golden coating of the noodles that completely transformed them.

François's foraging skills were not confined to the ocean (though he was preternaturally at ease in the water); he knew the land just as intimately. As the longtime viticulturist at the Domaine, he spent

his days among the vines, discerning their moods, their needs, their proclivities—a kind of agriculture literacy I've witnessed very rarely. My dad always said that good wine is made more in the vineyard than in the barrel, and if that's truly the case, François was disproportionately responsible for the quality of Domaine Tempier's wines (though I shouldn't discount the critical influence of his brother, Jean-Marie, who became the winemaker when Lucien retired). For at least a handful of decades François tended to the family's estate, made up of a patchwork of plots, spread between the main site of the Domaine and up into the surrounding hills. The three off-site vineyards have wonderful Provençal names—La Migoua, La Tourtine, and Cabassaou—and are made into distinct wines with eponymous titles. I never understood exactly what distinguished the vineyards—they all grew out of the same craggy soil, if at slightly different altitudes—but they somehow produced tangibly different elixirs (and were assigned escalating prices that seemed also to be relative to scarcity). It was my father who explained a lot of this to me and who took me along to wine tastings—whether at the Domaine or on visits to other venerable châteaux—so that I could learn how to discern the nuances of flavor from one prized liquid to the next. At these tastings, often held in musty cobwebbed caves, I was always the only kid. Hardly a budding oenophile, as an eight-year-old I just loved being with my dad, who patiently taught me how to taste a wine by fluttering it on my tongue to saturate the palate with flavor before then rolling my tongue into a kind of tube to more expediently discharge the mouthful into a spittoon. I was quite adept at this maneuver, and I think, in those moments of wine tasting with a distinguished set of older male vignerons, I made my father about as proud as he's ever been. But he also taught me to cup the bowl of the glass in one hand to warm the red liquid while trapping its aroma beneath the other, which was to stay firmly pressed to the glass's mouth. "Swirl it gently," he would instruct, "then bring it right up to your nose before you lift your hand.

Then inhale." He would always ask me to tease out the smells—this one tinged with the smell of overripe berries, this one with wet earth, another with dry hay, and so on. Whether or not he knew it at the time, he was training me to have a degree of olfactory sensitivity that would eventually torture everyone in the household, unless, of course, the subject under discussion was wine.

· · ·

Though, on a given day, Lulu will open at least a few bottles of the wine produced from the most immediate vines on the property—called Cuvée Classique—only very, very rarely would a bottle of Cabassaou see the light of day, even in the matriarch's house. I suppose the family couldn't afford to keep up with Lulu's habit if they were furnishing her daily with bottles of their rarest libation. My whole life I've known Lulu to easily dispatch at least a bottle of red wine on her own, though without ever seeming in the slightest bit cognitively diminished. My mother is convinced it's the key to her longevity, and I'm inclined to agree. The wines of Domaine Tempier, especially when consumed at the source, have a way of disguising themselves as health tonics—the more you drink, the better you feel. When I was younger I asked Lulu once why she never drank water—I had seen her drink little other than red wine, an occasional glass of champagne, and a scant cup of herbal tisane before bed. She turned to me, her hazel eyes glinting with mischief, and said, *"Je ne bois jamais d'eau! Si tu bois de l'eau, tu rouilles!"* ("I never drink water! If you drink water, you rust!")

It wasn't just the vines that François knew; he was likewise a connoisseur of the wild edibles of the region and, like his mother, was adept at corralling the robust flavors of the Provençal wilderness in his home cooking. Wild savory, say, or the green seeds of roadside fennel, the innermost kernels of wild cherries—these things were at home in his kitchen. He was also, incidentally, one of the best cooks in my early childhood. I yearned to be invited to his house for an aperitif, and a daytime visit meant he might have a fire going to grill mussels, which I love more than anything. I don't think there's a more delicious way to prepare them. He used something like my mother's Tuscan grill—a flat, simple square grill—placed low over the coals of a fire made from vine shoots (called *sarments* in French), which keep their slender vegetal form even after they've been transformed from wood to ember. François would shuck the mussels and set them down open-faced on the grill, dousing them in a bit of the olive oil he made from the Domaine's old mangled olive trees, and adding a quick grind of black pepper at the end. As we waited, we ate the green *olives cassées* he'd cured himself, using the ash from his wood fire and the green flowers and seeds of blossoming wild fennel. The mussels would begin to whistle from the grill as each one came to a boil in its own brine. At just the moment when they were completely cooked through, François would pluck them from the grill and his adored wife, Paule, would offer them to us on a platter, along with the sliced heel of a loaf of bread she had made. The taste of the sea; the flavor, almost figgy, of the vine fire in the smoke infusing the flesh; the oil mixing with the broth cast from the mussels as they cooked, each one a soupy and smoky delight.

Fennel-Infused Olives

CURING OLIVES the way François does requires harvesting or buying small raw green olives, breaking them open slightly with a hammer, doing something inscrutable with grape wood ash and sea salt brine to leach out the acridity from the flesh, locating fresh green fennel flowers to season them, and a lot of waiting. There was a fair amount of experimenting with curing olives in our family (with our Sicilian blacksmith friend, Angelo Garro, leading the efforts), but never much success. It's hard to rid an olive of its native bitterness and difficult too to infuse it in the curing process with the correct balance of flavor. Below is a shorthand method that approximates the effect of eating François's special olives.

PEOPLE RARELY THINK to marinate or additionally season olives bought at a grocer or market, but it's amazing what you can do to enhance the flavor of an already cured olive with a bit of spice and warmth, to make it that much more lovely a thing to begin a meal with or present with a drink. Start with about a cup of olives, preferably a green variety like Picholine, Castelvetrano, or Lucques. Drain them from their brine and place them in a sauté pan with a big sprinkle of fennel seeds, a couple of sprigs of thyme, a glug of extra virgin olive oil, and a few long, flat strips of zest, cut from the outermost peel of both an orange and a lemon using a sharp paring knife or a vegetable peeler. Warm the olives gently over low heat for a few minutes and serve while still warm.

Grilled Mussels   IT'S HARD TO FIND good fresh mussels these days. My mom and I have virtually stopped eating them because they're especially susceptible to pollution—it always feels like a risk. Still, it's impossible to resist François and, moreover, this particular preparation—which is about as simple as they come. If you make this dish, be exceptionally confident in your mussel source and ask your fishmonger questions about provenance and freshness (they shouldn't be more than a day or two old and preferably from a clean local place of origin). These can be made, as François does, on a grill outside over a wood fire, but they can also be prepared on a barbecue grill. Be sure, however, to use wood that will burn cleanly, and whose aroma will complement the mussels—they will take on a lot of the flavor of the woodsmoke. François uses old grapevine wood, which is ideal, but fig or apple wood work well too, as does oak if you can't find anything fruitier. Clean your mussels thoroughly in cold water and, using an oyster knife and a glove, shuck them, discarding the top shell. Make sure to smell each mussel as you open it; if it doesn't smell quite right, toss it. Set the shucked mussels aside on a large platter, drizzle a little extra virgin olive oil into each, and season with freshly ground black pepper and a tiny sprinkle of sel gris. Once your fire has died down to very hot, glowing embers, adjust the grill to sit just above the coals. Place the mussels one by one on the grill. I like to have a few slices of good levain bread to grill alongside the mussels. When the slices have some color, rub them with a fresh garlic clove cut in half, drizzle with olive oil, and serve alongside the mussels when they're ready. You'll know the mussels are done when they begin to sizzle, contract, and grow opaque. Pull them off the grill and serve immediately.

•　　•　　•

Most of the big meals that I remember from our summers in Bandol took place at the Domaine, but on a few occasions my mom would get everyone to come over to Mouettes for dinner. This usually happened toward the end of the summer, once our rental house had begun to feel like our own—had become patinated, so to speak, by our having cooked prolifically and burned rosemary indoors and trailed sand and seawater through every room and sat for too long on the sofas in wet bathing suits. If you visited us in the final days of our vacation, you'd also find drifts of notebook paper covered in drawings. Bob would have transformed our living room into an improvised studio, and the evidence of a creative summer would be conspicuous: piles of oil pastels, a makeshift easel, heaps of colored pencil shavings. I'll never forget one summer when we stayed in a house with a wide upstairs veranda that looked out directly over a proud, immense palm tree. Every morning Bob and I would sketch this tree, each time according to a different rubric. "This time, draw only the part of the tree that's in the sun," he would say; the next morning, "Draw only what's in shadow." My favorite prompt was being told to draw the tree according to the path an ant would take if it was exploring it. There was no one more compulsively creative, or more patient, than Bob.

Anyway, for the big meals at Mouettes, my mother would summon not just a handful of the Peyrauds but also my godfather, Kermit Lynch, and his wife, Gail Skoff, who lived nearby in Le Beausset during the summers; Richard Olney, from his paradisal culinary oasis up in the hills of Solliès-Toucas; my godmother, Martine, and her husband, Claude, from Vence, a tiny town near Nice; and even Nathalie Waag from Bonnieux, who was an old friend of Martine's and Lulu's and also the mother of Alexandre and Jérôme (the latter of whom would, two decades later, become the chef of Chez Panisse).

Everyone gathered on the expansive back patio littered with long brown pine needles to have an aperitif, and Martine would mix me my own "cocktail": a splash of red wine vinegar in a glass of sparkling water. Over the course of the afternoon, the aperitif hour would more or less morph into the meal itself. Claude and Martine would smoke cigarettes with Richard, who no matter the degree of solemnity of a given occasion was perpetually clad in little other than a miniature pair of jean cutoff shorts, flat espadrilles, and a short-sleeved button-down shirt left agape to reveal his convex bronzed belly. Richard was by this time already a very established culinary figure, having written *The French Menu Cookbook* and *Simple French Food*—both of which deeply influenced my mother—and in 1977 having been appointed editor in chief of the twenty-eight-volume Time-Life Good Cook series. Together with Julia Child's efforts, these books were part of a push to codify and familiarize the anglophonic public with French cuisine. He'd also collaborated with Lulu to transcribe and publish all of her regional recipes in what was in our house a Bible-like text called *Lulu's Provençal Table*. To me, at age nine, he was a sort of grudgingly kind, largely disinterested (in me, anyway) older gay man with sartorial flair who happened to make terrific omelettes. My mother, on the other hand, treated him like a deity. These meals were usually not designated potlucks but in some fashion ended up emulating the form. It was virtually impossible to have so much culinary talent concentrated in such a small space and not have everyone wanting to pitch in, or at least editorialize. For these occasions Nathalie would often bring the ingredients for one of my favorite salads—she knew how much I liked it—and I would help her prepare it. It was a salad of blanched small green beans, strips of roasted red bell pepper, tiny chanterelle mushrooms, toasted hazelnuts, torn parsley, and a vinaigrette made with walnut oil.

First, we topped and tailed all the beans together, tossing the little pile of ends over the patio railing into the sea. Next, we emptied the beans into a pan of heavily salted water, letting them very quickly blanch before spreading them out on a *torchon* to arrest the cooking and allow them to dry. We roasted the peppers over the gas flame of the stove until they were thoroughly blackened and so fragrant that everyone stopped smoking and chatting and became pleasantly aware of their hunger. "They are not too burnt?" Martine asked from over my shoulder as I turned the peppers with a long-handled pair of tongs.

Nathalie quickly transferred them into a bowl and covered it with a plate to steam their skins so that they could easily be scraped away from the flesh with a paring knife. After the peppers had cooled, I carefully cut them into ribbons on the bias, making sure that all their pale confetti-like seeds had been cleaned from them along with any remaining bits of integument. Nathalie tossed the chanterelles with a bit of minced garlic and olive oil in a sauté pan to *just* warm them through, to open their flavor and make them tender, without cooking them to the point of casting off excessive moisture.

Meanwhile, my mom toasted the hazelnuts in a cast-iron pan set atop the highly provisional and no doubt rental-house-deposit-forsaking grill she'd erected on the tiled patio, using just a few fire-proof bricks and a grill she'd found at a secondhand store. Finally, I pounded a clove of garlic with salt for Nathalie to make the sauce, dousing it in lemon juice and red wine vinegar to macerate for a few minutes. She always brought a little flask of walnut oil along, since she knew my mother never kept any, and would slip it into the bowl as if it were contraband. My mom's aversion to nut oils generally lay in the incontestable fact that they spoil very quickly. You had to use a lot of walnut oil in your cooking to rationalize its purchase, and even then you had to taste various brands and be willing to toss out or return just-opened bottles if there was even the slightest hint of rancidity. Needless to say, the oil Nathalie procured from her *épicerie* in Bon-nieux was exceptionally fresh and nutty—I loved the unusual flavor it imparted, especially as a complement to the distinct but related flavor of the toasted hazelnuts. While Nathalie assembled the salad, using her hands to coat the mix of beans, mushrooms, nuts, parsley, and peppers in vinaigrette, my mom was just pulling off a perfect rack of rosemary-strewn lamb chops from the grill—always less trimmed and shorn of fat by the French *boucheries* than by our American ones. At age nine I still recoiled at the thought of eating the thick pearlescent rind of semi-rendered fat that rimmed my chop. My mom plucked it from my plate with gusto, pronouncing us a reincarnation of Jack Sprat and his wife (he who consumed no fat, she no lean, so that "betwixt the two of them, they licked the platter clean").

As the night fell and the mosquitoes began to rise out of nowhere, my mom would light those coils—made, I believe, from the powdered extract of an insecticide found in daisies—at the distant reaches of the patio. I'd watch the smoke snaking from them, and like a serpent in a trance would start to sink into my seat. I never remembered the ends of these long summer meals, no doubt because someone—likely my dad, or Bob—would have plucked me from my post and carried me upstairs, where I'd sleep more deeply, from within the safety of my draped muslin net, than I would almost anywhere else in world.

CHAPTER 16

La Villa des Clairs Matins

Though Martine and Claude were friends of my mother's from Berkeley (dating back to their extended 1970s residency during Claude's mathematics postdoc at the university), by the time I arrived, they had moved back to France and were living in a small southern town called Vence. They have since moved from Vence to the outskirts of Montpellier, and in fact have always had a small apartment in Paris, but I only ever visited them at La Villa des Clairs Matins. Many beautiful homes populated my childhood—memorable places inhabited by the more eccentric or artistic friends of my parents—but there was really nowhere else like Martine and Claude's.

To get there, I remember you had to brave a long driveway that rambled down at a forty-five-degree angle barely navigable by Claude's old pale blue and cream-colored deux chevaux. On our way there my parents would fret sotto voce about whether the rental car could survive the rough declivity, and moreover whether it would prove capable of mounting the incline upon exit. Needless to say, there was no Waters-Singer rental vehicle that ever made its way back onto the Hertz lot in pristine condition. Even if it didn't fall prey to the driveway at Martine and Claude's, at some point in the season my mother was sure to run it slightly off the side of the road, skimming a cypress hedge or scraping it through a choked opening in a vineyard. La Villa des Clairs

Matins definitely *had* a front door, but at the bottom of the hill was a garden whose lawn sublimated into the gravel of the drive. It was exclusively through this semi-cultivated sward that we would enter the house—up the back steps and into the kitchen directly (which in any event was where you wanted to be at Martine's). Because even though Martine is a practicing artist, she is, as much as any of the other culinary greats I've encountered in my life, an irreducible force in the kitchen, as inventive there as she is before a sheet of paper, a set of watercolors in hand.

We never stayed for very long with Claude and Martine, whose hospitality was always limned with something approaching contempt. Which is to say: we were admitted warmly, with the greatest love, but not long afterward were willed gently back onto the road, once our American appetites for certain conveniences (excessive use of hot water, say) had begun to abrade the sensibilities of our more provident hosts. There was an order to things, and we were foreign agents of disarray. Martine's "official" role as my godmother did little to soften her emotional parsimony—I knew that she loved me, but she was almost cartoonishly withholding (some, I'm sure, would just write this off as "being French"). But, over time, the consistency of her rigid demeanor was itself a kind of comfort, indeed an attitudinal disposition, I came to depend on, and anyway it was offset by Claude's congenital conviviality, a warmth I always think of in relationship to the French adjective *chaleureux* (which despite being the literal translation of *warm* contains a necessary element of onomatopoeia the English lacks).

Martine is tall and angular and extraordinary looking. She has always worn her dark hair in a short curly bob with straight-across bangs, her lips painted in maroon, a mouth eternally etched in a 1930s silver-screen pout. Her clothing was always vintage: exquisite crepe de chine ankle-kissing florals, her feet bound in the ribbons of flat espadrilles, bangles jangling at her wrists while she cooked.

Sometimes she'd throw on an architectural jacket, block-printed by her Venice-based textile designer sister, Hélène, or a pair of trousers whose tailoring felt vaguely Japanese. She was chic but also irrepressibly bohemian, and the confluence of those things gave her a style completely her own. Claude was her counterpart in this respect too: a shorter, rounder, less refined figure, but possessed of a kind and open face set with enormous eyes whose movements during storytelling often became their own plotline. Photos of the two of them in their youth were beguiling. Martine could easily have been one of the film starlets whose lip line she mimed; the glamour she embodied seeped from the frames of photographs. Claude back then—a svelter version of himself, his jaw defined and set—would bend to the sobriety Martine's implacable gaze mandated; serious, frozen in black and white. They were beautiful.

The house was Martine's masterpiece. She is that type of artist whose practice is more a compulsion than an art form; it suffuses everything she touches. In this respect, she resembles my mother (or perhaps my mother resembles her?). The house had no doubt been inherited with existing centuries' worth of patina (floors lined in foot-worn tiles, louvered shutters a pale shade of sun-bleached blue, etc.), but Martine had—in the forty-plus years of renting the villa—left no corner untended. Because Martine was the *Reine des Brocantes,* the *Impératrice des Marchés aux Puces*—no one could find treasures like she could. No one could thrift with such intuition, such success, with that balanced mix of investment and indifference that yielded the most covetable finds at the most bargain prices. My mother always said it was Martine who taught her to shop for antiques. It was hard to fully believe that, since my mom is known for her eye and her beautiful collections of things, and of course for her unwillingness to compromise on aesthetics. But watch the two of them poke around a *brocante* together and it's clear who's the student and who's the teacher. Martine can case a joint in a glance; fifteen minutes later my mom will still be ogling a set of champagne coupes Martine has already pronounced as "*Trop cher, Alice! T'es folle, quoi?*" And she's right, because the next vendor will have an even better set at a better price, and those will be the ones worth carrying home to the States in our luggage, wrapped in all our clothing like eggshells.

Martine's gift—both in antiquing and crafting—was evident in every room of Clairs Matins. Each one contained a lamp, or several, whose paper shade was printed or painted by hand. Each salvaged sofa or bed frame, chair or divan (little was ever bought new), contained a cluster of pillows hand-sewn from her sister's printed textiles or ones she'd painted herself. Art nouveau wallpaper, beaded silk curtains, collections of cloudy blue bottles poised on the windowsill near the lip of the bathtub, a plant with serpentine tendrils hanging from above—the place felt like a lived-in theater backdrop for a play set in Weimar Germany. There were candlesticks mounted to certain walls, brass-rimmed mirrors on desks or chests of drawers, their glass smoky and flecked with age spots; in that house of permanently low light, your reflection was always its most flattering. I loved to dwell in the downstairs toilet a moment longer than necessary just to gaze at the selection of clippings and ephemera pinned to its walls. Dozens of bits of paper, their edges curled but not degraded beyond legibility: a black-and-white advertisement featuring a beautiful model in high-cut underwear, a paper valentine, a *carte postale* from an anonymous beach town, a family photo.

The garden was a mix of flowers and vegetables, cultivated patches with wild edges and a stretch of pleasantly neglected grass studded with fallen plums or other overripe fruits of the season. In the later summer, several herbs would be going strenuously to seed; a few lettuces with bolted cores, like vegetal skyscrapers, stood amid the low-rise clusters of fraises des bois or ground-hugging *courgette* with its tortuous limbs. Edible things were interspersed with roses, but only the most heirloom of varietals, with a proliferation of a certain heavily scented rose my mother called "Tango," a flower used in the manufacture of perfume, whose splayed petals were the melded colors of a Los Angeles sunset, a deep tangerine edged in pink—it was my mother's favorite. These roses seemed to bloom endlessly, from the late spring through to the beginning of autumn, and Martine would arrange jars and vases of them throughout the house, often at an open window so that any movement of the air would carry their scent into the room, giving the illusion that the breeze in Vence smelled exclusively of roses.

My mother has written about how Martine changed the nature of her palate, and maybe the course of her career, with her attention to flavor and her uncompromising approach to cooking. Meeting her was very possibly the fulcrum in Chez Panisse's conception—in the late sixties, no one else in Berkeley was cooking like her. Martine had and still has a way of thinking up new things to do with flavor that fit neatly into her southern French repertoire. Radical simplicity, shot through with innovation. The perfect mesclun salad, say, laced with a pounded tarragon dressing. A dish of rabbit braised with grapefruit peel. A lemon tart made with candied bergamot in the curd, its crust cut with buckwheat flour.

One summer, when I was fifteen, I was visiting with my best friend at the beginning of a long European trip. We'd spent the first two nights in London, but when we arrived in Vence, we were still jet-lagged and delirious. Scarcely had we deposited our bags in the downstairs bedroom than Martine had shooed us out into the garden, a chipped enamel colander in hand, and asked us to pick what remained of the cilantro. By this point in the summer it was already beyond blossom: a small thicket of spindly umbelliferous green stems ending in tiny, fresh, and exceptionally pungent seeds. We picked it all. Every last little leaf, every gleaming little emerald sphere. I have never forgotten what Martine prepared with those cilantro remains, in part because the flavors struck me as vaguely incongruent with her cooking, and certainly with French cuisine more broadly. But also because she made something out of what was next to nothing: cooked bow-tie pasta, mixed with cream, butter-softened onion, a little nub of Parmesan, grated, and all of our green harvest, chopped and folded in, salt, pepper, and a blanket of crispy bread crumbs to form a crust. It was a simple pasta gratin, really, but like nothing you'd ever tasted in that vein; the cilantro a new perfume that added a reverberating set of flavors to something homey and familiar, rendering it so much more delicious.

Green Coriander Seed Pasta

THOUGH I AM CERTAIN that the *pasta gratinée* Martine made for us that night was not particularly complicated, I have never been able to satisfactorily re-create it—and believe me, I have tried. Somehow, between a béchamel and cheese and melted onion, something of the fresh green coriander taste is lost. I've asked Martine about it, but she has not the faintest memory of the preparation—amazing, really, how certain flavors lodge in the minds of some but not of others. Then again, Martine is a prolific author of delicious dishes; I'm not surprised this one didn't become a fixture. It is, after all, quite difficult to find green coriander seeds. They require that a farmer allow a portion of her plants to go to flower and then to seed, a process that takes a fair amount of time, as nature completes her ponderous cycle. Still, we're seeing them more and more in the farmers markets in California, and if you find a farmer selling bunches of cilantro, why not ask them if they'd consider allowing some of their crop to progress to the next phase? The best solution, however, if you have access to a patch of garden, is to grow some yourself, planting twice as much as you think you need, letting half of it go to seed. The tiny white flowers are as worthwhile as the seeds and should be used liberally to garnish soups, salads, or this pasta—my version is inspired by Martine's, but borrows from the Roman classic *cacio e pepe*. It is *very* different from Martine's method, but alike in spirit. I've used bow-tie pasta here in homage to the original, but this bright, creamy sauce would be wonderful on spaghetti or bucatini.

BEFORE MAKING THE PASTA, which takes just minutes to prepare, start with the bread crumbs. These are by no means necessary for the dish, but they add a burst of flavor and crunch, reminiscent of Martine's gratin topping. Preheat the oven to 350°F. Pare away the crust from a slightly stale country-style bread, such as a levain, and cut the bread into cubes. Tear into smaller irregular pieces until the crumbs are about ¼ inch around.

COMBINE OLIVE OIL (about 1 tablespoon for every cup of bread crumbs) with garlic grated on a Microplane grater. Pour this over the bread, along with a large pinch of salt, and toss until evenly coated. Bake on a sheet pan until golden brown, stirring every few minutes.

TO MAKE THE PASTA, pick the umbrellaed cilantro stems clean of the bright green seeds until you have about 2 tablespoons, setting aside any flowers for later. Place in a mortar and add a generous pinch of salt along with a handful or two of roughly chopped cilantro leaves. Pound for several minutes. The leaves will disintegrate, but the seeds themselves are too fibrous to turn into a paste. Pound until they break into much smaller pieces (younger seeds will pulverize more easily). Add 3 cups of bow-tie pasta to salted boiling water. While the pasta is cooking, transfer the crushed coriander to a bowl, adding a little less than 1 cup of grated Parmesan, a teaspoon of coarsely ground black pepper, 2 tablespoons of butter, and 2 tablespoons of olive oil. Just before draining the pasta, steal about ½ cup of the pasta water. Drain the pasta and let it sit briefly in the colander while you finish the sauce by adding half of the pasta water to the coriander mixture. Stir quickly to melt the butter and cheese and emulsify the sauce. Add the pasta and stir to coat it. The green coriander seed sauce should be slightly runny; if it isn't, add a little more pasta water and stir to combine. Divide between 4 plates. If after tasting, you want more cheese, grate Parmesan or pecorino on top. Finish with a sprinkling of the garlicky bread crumbs and the plant's white flowers.

Buckwheat "Tarte au Citron"

ON A MORE RECENT VISIT to Martine and Claude's house—before they gave it up—Martine served my mom and me a lemon tart at the end of dinner. I remember there being something different about it. For starters, the flour was cut with a measure of buckwheat, which made the taste of the crust that much more complex. The shape too was slightly irregular, as if the dough hadn't quite reached to the edge of the pan. This really struck me: an oblong tart, more wonky ellipse than circle. Its imperfection was not just beautiful in the moment, but also memorable. And it seemed a kind of object lesson in hospitality: one need not churn out magazine-perfect dishes to make an impression; something clearly handmade is much more special. And of course the lemon filling, unctuous and yet barely sweet (Martine's palate bends more toward savory than sweet). I feel certain she used a bit of fresh bergamot citrus juice and zest in her curd—it was so floral. Needless to say, the following is entirely an adaptation, and while I did try to mimic her buckwheat crust, the filling is a pretty classic lemon curd (alas, without bergamot, which is especially difficult to source).

THE DOUGH for this tart is a riff on the *pâte sucrée* used in the restaurant for fruit tarts. Though it's not quite as rustic as Martine's, I wanted a reliable dough that could be managed without decades of experience improvising in the kitchen. Start with 8 tablespoons (1 stick) of room-temperature unsalted butter. Beat that together with ¼ cup of sugar until the butter mixture is creamy and light. Add a large pinch of salt, 1 egg yolk, and ¼ teaspoon of vanilla, mixing until completely combined. In a separate bowl, mix together ¾ cup plus 2 tablespoons of all-purpose flour and 6 tablespoons of buckwheat flour. (If you feel confident in your pastry skills, you can up the buckwheat to ½ cup total and decrease the all-purpose flour to ¾ cup. The dough will be more friable, but if you're practiced at rolling pastry dough, I recommend trying it.) Add the flours to the butter, mixing with a wooden spoon until the flour is completely incorporated. Gather into a ball and wrap in plastic, pressing down on the dough so that it flattens into a disc. Refrigerate for an hour, or until firm.

TO MAKE THE LEMON FILLING, grate the zest of 2 lemons into a bowl. Place a strainer over the bowl and juice two lemons into the zest, pressing the pulp against, or even through, the strainer (you'll need about ¼ cup of juice). In a small, heavy-bottomed saucepan, whisk together 2 eggs and 3 egg yolks, 5 tablespoons of sugar, and a pinch of salt. Add 2 tablespoons of milk and 6 tablespoons of chilled butter, cut into cubes. Cook the mixture over low to medium heat, stirring constantly until the butter is melted and the lemon filling thickens, resembling crème anglaise. Remove from heat and let stand for 5 minutes to thicken even more. Whisk lightly to smooth the mixture out and pour into a bowl. Cover with parchment paper and refrigerate until ready to use—the filling can be made a few days ahead.

TO ROLL OUT THE DOUGH, cut two 14-inch pieces of parchment paper. Sprinkle one lightly with flour and then place the disc of dough on top, sprinkling the dough with flour too. If it's still quite stiff from the fridge, let it soften for 15 minutes or so. Lay the other piece of paper on top of the disc and roll out the dough until it is about a 12-inch circle, dusting the dough with flour as needed to prevent sticking. Transfer the parchment to a sheet pan and chill in the refrigerator for 10 minutes.

REMOVE THE TOP SHEET of the paper and invert the dough into a 9-inch tart pan. If this feels too terrifying, try removing the bottom parchment too, which should easily come off after refrigeration. Use your hands to swiftly move the pastry over the tart pan. Press the dough into the corners of the pan, and pinch off any overhanging dough. The buckwheat makes this dough more fragile, so patch any holes with dough scraps. Don't worry if the dough looks a little beat up; it will be covered with the lemon filling. Place the tart shell in the freezer for 10 minutes before baking.

PREHEAT THE OVEN TO 350°F and bake the tart shell (and any scraps rolled into little cookies) for 15 minutes. Remove from the oven and let cool, then add the chilled lemon filling and bake at 375°F for 15 to 20 minutes, or until the filling is just set. (If during this time the crust's edges look in danger of burning, cover the crust with a long strip of foil and continue baking.) Serve in small wedges, as is, or with lightly sweetened whipped cream.

· · ·

Because Martine and Claude lived so near to Nice, there was always a temptation to make a salade Niçoise whenever we were in the vicinity or, if we were back in California, to make a version of it to conjure Martine and Claude and the aridity of the southern summer. This is a "deconstructed" version of the French classic, a favorite hearty salad we serve for lunch in our house. It's got a bit of everything, but it isn't tossed and eschews some of the conventions (I'll put lettuce in everything I can get away with putting lettuce in, whether or not the French would approve).

Deconstructed Niçoise Salad	A GOOD SALAD depends on the vinaigrette, and a Niçoise, more than others, needs an assertive, garlicky dressing to stand up to the textures and flavors of its varied ingredients. The vegetables I mention here are mostly traditional, with the exception of lettuce, but feel free to improvise, taking the concept of a cooked vegetable salad fortified with fish or egg (or both) and dressed with an assertive herbaceous dressing to whatever season and configuration you like.

TO MAKE THE VINAIGRETTE, first pound 3 garlic cloves and a generous pinch of salt in a mortar until pureed. (The amount of garlic depends upon your preference, and the season. Winter garlic tends to be more pungent, so just 2 cloves will suffice, whereas spring and summer garlic is fresher, brighter, and, in my mind, tastes great in copious amounts.) Shred or finely cut 2 cups of basil leaves and add them to the mortar, along with another modest pinch of salt, and pound until the leaves break down to form a

verdant pulp. Add 1 tablespoon of Dijon mustard, 4 teaspoons of white wine vinegar, and ½ cup of olive oil. Whisk together and taste. It should be slightly saltier, more acidic, and more garlicky than you think decent for a dinner party—the salad's ingredients absorb the flavors readily and counterbalance any pungency that threatens to overwhelm.

BEGIN BY CHARRING a whole red pepper over a gas flame or medium-hot coals (this can also be performed under the broiler of an oven), rotating it until the pepper's skin is blackened and the flesh is entirely cooked and soft. Remove from heat and place the pepper in a small covered bowl, allowing it to continue to steam, which will make slipping off the skin with a small paring knife easier.

MEANWHILE, boil two large handfuls of small potatoes in salted water until tender. In a different pot, blanch a modest pile of small green beans or haricots verts in salted water until they are cooked through. Slice several small tomatoes or a couple of large heirloom tomatoes in half or quarters, depending on their size. Wash and dry 2 heads of a crispy lettuce, like Little Gems or hearts of romaine.

TO COOK 4 EGGS, bring a pot of water to boil. Turn the flame down so that the water simmers, and gently lower the eggs, one at time with a slotted spoon, into the water. Cook for 8 minutes. Remove each egg from the water and place in a bowl of ice water.

WHEN READY TO ASSEMBLE THE SALAD, peel the eggs and slice in half. Take a jar of the best-quality tuna you can find, preferably packed in olive oil, and divide it into handsome but approachable chunks; set aside on a plate along with the halved eggs.

REMOVE THE SKIN AND SEEDS from the red pepper and cut it into slices. Place the peppers, potatoes, green beans, tomatoes, lettuce, and about ½ cup of whole Niçoise olives into a wide, shallow bowl (I prefer a shallow bowl for this salad because it shows off the beautiful ingredients).

BEFORE DRESSING, squeeze a halved lemon over the vegetables and sprinkle with salt. Toss gently. Whisk the dressing to emulsify it and pour half over the salad. Toss gently to coat and then taste for seasoning. Add salt, pepper, or more vinaigrette if necessary. Once it is seasoned to your liking, arrange the tuna and halved eggs on top of the salad. Season the eggs with sea salt and drizzle vinaigrette over the tuna. For color and a hint of heat, garnish the eggs with Marash pepper flakes. If any vinaigrette remains, save for tomorrow's salad. And if your gathering grows in numbers, add a few more eggs, tuna, or any of the vegetables to the bowl.

CHAPTER 17

The Pyrenees

Though our typical family trips to France took us to the South and to the well-traced vineyards and beaches that skirted Bandol, there was one trip when my parents, as well as a few other families, put our fate into the hands of the chef of Chez Panisse, Jean-Pierre Moullé, and his wife, Denise. The idea was for them to take a group on a tour of different culinary producers—from wine to foie gras to cheese—in and around the Pyrenees region. We began in Bordeaux, where Denise's family owns a considerable vineyard and winery. I remember only a few snippets from most of these visits, but one such vignette is especially memorable, if only for the unease that suffused it. This was the foie gras demonstration, in which we gathered in a round to watch a woman force-feed a goose. Throughout the duration of this feeding, the bird's periodic efforts to prize itself from between its master's clamped knees elicited a sort of sympathetic queasiness, and yet all we could do—short of mount an unexpected animal welfare protest—was to watch on as a seemingly endless stream of grain poured from a small burlap sack into the yawning metal funnel. The goose fanned its wings in an act of defeated demurral, showing us the soft gray-brown feathers of his undercarriage, before finally folding them up in weary submission. Feeling a young person's confusion over something registering more as violence than nourishment, at one point I turned to

my mother to ask her whether all of this was "okay." I was twelve, still tender, and needed badly to receive parental confirmation. My mother is no great defender of the type of soft abuse that foie gras entails (and the ingredient is never on the menu at Chez Panisse), but in an effort to assuage my anxiety she replied peppily, "The geese love it! They get to eat as *much* as they want of all those tasty grains, and look how their owner is massaging their necks so lovingly. It must feel like heaven." I was not exactly convinced, but neither was I in a position to argue— I let it go.

The chapter of this trip that would prove most memorable—and far less traumatic—was a jaunt high into the mountains to sleep amid a flock of sheep. I should preface this story with the well-known fact that my mother is not a camper. The idea of sleeping outdoors in a small nylon pod, encased in a synthetic wad of insulation and on a potentially uneven surface, has never appealed to her. In fact, I would go so far as to suggest that for her, camping is anathema. I do, however, think that if she'd been born into a different era of camping, it might have held greater intrigue—say, British Raj–style digs in a warm and insectless meadow, on a tufted silk mattress under the stars . . . with really good curries and breads and raitas and pickles, of course.

We hiked for hours into the hills—through the lushest grass I have ever seen, strewn with wildflowers, little flecks of color like ragged daubs of paint. The mountain peaks were still capped in unblemished snow. At last we arrived at the small wooden hut belonging to a man I believe was named André, the shepherd and cheesemaker Denise and Jean-Pierre had planned for us to visit. On very few occasions have I met someone who so conformed to an archetype. He could have been forty-five or sixty-five; his ruddy, weathered appearance belied his actual age. He wore a sort of beret and a rough, woolly hand-knit sweater over patched trousers tucked into knee-high boots. In my memory, though surely not in reality, he was smoking a pipe.

We scattered to set up tents nearby. Together with Jean-Pierre and Denise's daughters, Elsa and Maud, I started in on the fiddly process of pitching our shared tent. I had so infrequently been taken on camping trips as a child that the prospect was thrilling. My mom and dad's tent was close by. The gloaming fell suddenly, steeping the mountains in cooler light, and André whistled to his dogs—a strong, clear whistle whose penetrating peal was amplified by the mountains tossing it back and forth. His herd dogs came alive, bolting into faraway folds of hillside, dutifully unearthing stray sheep and bringing together their cottony bodies into a stream of animals, forming something like a skein of wool flowing down the mountain. André's calculated whistles prompted his dogs to stay on task, nipping at heels whenever a beast left formation, firmly checking their flanks to keep them in line. Once the entire flock had been gathered into the barn, we clustered around André to watch him milk his ewes, one by one. The children all took turns. When it was mine, I remember reaching under the animal, groping for the udder beneath the weight of its taut, pungent-smelling belly, its body warmer and twitchier with anxiety than I had expected. André helped me to pull in the right place, with a balance of force and care. A jet of steaming milk shot into the pail.

Once all the animals had been tended to, we helped him carry the milk in large metal canisters up the hill to a stream of freezing runoff from the snow cover. It would cool there until morning, when he'd begin the process of making cheese. That night Jean-Pierre cooked dinner over a fire outdoors. We ate at an improvised table beneath a canopy of stars, whose glister was more apparent at this altitude, I thought, than from any other vantage. The Milky Way was, rather appropriately, at its milkiest, like a liquid splash of astral matter extending across the entirety of the sky. All the kids lay in the damp grass and watched it like television. Our tents, each illuminated with a hanging lantern, glowed warmly, appearing suspended in the liquid blackness of night like a swarm of outsize fireflies.

In the morning, we woke to the dissonant jangle of the sheep's bells as they rambled up the hillside in pursuit of fresh grass—a chorus of tinny bells and baying. It was early and still very cold; the tent was drenched in dew. Morning light was only just beginning to gather around the edges of the mountains. We remained in the cool blue dark for some time. With sleeping bags around us like shawls and socks so sodden we might as well have walked through a river, we sleepily migrated toward the shepherd's hut. To no one's surprise, we discovered my mother had slept in there . . . with the shepherd! She had thrown in the towel on tent sleeping more or less the instant she had lain down on the thin film of "mattress" under her sleeping bag and discovered that the tent was canted on the hillside such that the chance of rolling down seemed not just possible but likely. André had taken pity on the urbanite and proffered her some sort of surface in his loft. Needless to say, the punishment for her faintness of heart was to be mercilessly teased, for the balance of the vacation, about her new love affair with a cheesemaker.

André had already retrieved the milk cans from the stream and had begun to warm a batch in an immense copper pot over a gas burner. As the milk heated, he lowered the flame, stirring the liquid, a color brighter and more densely white than anything I'd ever seen before. I remember being struck by the strange incongruence: that something so clean and pure could be excreted by the muddy, matted beasts whose gamy odor permeated the hut, even in their absence. We watched as the curds separated from the whey, as if by magic. From time to time, André would plunge his immense hands into the milk—his pink fingers calloused and tumid from years of use—to agitate the curds and coax them slowly into a soft mound of cheese. He gathered this mound into a length of fresh muslin, shaped it into a loose round, and pressed it into a metal colander to further drain. We were offered cups of steaming whey. The flavor was salty and grassy, almost to the point of tasting the way the air smelled, wet and pregnant with the scent of earth. Though most of the curd would be stored for months to become hard rounds of cheese, André sacrificed one of the fresh batches for our breakfast that morning. He offered us a pot of rose hip jam made after his grandmother's recipe, using the roses that grow wild in the mountains. The earthy ricotta-like cheese, still warm, spooned over with rose jelly . . . it was delicious. Even my mother, underslept from her night of changing venues, was moved by the flavors. I remember her pronouncing it the most delicious breakfast she'd ever had. Absolutely no one disagreed.

Rose Hip Jelly   ROSE HIP JELLY is one of those things you don't readily find in grocery stores. It's too difficult to cultivate rose hips in any quantity, and the flavor of the jelly itself, though delicious, is something of an acquired taste. In fact, the word *rose* is misleading. The jelly doesn't taste so much floral as it does earthy and acidic, a bit like dried hibiscus flower tea. This is in part due to its extraordinarily high levels of vitamin C (about twenty times as much as an orange), which makes this jelly, though sweet, not entirely unhealthful. With any extra hips, I like to make a simple tisane: just sliver the seedpods and steep in boiling water for a bright, tart, and nourishing brew.

TO MAKE ROSE HIP JELLY, you'll need a pretty considerable quantity of rose hips, and while they're not exactly easy to buy commercially, they're not as rare as you might think. Several varieties of garden rose yield the types of hips that work for this recipe, and you can also find wild bushes filled with hips at the edges of sand dunes, in the foothills, or in forests and parks. They are also absurdly easy to find on the greener blocks of small towns like Berkeley (but also in cities as massive as London). In other words, this is not a recipe to premeditate so much as to make if you happen to come across a particularly laden bush, at the right moment in the season.

ALL ROSES PRODUCE HIPS, and all are edible, but certain varieties produce the type of hips that make for the best eating. They're ripe for harvest only once the flowers themselves have faded and died. A favored variety is *Rosa rugosa*, a bright magenta rose that grows wild but can likewise be cultivated. Any time you encounter a large naked bush covered in bright orange little seedpods, harvest them, though they will be a bit sweeter after a first frost.

TO MAKE ABOUT FIVE TO SIX 8-OUNCE JARS OF JELLY, you'll need about 8 cups of rose hips. (Whenever I undertake canning, I resist the temptation to make a super tiny batch. The slight extra fuss to make a bit more seems worth it, given how rarely I feel like sterilizing jars and making jam.) Start by rinsing and trimming the rose hips thoroughly, making sure to cut off and discard the scraggly tops and tails. Place them in a large stainless steel (or other nonreactive metal) pot and add 6 cups of water and the zest of one lemon. Bring to a boil and reduce the heat to a simmer, then cover and cook for 1 hour, or longer, until the rose hips are very soft and easily mashed.

USE A POTATO MASHER OR FORK to break up the hips into a rough purée. Set up a jelly bag (or a large fine-mesh strainer lined with several layers of cheesecloth) over a bowl or large pot. Transfer the mixture into the jelly bag or cheesecloth-lined strainer and allow to drain into the bowl for at least an hour. Squeeze the jelly bag or cheesecloth to get as much of the remaining juice out as possible. While the juice drains, prepare your canning jars. You'll need to sterilize 6 half-pint canning jars and lids by either running them through the dishwasher on a hot cycle just before canning or bringing them to boil for ten minutes on a rack in a large pot of water.

YOU NEED 3 CUPS OF ROSE HIP JUICE for this recipe, so if you have less than that, add a touch more water to the strained mixture. Place the juice in a large, wide pot. Add the juice of ½ lemon and 1 packet of powdered pectin. Bring to a boil, dissolving all of the pectin. Add 3 cups of sugar, and, once it's dissolved, add ¼ teaspoon of butter. Taste for sweetness. If the mixture needs more sugar, add a little at a time, tasting continuously. Bring to a hard boil and allow to bubble for a full minute. Remove promptly from the heat and pour the hot liquid into your prepared canning jars, leaving a bit of headspace below the rim. Place lids and rings on your jars and secure them firmly, before processing them to ensure a seal. Put your jars on a rack in a large, tall stockpot, cover with water, and bring to a rolling boil for 10 minutes, making sure the jars are submerged. Turn off the heat, remove the jars from the water, and allow them to cool.

THIS JELLY IS WONDERFUL as breakfast or a very simple dessert: just spoon over a lovely fresh ricotta and serve.

CHAPTER 18

Lobster Salad

The scene unfolds in Alsace in the summer of 1993. My parents had decided to undertake a "research" tour of France's great restaurants and wineries that year, and I was along for the ride, perhaps because I could, at age nine, finally be trusted to sit uncomplainingly at the table for the duration of a meal. Also, thanks to the bilingual French American education they'd insisted on—despite neither of them being or speaking French—I had established myself as their indispensable interlocutor.

On this particular day, we would be driving from Alsace to Reims, where at noon on the dot, my father had arranged a special tour and tasting in the caves of Krug, the illustrious champagne house. His guide was to be none other than the heir of the estate, Rémi Krug. Needless to say, my father, a committed oenophile and professional wine merchant, was *very* excited about this engagement. This had been a topic of conversation for weeks, a hotly anticipated event.

Because my mom does not subscribe to the notion that one can ever *not* be hungry, my complaints that morning of not wanting to eat before we struck out fell on deaf ears. I was fed a large portion of scrambled eggs and orange juice, maybe even some toast with butter (butter a luxury I identified mainly with Europe). In my memory the car journey between Riquewihr and Reims was forty-five hours and

the road more tortuous than Wisconsin's famously crooked Pecatonica River. In reality, I gather, it's under four hours and mostly a straight shot.

We said goodbye to our friends John Meis and Jacques Feger (who paints meticulous oil still lifes of vegetables reminiscent of the Dutch Masters—my mom has two in her kitchen still) and loaded ourselves into the rental car. Bob was with us—of course—and was singing a made-up show tune called "Jacques from Riquewihr." Whether or not the road *does* eventually straighten out is, to my mind, immaterial: the first dozen or so miles of the drive felt like tracing the tracks of a professional skier carving out hairpin curves in fresh powder. Within minutes of winding through the sylvan but increasingly sinister national park, Ballons des Vosges, I felt queasy. A moment later, I started to moan from the back seat like a woodland mammal wounded in a hunting trap.

Even though we had left with enough time, we had not allowed for delays greater than the window required to consume a roadside *sandwich* (spelled the same but pronounced *sahndweech*), should our blood sugar levels dip too precipitously. In other words, there was not a sick-child contingency plan. My parents were not the types to equip themselves with a utility bag containing a variety of emergency vomit receptacles or Handi Wipes or antibacterial solutions or anything else that would have proven useful once it became clear that we were going to be reacquainted with my breakfast sooner rather than later. The nausea was mounting. Even with Bob's plastering himself against the door as far from any possible vomit trajectory as could be negotiated in the smallish back seat, and my mom's sympathetically furrowed brow, none of the adults in the vehicle were willing to pull over: the promise of endless champagne was too great a prize to forsake. "Daaaaaaaaaaadddddd," I whimpered. His strained reply: "We'll be on the autoroute any second, Fan! Then it's totally straight! You'll be fine once it's straight!" "Mooooooommmmmm," I begged, "pull over,

I'm gonna puke! It's gonna happen! It's about to happen! It's happening right now!"

This portion of the memory is largely defined by the trauma of a recalled sickness, a malady at once temporally remote but still excruciatingly tangible, and yet the most vivid detail—like a commercial break in the middle of an emotional drama—came in the form of my mom handing me, as a vessel for my forthcoming vomit, a *cone* fashioned from a *road map*. Though I'm sure it was not the case, I remember everyone in the car temporarily suspending anxiety in order to laugh hysterically at the fact that my mom had actually tried to "MacGyver" an airsickness bag *out of a map of France*. I did not throw up in the map cone, but by this point I was wailing enough that my dad did finally consent to pull the car to the side of the road. On a soft shoulder sloping down into a conifer wood, I stood on a lip of pavement covered in a carpet of brown pine needles and, in the deafening quiet of the forest, dry-heaved futilely. I could feel my father's frustrated glare boring a hole in my back, my mother fretting, Bob relieved that the drama had not reached its crescendo *inside* the car. And yet we were neither figuratively, nor literally, out of the woods.

Over the course of the next two hours, off and on, we pulled the car over to accommodate my urges, none of which—much to the dismay of the whole party—came to fruition. Only once it was guaranteed that we had missed the champagne tasting—apologetic calls had to be placed to Rémi from a gas station pay phone—did I finally manage to empty my stomach of its now-very-digested contents. Fortunately this occurred in an actual toilet, once we were on the autoroute, whose straightness, it transpired, had done little to quell the nausea. Now unburdened of my regurgitated eggs and toast, I was a picture of good nature. The adults, by contrast, were silent and surly. My father, for hours, refused to make eye contact with me.

Though we had failed to catch the tasting, we were still on time for lunch. Rémi had invited us to dine with him at the then-three-

Michelin-starred restaurant, Les Crayères, and by agreeing to meet him directly, we still stood to make the one-thirty reservation. We arrived, bedraggled, at an immense, gleaming château. There we were ushered into one of the most sumptuous interiors I'd ever clapped eyes on: a Versailles-worthy dining room, festooned with white and gold textiles, the crispest table linens, overheavy embroidered drapes spilling over floor-to-ceiling windows, Ingres-like portraits of nobility in gilded frames, gold things just *everywhere*. Rémi stood up from the table and greeted us, a beaming, charismatic presence, totally unoffended by our tardiness. He must have been maybe fifty at the time, but I fell instantly in love with him, believing him, I think, to be the prince of the castle we'd found ourselves dining in.

Minutes later, Chef Gérard Boyer emerged from the kitchen in the type of impeccable chef whites that seem to exist only within French borders, his longish brown-gray locks tucked neatly behind his ears. He greeted me first, as if I were the most important person at the table, and I returned the glowing attention with perfect French: *"Je suis enchantée, monsieur. Merci de nous avoir accueilli dans votre restaurant exquis."* To which he exclaimed, *"Mais elle parle parfaitement le français! Comment ça ce fait?!"* Before my mother could mumble something about my French education, or about how the very recent bout of carsickness probably meant I wouldn't eat much by way of lunch, he'd whisked me into the kitchen for a tour. In front of his crew of twenty-odd immaculately clad cooks, he announced that I could have whatever I wanted for a special customized menu. It turned out he had a daughter exactly my age, and the fact that a small American could speak flawless French (which, I hasten to add, is sadly no longer the case) had resonated deeply. Once he had returned me to the table, he asked, *"Alors, mademoiselle, qu'est-ce que tu prendras? Qu'est-ce que ton coeur désire?"* Without a shred of self-awareness, I replied, *"Tout simplement une petite salade de homard comme ils font à Chez Panisse, s'il vous plait."* ("Oh, just a simple little lobster salad

like they do at Chez Panisse, please.") Though Chef Boyer seemed rather delighted, if slightly perplexed, by my bold request, my mom's face flushed with red-hued shame. "What exactly does this mean?" he asked her, smiling. Head bowed: "Um, just, well, some salad leaves, like, um, some mesclun, you know, and then, well, of course, a bit of lobster meat, little tomatoes maybe, and, um, I guess just a very simple lemon-shallot vinaigrette," she managed by way of reply.

A while later, after everyone had been returned to good humor courtesy of Krug-brand libations, our food arrived. The plate set down before me contained the very platonic ideal of a lobster salad. Intermingled with the most pristine collection of sundry leaves was lobster meat so perfectly intact it looked as though it had never possessed a shell. Bruiseless edible petals were scattered throughout, as were the tiniest tips of feathery chervil, minute basil blossoms, peeled cherry tomatoes, all tossed in an ethereal, citrusy shallot dressing. It was the best thing I'd ever eaten. In that moment it trumped all previous iterations of salad, of lobster—indeed, of *food*. I don't think I let either of my parents taste even the smallest morsel. I was in a kind of sensory ecstasy, and this after one of the more harrowing episodes of carsickness in my short life. Rémi watched in awe as a child he'd been told might perish on the journey dismantled with gusto a pile of lobster.

As we left the restaurant en route to a rescheduled tour of the Krug cellars, I turned to my mom and told her that "Chez Boyer" (my immediate shorthand for Les Crayères) was my new number one favorite restaurant. Chez Panisse, I was sorry to report, had been knocked down to second place. I kept an informal tally, you see, a "Top Ten," and thanks to that lobster salad, Boyer occupied the top seed for at least another five or so years. The only thing that could have improved the day was seeing my adults (let's call them) being rewarded with yet further champagne, a liquid seemingly capable of dissolving even the foulest of moods. By four p.m., my father was an angel, Bob a comedian, my mom virtually somnambulant. Rémi had been told that my tenth birthday would be arriving the following month and, to mark the occasion, gave me a bottle of champagne from my birth year: a rare Blanc de Blancs from one of their small walled-in vineyards called Clos du Mesnil. By this point, some might already have begun to consider it "old" for a bottle of champagne, or at least this was the rationale used by the adults in their attempts to convince me to open it immediately: "Fan, you know, if you wait any longer, it could be off. And that would be a tragedy. We should probably open it now, don't you think?" Somehow I managed to fend off the vultures from imbibing my keepsake, not just for the next two weeks, but for the next eleven years. My dad, mom, and I drank it on the occasion of my twenty-first birthday, at Chez Panisse—just the three of us—and we all agreed that it was, in fact, aged to perfection.

Lobster and Lettuce Salad

LOBSTER SALAD, like so much crab salad out there, often means something swimming in mayonnaise. I like aioli as much as (or probably more than) the next person, and am not even totally averse to the store-bought varieties, but because lobster meat is so sweet and succulent, it always seems like a waste to drown out these finer qualities in a bath of jarred sauce. My favorite way to eat lobster—after simply boiling, which is always best—is in a bright salad of the best leaves you can find. Other vegetables, like sliced heirloom tomatoes or peeled cherry tomatoes (just blanch for a minute to slip their skins off) or tiny blanched green beans or avocado, can be added—though I tend to feel that less is more.

BOIL THE LOBSTERS WHOLE. Received wisdom suggests boiling them in 3 quarts of water per 1½ to 2 pounds of weight, with 8 minutes of cooking time per pound (with 2 additional minutes of cooking time for each extra ½ pound of weight, up to 3 pounds, and, after 3 pounds, an extra 2½ minutes per ½ pound). More detailed instructions for lobster preparation can be found on pages 201–202. Plunge the lobsters in ice water and let cool completely before using crackers to extract the meat, being careful to keep the flesh as intact as possible. I like more leaves than meat—so the lobster is almost more of a surprise than a main feature—which means that one healthy-sized lobster is plenty for 4 people. So although *lobster salad* might sound extravagant, it can actually be a pretty economical "fancy" dish to prepare for guests.

MAKE SURE THE LEAVES YOU CHOOSE are sturdy enough: Little Gems, chicories, and endive hold up better to the meat and other ingredients, but good butter or oak leaf lettuce is nice too. I like to make a dressing with a finely diced shallot macerated in champagne vinegar, lemon juice, and sea salt, and then whisked with olive oil, but this too can be embellished: add chopped basil or pounded tarragon or parsley.

CHAPTER 19

Potpie

There were many instances in which my overactive sense of smell was a source of both personal suffering and parental grief—my dad used to uncharitably compare me to the German shepherds used to sniff out drugs or weapons at airports. There was one particular episode, however, in which my nose turned my parents nearly murderous (or at least initially). It had to do with the time we were on our "Tour of Notable Restaurants of France," stopping only at more or less the fanciest, most renowned joints throughout the French countryside. I think my mom did this more out of a sense of professional obligation (and for research purposes) than for pleasure, since this has never been her favorite way to eat, but, either way, the journey was memorable, and of course there was plenty of incredible food and hospitality along the way.

This was toward the beginning of our gastronomic odyssey, and I was just starting to warm up and stretch my menu-ordering legs. Basically I was allowed to order whichever starter and main I wanted as long as I promised to actually eat them. We arrived at a multiple-Michelin-starred restaurant situated on the grassy sloped bank of a small but elegant river. The main dining room, I remember, was made almost entirely of glass, so diners could look out directly onto a Monet-like scene of weeping willow curtains and swans, magical snow-white birds with calligraphic necks who floated languidly back and forth like paid entertainers throughout the meal.

We arrived at this bucolic luxury dining outpost at some point in the early afternoon, and as is typical of our family—Bob included—were by this point quite hungry and therefore more than a bit ornery. The minute we stepped through the front door, however, I stiffened, scrunching my nose, and began to tug on my mother's sleeve. "Mom, it smells like rotten fish in here," I said in something more audible than a whisper. My mother's eyes became small. She opened her mouth to tell me something—presumably some form of scolding—but before she could utter a word the maître d' had appeared and was suddenly ushering the *Table Watèr-zzz* (my best approximation of the spelling of how *Waters* sounds spoken in French) to its prime location before the living Impressionist tableau beyond the glass. We sat. Though the pronouncement had been unpopular during its initial trial, I decided to reiterate my complaint: "Don't you think this restaurant smells sort of like bad fish?" This time I was met with the scowls of two of the three adults. (Bob always managed to hold himself largely apart from family altercations—a kind of Switzerland, if you will, if Switzerland had been prone to occasionally mooting opinions on intuitive parenting such as "She says she's ready to watch David Lynch's *Fire Walk with Me* even though she's only nine—I think you should let her." Cue a five-month period of nightmares that had me sleeping in my parents' bed more nights than not.)

"Fan, this is one of the nicest restaurants in France. I'm *sure* the fish is not bad," my mother ventured in a tone at once conciliatory and irritated. "Fan, would you cut it out with your goddamn nose?!" my dad rejoined before being happily distracted by the arrival of a Torah-length wine list and the task of choosing the meal's refreshments. Shortly following the selection of wine came the distribution of menus. I was nine at the time and qualm-free when it came to reading and ordering on my own. I have no idea what I elected to eat by way of appetizer, but my eye was drawn, as ever, straight to the lobster dish listed under the mains. In my memory this dish was *homard truffé en croûte*, but that translates roughly to "truffled lobster potpie" and I feel fairly certain it would have been a preparation more painstakingly nineties, like "100-layer lobster and truffle mille-feuille." In any event, the dish was the most expensive item on the menu by a considerable margin. Something like 700 francs, maybe more, though of course I had zero conception of money and its value, least of all in francs, of which many hundreds had to be associated with something before my parents would begin to feign, or feel actual, shock. I believe my insistence on eating the *homard en croûte* did provoke shock of the genuine variety, but Bob hastened to come to my defense: "Hey, guys, you *did* say she could order whatever she wanted off the menu, so long as she ate it." The lobster was ordered. The swans sailed frictionlessly by.

Appetizers came, were dispatched, and cleared, without event. Then, however, after a few fine bottles of wine had been ordered and enjoyed—I drank a goblet of that semi-sulfurous French sparkling water called Badoit—the main courses began to arrive at the table, each carried by its own server, working in the type of choreographed ballets unique to the overstaffed environs of the chichi-est restaurants. The lobster was ceremoniously placed before me. Scarcely had the waiters moved from within earshot, however, when I said, a faint vein of vindication undergirding the delivery, "This is it. This is the rotten fish. This is what I was smelling before. I told you so." My dad's initial look from across the table telegraphed pure exasperation. My mom—though no one beyond our table had overheard my opprobrium—looked mortified. Bob, as ever, was bemused. I poked the croûte with a fork and leaned in for a more intimate whiff. There was no doubt in my mind: this was the culprit. My mom, seated to my left and obviously unable to enjoy the portion of *viande* sitting blamelessly on her plate, had her eyes closed, as if she were willing herself to tele-transport to a childless island. "This is not happening,"

I heard her mutter. Then she opened her eyes and slowly dragged my immense gilt-edged dish toward her. Tentatively she leaned in for a sniff. "Goddammit, she's right. It's no good," she corroborated to the table. And then to me, "Fan, you don't have to eat it." The subtext, however, was *You DO have to do enough damage to it with your fork so that you could have plausibly taken at least a few bites.* Despite my best effort to disturb the ingredients, our waiter had cottoned on. *"Tout allait bien avec votre repas?"* he asked my mother accusatorily as he picked up my plate. "Fickle children." She rolled her eyes performatively. "They think they want something. Then it arrives and they decide they don't. What can you do?" My mother has never to my knowledge returned a dish or registered a complaint at a restaurant. She may dislike something from time to time, but it was not in her nonconfrontational nature—nor in her moral code, it would seem—to disrupt the peace at institutions in which she always thinks of herself as a guest, even if she's paying full price. I've always appreciated this stance and largely hewn to her example, though her respect for order has struck me as a bit old-fashioned, if not somewhat self-abnegating. (It remains a challenge for her to accept the notion that a chef might actually be *craving* the thoughts and feedback of Alice Waters, and would most definitely want to know if she violently disliked something.) From time to time in my adulthood, if a dish really does taste wrong, I've sent it back—in silence asking for my mother's forgiveness, as if she were the Patron Saint of Politesse. No one on the waitstaff, however, is reporting to the chef that "Fanny Singer didn't think the mussels were quite fresh enough," and that is completely fine by me.

Anyway, at this particular fine dining station, the bill could not come soon enough. Bob paid. For the purposes of disambiguation, I should explain that my parents had struck a deal with Bob that pertained to any of our joint travels: so long as we ate out somewhere delicious, they'd pick up the bill; if the food was bad, however, Bob had to pay. This mostly worked out in Bob's favor, since my parents never wittingly selected dicey or inferior restaurants, but from time to time, the reservation would be some multi-person table at an especially upscale joint and Bob would find himself liable for a bill of crushing and incomprehensible proportions. For the record, though, this foul lobster episode did not in any way affect my love of or propensity for ordering dishes containing the beloved ingredient. A little portion of foul potpie could hardly get in my way.

CHAPTER 20

Puteaux

When I was ten years old, my French American elementary school in Berkeley organized to send my fifth grade class to Paris—or, more specifically, the outskirts thereof—for a period of more than two weeks. When you are ten years old, two weeks might as well be a year; there's no intellectual apparatus governing your understanding of how time functions. And up to that point, I had never been on a trip without my parents for more than a day or two, and certainly not one that entailed international air travel. Nevertheless, this was my school's custom, to send the tender indoctrinated flock over to the motherland to embed with *real* French families. In preparation for this adventure, we had each been in correspondence with a child of about our age belonging to the family in which we would be placed. This was achieved primarily by letter: painstakingly executed French-cursive orthography (lowercase *p*s with open bottoms, uppercase *T*s that looked like *C*s, etc.) in the service of numbingly banal content (*"J'aime les bananes. J'ai une paire de baskets roses. Aimes-tu lire?"* "I love bananas. I have a pair of pink sneakers. Do you like to read?"), but occasionally it also involved the use of the Minitel. For those of you either too young or too old to know what a Minitel is, let me assure you that in the early nineties this piece of French-invented equipment represented cutting-edge telecommunications technology. Using this rudimentary boxlike computer, we were able—before the invention of the World Wide Web!—to communicate with children on the other side of the world! To tell them that "Yes! I too love bananas! Pink sneakers are super cool! And reading is, well, okay, I guess."

After several months of planning and a few reassuring international phone calls between my "French mom" and my biological one, my class was dispatched to Paris under the supervision of our flamboyant fifth grade teacher, Yves. The first crushing blow was the discovery that we were in fact not going to be stationed in Paris proper—i.e., in the immediate vicinity of the Tour Eiffel—but rather in one of its sleepier suburbs to the northwest. This was a place called Puteaux, whose most notable feature was something called the Grande Arche, a Brutalist-looking square-edge monument erected in 1989 to mark their business district of La Défense. Some of us had been to Paris before, and others had seen it romanticized in picture books; we were not immediately impressed by Puteaux's offerings. The family I was staying with lived in an enormous apartment block, with views as far as the Bois de Boulogne. From their balcony, I could pick out the Grande Arche (looking not particularly *grande* from there). Theirs was a modest flat—two bedrooms, a sitting room, a small kitchen— but it was very tidy and lovingly maintained. The two daughters had transformed their shared bedroom into something of an early adolescent oasis the likes of which I had never seen before: posters of French and American pop cultural icons, a multicolored plastic boom box, piled CDs of the French rapper MC Solaar. They even had a small TV and VCR *in their room*. As their guest, I was given one of their two bunk beds; Marie-Laure, my pen pal, surrendered her bed and slept on a pallet on the floor for the duration of my stay. I was not an impolite or ungrateful child, but there is no way I was at the time aware of the extent of this family's sacrifices when it came to providing me room and board.

For starters, I didn't sleep. When there are no biological parents around to enforce sleeping patterns, jet lag has its most prolonged, deleterious effects. I won't say that I *loved* my jet lag, exactly, but I certainly coddled it. In fact, I did next to nothing to force myself to conform to the rhythms of my adoptive home, not so much out of insolence as out of sheer inexperience when it came to solo travel. The nine-hour time difference, coupled with an unreceding flood of homesickness, created the sensation of being on an amphetamine I couldn't come down from. After a few nights of my reading through the night with the lights on, my French "mother" bought me a headlamp so that I could continue with my insomniac schedule without disrupting her own children's sleep. Over the course of two weeks of sleeplessness, I read every book listed on our syllabus for the entire year—*Johnny Tremain; The Diary of Anne Frank; Candide;* etc.—and I am *not* a particularly fast reader.

Secondly, I am almost impossibly averse to the smell of cigarette smoke. My French "father" smoked like the proverbial chimney, and almost exclusively indoors. I can't remember in what no doubt painfully uncouth way I let it be known that this smell, for me, was tantamount to being poisoned and dying a horrible and protracted death, but it was quickly resolved. The next day, I was presented with a few freshly purchased handkerchiefs (to strap around my face like a bandit) and a couple of cans of citrus-scented aerosolized air freshener, which I discharged liberally. Thinking back, I am convinced that the chemical perfume enlisted as remedy did more harm to our fragile human bodies than the offensive tobacco fumes it was intended to mask. Alas, at age ten, I wasn't working from a vast set of data points on the subject.

Lastly, I was, well, not particularly versed in the elegant use of cutlery at the dinner table. There are no people more committed to the etiquette of flatware than the French, not just as to which implement is designated for what use but also as regards the balletic movements one must undertake to avoid the slightest chance of directly touching your food. Eating at least part of a meal—salad, say—with one's hands was de rigueur in my Berkeley household, and I had taken the culture of our table as the norm. It had not occurred to me to brush up on my fork and knife skills prior to setting out for France. One of the first meals I ate with my French family was pizza, takeout pizza from a neighborhood pizza joint. I grabbed and began devouring a slice, holding the sagging triangle to my face without pause as I munched my way to the crust. About midway through, however, I became aware that I was the only person at the table behaving in this manner. They had each placed a slice on their plate and begun meticulously cutting away small bits with knife and fork to convey daintily to their mouths. Eating pizza with a fork and knife?! I would have conceded that, in general, greater fluency in cutlery manipulation would have been welcome, but this was unthinkable! I continued with my hands. As much as I tried to adapt my behavior at the table going forward, I still found heavy use of my napkin to be inevitable. While napkins seemed to serve a mere decorative purpose in this household, mine got a considerable daily workout. Every night, while the rest of the family's serviettes were placed neatly into labeled rings, my French mother would—without issuing the slightest reprisal—wash and rinse mine out and hang it up to dry. Even through a muddling prism of shame, I recognized at the time that this was an act of supreme kindness.

Marie-Laure and her sister were not interested in food. Or rather they were not interested in the kind of food their mother made. This was the era of the absolute supremacy of McDonald's, both at home and abroad. A time when America was still impossibly cool, perceived from overseas to be a land of cultural and political preeminence, of unparalleled pop music, cutting-edge fashion, and, of course, fast food. The only thing the daughters wanted, and in fact would routinely beg for, was "Macdo" (pronounced *Mack-dough*). I was horrified. I'm not sure if at this juncture I had yet sampled anything off a McDonald's menu, but, unsurprisingly, I was nonetheless thoroughly convinced of its malignancy. So much so, in fact, that a few years earlier, when our family was flying down to Florida to visit my paternal grandparents in West Palm Beach, I staged a one-person hunger strike rather than consume a McDonald's drive-through cheeseburger. Yes, my mother did, circa 1990, patronize a McDonald's. In her defense, however, our flight was four hours delayed, it was one o'clock in the morning, she and my dad were starving, and there was actually no alternative to be found. If there's one thing that might occasionally force my mother to compromise on her morals, it's her blood sugar. Its fluctuating levels are not just responsible for her famous refrain of "I'm having a blood sugar crisis!" but have been the driving rationale behind some of our best, and also worst, culinary escapades. I'd say that the visit to the West Palm Beach McDonald's franchise was a low point. But even at this familial nadir, I remained maddeningly inflexible. So effectively had my mother inculcated in me the evil of the fast-food industry—despite being an only slightly abashed lover of the airport and/or ballpark hot dog—that I was willing to go to sleep that night with little in my belly other than a blueberry Nutri-Grain cereal bar foraged from the hotel minibar.

The first few meals that my French mother cooked for me have since faded from memory. In the pre-Google era, she hadn't been able to research my mom in advance of my arrival and had therefore assumed that I too preferred the bland white-food dinners that her daughters favored. At some point, however, I managed to insinuate that I was in fact a great lover of good food, a fledgling gourmand even, and that I would be eager to help her in the kitchen. We started to talk about what foods we liked and disliked. I told her about Lulu Peyraud at Domaine Tempier and her Provençal-style cooking, her bouillabaisse with its rich fish stock and spicy garlic aioli. I told her how much I loved salad, and the mesclun grown by my godmother in her garden in Vence, whose seeds my mom imported to America to grow in our own backyard. And of course I began to describe Chez

Panisse. I explained how the kitchen looked when you walked in for the first time, the coruscating luster of the copper that clad everything, the low, warm light, the immense open hearth in which at least one ingredient in a given meal would be cooked. I spoke of the platters displaying whatever it was that featured on the menu—glossy eggplants and squash blossoms arranged with enormous heirloom tomatoes, say, as a deconstructed ratatouille; baskets of fresh herbs and multi-colored gypsy peppers—and the flower arrangements that looked like cascades of tangled blooms only loosely contained.

When I came home one afternoon from a class excursion to Versailles, she took me by the hand and said we were going to head out on a few errands together. We left her family behind. I asked where she was taking me, but she just smiled and declined to answer. We wove between buildings, up narrow streets, around enough corners to completely scramble my inner compass, before finally arriving at her local outdoor *marché*. I had been to many markets, indoors and outdoors, in both America and France, but it was still a shock to see the rawness of it here. This market lacked the prissy merchandising of American farmers markets, as if to suggest that the French didn't need to be persuaded to eat decent food. There were, of course, as in any industrialized country, plenty of vendors whose product is largely imported: grapes from Italy, figs from Greece, avocados from Africa—these were to be avoided. She took me instead to her favorite vendor, a woman who brought things to her stall that scarcely looked cultivated, but rather plucked from the wild. We bought a cluster of freshly dug potatoes, mud-caked and still strung together by tuberous strands, several heads of pink garlic, white onions with beard-like roots, a bunch of parsley pulled from the earth with radicles intact, and several bunches of watercress. I'd never seen watercress like this before, glossy and dark emerald green, and so peppery you could almost smell the spice.

That night she cooked a *potage de cresson,* a soup made with more watercress than any other ingredient (although I was impressed to

discover that she also included the scrubbed, finely minced roots of the parsley, which tasted something like a cross between parsnip and celery root). When it came to the table, the soup was a puree so vibrantly green-colored it was almost hard to believe it was edible. The flavor of that soup remains one of the most indelible tastes I've experienced in my life. Even her children, the staunchest upholders of the wan food regime, caved, ate it, swooned. On one of the 3,500 long-distance phone calls placed to my parents during that stint—made at great expense on prepaid phone cards—I spent at least ten minutes describing the soup to my mother. When I returned to California, she and I tried to make it together, according to the exact method I had observed in my French mother's Puteaux kitchen. It was good, but not *as good*—it lacked a certain something. Terroir, my mom would say whenever an ingredient we were eating in Europe was unmatched by the version we'd been cultivating back home. Hundreds of years of growing varietals, selecting for flavor, for resilience, for beauty—this was the taste of the land, of a very particular place coming through. And it was something that Californians necessarily lacked the depth of experience in, having only recently brought Old World seeds to the frontier. We've got a lot of variety, she would lament, but not the complexity of flavor, the taste of the centuries. Though I've still never tasted a watercress soup as spicy and verdant as the one I had in fifth grade on the outskirts of Paris, it's a recipe I love to make if I can find good watercress in the market.

Potage de Cresson

MELT A COUPLE OF TABLESPOONS OF BUTTER in a large, heavy-bottomed pot. Add a glug of olive oil, a chopped white onion, a thinly sliced leek, and a finely minced tiny Thai chili. (The chili is optional, but when it comes to capsicums, I'm my father's daughter, and my father is someone who will put jalapeño in risotto.) Sauté until soft. Throw in a couple of minced cloves of garlic, a handful of roughly chopped parsley leaves, and two big pinches of salt, and stir for a minute, being careful not to burn the garlic. Cut a peeled large potato (or a couple of smaller ones) into ½-inch chunks and add it to the pot along with 4 cups of water or chicken stock. If you ever happen to find parsley roots in your farmers market, mince them and add them here—it's a deepening supplemental flavor here and in many other soups. A bit of celery root is a nice alternative, but both are optional.

BRING TO A BOIL and turn down the heat to a simmer until the potato is completely tender and easily broken apart (about 10 to 15 minutes). Take the pot off the stove and add about 6 cups of coarsely chopped watercress and a big pinch of freshly ground black pepper. Use an immersion blender to puree the soup until uniformly green (this can also be done in batches in an upright blender). Reheat, adding a little water, if necessary, to achieve the desired consistency, and tweak the seasoning with additional salt or pepper. Sometimes I have this soup in a heartier unblended form, but you really unlock the intensity of the watercress flavor when you process it. Add a dollop of thick yogurt, a sprinkle of Marash pepper, and a drizzle of good olive oil, or just serve it as is.

CHAPTER 21

Le Twix

Even after my French mother had begun to adapt her dinnertime repertoire to cater to my ten-year-old culinary intrepidness—which, I have to believe, was a source of great joy and pride for her; she was a fabulous cook—she continued to furnish all three of us children with packed lunches containing exceptionally humdrum fare. Every single day for two weeks: a sandwich of sliced crustless white bread, spread top and bottom with a quarter inch of (granted, super delicious French) butter, between which lay a single flaccid piece of *jambon;* a bag of Lay's potato chips; and "le Twix." Thanks to my erratic circadian rhythms, I spent most of the morning sleeping on the bus to wherever we were being taken (Versailles; the Louvre; le jardin du Luxembourg; the Pompidou) and would awake, ravenous at eleven a.m., to a bag containing a disappointing triad of comestibles. Sorry, I should say disappointing *duo,* for it was on this trip that I ignited a deep, if too-brief, love affair with Twix. Once I had washed down my sandwich and chips with a Coke (another thing I was scarcely permitted to look at back in the States), I spent a serene and grateful moment with my fun-size Twix bar.

Candy was, needless to say, not a particular feature of my childhood. I don't think I had actual *candy-candy* until I was maybe six years old, and then only on holidays like Easter and Halloween and

only under intense parental scrutiny to ensure intake was minimal. I was allowed those perennially disappointing flavored honey sticks from the health food store and maybe a handful of carob chips, but I mean, who are you trying to kid with those things? They taste *nothing* like chocolate. Specialty fruits were also sometimes pawned off on me as an equivalent to candy—for example, "You can have *one* passion fruit if you're really good today." The latter has resulted in regular episodes of profligate expenditure on passion fruit now that I'm an adult and in charge of my own finances. Desperate for the experience of eating sugar, I remember at one point begging babysitter Mary Jo (conveniently also the pastry chef of Chez Panisse) to undertake the project of homemade lollipops. They bore an impressive visual resemblance to the real thing, but tasted altogether too much like fancy plum jam to be passed off as candy.

About midway through the first week of the French sojourn, however, it occurred to me that somewhere in the house from which the Twix ration sprang, there must be a font of individually wrapped caramel and chocolate–covered biscuits. Emboldened by jet lag, I donned my headlamp and went in search of the stash. After a short hunt, I located it on the upper shelf of the hallway cloak closet. I went into the kitchen to retrieve a small step stool and padded back to the closet as silently as possible. There I pillaged the Twix repository in what would become a nightly routine. Despite the Costco-like proportions of the box, I was nonetheless scrupulously measured about my middle-of-the-night candy consumption. To avoid detection, I never purloined more than one bar at a time, secure in the knowledge that another would be delivered to me come lunchtime. This, I would eat back in bed with as much pleasure as I've ever derived from eating anything, scraping the chocolate and caramel from the cookie using my front teeth, then slowly and noiselessly making my way through the saliva-saturated base.

•   •   •

When I returned home after two weeks away, I was at once so weary and so relieved that all I could do was sit slumped in the back seat on the ride home from the airport. My parents knew they'd eventually extract all the stories and, inevitably, also be privy to the glut of grainy, poorly composed photos I'd taken with a bunch of disposable cameras, so they didn't press me. When my mom opened the front door to the house, however, I was instantly reanimated. I ran straight through the kitchen, flung open the back door, leapt down the back steps three at a time, and threw myself onto the grass that unfolds from the foot of our towering, ancient redwood tree. I lay that way for an hour, my mom remembers, legs and arms spread out wide as if I were floating: the grass a placid lake, my body buoyant on its blades. In retrospect, this was not just a performative expression of homecoming—though two weeks of solid rain and jet lag in the outskirts of Paris had shone a light on a very different type of experience. Rather, this was a communion with nature—which as a Berkeley kid I took for granted. There was no place like home, no place I'd yet been where you could fill your view with nothing but the evergreen branches of a majestic tree, the blue of the sky just a flat, brilliant color to frame it.

CHAPTER 22

Bolinas Birthdays

When I was very little, my mother always threw my birthday parties in our spacious backyard, a now-quite-feral and beautifully overgrown mix of edible plants and roses that at one time in my youth was striated with rows of lettuce destined for the restaurant's kitchens. A mix of my parents' friends would show up to drink, nibble at my mother's spread, and mingle between rows of mesclun. On these occasions I was even allowed a slice of Mary Jo's applesauce cake, though it was a basically unsweetened, salubrious-looking thing most children wouldn't have considered a dessert. (Still, I have such fond memories of it that I recently attempted a version for my goddaughter's first birthday—she seemed as pleased with it as any one-year-old could be.) The most memorable of these backyard parties was my fifth birthday, about a month before I started kindergarten at a new school. A few weeks beforehand, I had evidently started to express desires for "a birthday parade." My preschool friends would be in attendance, including my "boyfriend" Cole, and I had it in my mind that we would experience some type of grand procession. I have no idea how this idea came to me.

As Bob tells it, the day arrived and my mother still hadn't created or organized any such event or happening, though I was talking about it excitedly to my friends as if it were all but guaranteed. Bob, I think, was suffering from more absence-of-parade anxiety than my mother, no doubt aggravated by my increasingly vexed parade-related inquiries as my friends began to trickle in. My mother shooed us into the backyard with snacks and juice and disappeared for twenty or so minutes, only to reemerge with armfuls of treasure: costumes, face paint, colored paper for making hats and crowns. Though I think I'd been imagining *seeing* a parade, she turned us into one instead, adorning us with headdresses, affixing colorful paper shapes to sticks for us to hold in the air, tying an old sheet around my neck to make a train. She gave us glitter for our cheeks and red lipstick for our pouts, placed flowers in our hair, tied silk ribbons around our waists like festive cummerbunds. First we paraded around the lettuce patch and then we struck out farther afield: taking our procession to the streets, circling our Berkeley block dozens of times, cheering and waving our nonsensical heraldry in the air. Cole was at my arm, his paper crown hanging low over his dark locks, the two of us at the front, delighting in our makeshift cavalcade.

From when I was about ten or so, we started to spend at least part of the summer in Bolinas, a small beach town in Marin County, about an hour northwest of Berkeley. My mother's close friend Susie—a sort of "fairy godmother" to me—had grown up spending weekends in Bolinas in the fifties, and decided many years later to buy a parcel of land there and enact a kind of homecoming. The land was sold with an existing cottage that Susie restored and stayed in while a more permanent house was under construction. Thanks to this little cottage, I began to regularly visit West Marin, often just the two of us: Susie and me. At age ten, I remember reporting to my friends at school that my *very best friend*, Susie, was fifty years old. This, I'm afraid, is what happens when you raise an only child among adults. I've been age-dysmorphic ever since.

Anyway, once Susie's house was finished, she began to invite friends to stay in the cottage whenever they wanted. Though many people vacation in that place besides us, I've heard Susie and her husband, Mark, at times refer to it as "Alice's cottage" or "Alice and Fanny's cottage," and, if you were to poke around its four generous rooms, you'd find more photos and memorabilia of and relating to me and my mom than we have on display in our own Berkeley house. I think it was Susie's way of telegraphing to us that it really was a home away from home for us, and that we should treat it as such and feel able to escape to it whenever we felt the urge.

Years later, when I was still living abroad, I often wouldn't feel oriented back in California until I had visited Bolinas; until I had passed over onto the Pacific Plate from the North American one, traversing the upper edge of the bay and over the invisible San Andreas fault line at the apex of the lagoon. This may sound a little abstract, but I swear I can sense a difference in that moment of crossing, as if the geological makeup of the territory could be sensed immediately, even just in the quality of the air. I don't think I'm an utter fabulist, though; the trees, the landscape, the texture of the light, even—wouldn't those things change if the minerals in the soil had been imported to this coast from another part of the earth, jammed together with this one over the course of millennia, until just a seismic fissure remained? Regardless of what ineffable forces are at work, when I arrive in Bolinas I do suddenly feel "here," or, perhaps, at home. And that almost cosmic feeling has tethered me to the place in both concrete and spiritual ways for the better part of my life.

For at least the last twenty years, even when I was living in England, I celebrated my birthday in Bolinas and, more often than not, in Shed Panisse, which sits across the small patio from the cottage. Maybe ten years ago, Mark, an amateur but very competent woodworker, made a sign for this outbuilding—in which an enormous table is installed for festive occasions—that reads SHED PANISSE in a simulacrum of the original Chez Panisse font, recalling, in its humble materials, the painted sign that graced the wooden facade of the restaurant in 1971.

Shed Panisse has a wood-shingled roof and plain sun-bleached siding made of rustic wooden planks. A large Cecile Brunner rosebush arcs over its front, more a thicket than a bush, studded with small, pale frilly flowers throughout the spring and summer. A custom-built table fills the entirety of the inside of the shed; barn doors swing open onto a stone patio where an outdoor fireplace is outfitted with a slightly rusty pair of my mother's favorite cast-iron Tuscan grills. Two wide benches with upholstered cushions running their length bracket the width of the table. Smaller cushions in a fabric whose color and striped pattern I associate with the bistros of the South of France are scattered against the wall, allowing for comfortable postprandial slouching. Above the banquettes, and between each stanchion, the walls are covered in antique mirrors, their glass wobbly and chipped and in some

instances nearly opaque with age. A huge wire chandelier, into which votive candles in tiny tumblers can be slotted, hangs above the table. When the sun sets and the candles are lit, each mirror throws back the light of dozens of small flames, and the whole little shed is filled with the golden warmth of candlelight, a glow so atmospheric it almost has a texture. There's nothing particularly extravagant about the space, but, with the candles lit and the table spangled with small vases of Susie's brilliantly colored garden dahlias and plates of beautiful food, it does feel otherworldly.

For as long as I can remember, my mom has asked me what I wanted to eat on my birthday. I'm a little ashamed to admit that from the time I was able to articulate my culinary desires, this usually included lobster. In my defense, I didn't learn how expensive or rarefied an ingredient it was until much later (although the acquisition of said knowledge did not *exactly* precipitate a reassessment of the menu). I do, however, also take comfort in the fact that, no matter how upscale a reputation lobster has acquired in more recent decades, in the colonies of the 1700s being forced to eat the ubiquitous crustaceans more than a couple times a week was considered by prison inmates to be a cruel and unusual punishment.

Because lobsters are not native to California, there was a feeling of reverence when it came to this ingredient, and its inclusion on a birthday menu was treated with an air of exception. Over the years, we've made many delicious lobster-themed dishes, from my godbrother Nico Monday's lobster paella to Sylvan Brackett's lobster miso soup, even lobster tail and steak for a lavish "surf and turf" spread at my twenty-first birthday. Yes, I did provocatively request surf and turf for this birthday, and yes, despite her reluctance to "Sizzler-ify" the menu, my mom did deliver. The most memorable preparation, however, was the green goddess lobster roll. Despite my love of lobster, I've never been particularly partial to the lobster roll. My favorite way of eating lobster is very simply boiled, and served with a bit of melted butter and some large wedges of lemon. When it comes down to it, what I like most about these creatures is the meat itself, differently textured at claw and tail, with a concentration of sweetness sometimes hiding in the meager flesh of the legs, which as a child I would enthusiastically suck as if they were straws.

That said, on this one birthday, I requested lobster rolls to mark the occasion. Alongside these, I asked that we have a green goddess salad—which is to say, a salad of Little Gems lettuce dressed in an exceptionally herby and avocado-y dressing (not the thin, uninflected mayonnaise-like thing that contains more food dye than seasonings, nor the version created at San Francisco's Palace Hotel in 1923, a base of mayonnaise and sour cream, blended with chive, parsley, and anchovy).

At some point in the preparations of this meal, my mother decided on a critical change of course: to toss the salad greens in a simple vinaigrette and use the green goddess sauce to dress the lobster instead. The product, Green Goddess Lobster Rolls, was so insanely inspired it seemed obvious. Of *course* lobster would taste incredible suffused with the scent of basil and tarragon and cilantro and parsley, and be complemented by the richness of the aioli and mashed avocado at the sauce's base. Add pungent chives, diced shallots, and the juice of lemons and limes, and the flavor became that much more complex and rewarding. The rolls were a revelation, and have since supplanted the ordinary version in our repertoire. If you're going to make lobster rolls, try this slightly more prep-intensive method.

Green Goddess Lobster Rolls

TO MAKE LOBSTER ROLLS for four people, start with two lobsters, weighing about 1½ pounds each. Bring abundant salted water to a boil in a vessel large enough to hold the two lobsters. Refrigerate the lobsters until the moment you're ready to drop them into the pot, which is best managed by grabbing the body and putting each lobster in headfirst. At the moment the first lobster enters the water, start a timer for 7 minutes and then prepare an ice bath. Adjust the flame in order to maintain a simmer—boiling water will toughen the meat. As soon as the timer goes off, remove the lobsters from the water and drop them into the chilled water to cool.

TO MAKE THE GREEN GODDESS DRESSING, have a batch of aioli, redolent with garlic, ready (page 69). Macerate a minced large shallot and a generous pinch of salt in 2 tablespoons of champagne vinegar, ½ tablespoon of lemon juice, and ½ tablespoon of lime juice. In a bowl or a mortar, use a fork or a pestle to break down a medium-sized avocado until it is a smooth puree. Place the avocado and ½ cup of aioli in a bowl. Add to it ¼ cup finely chopped parsley, 3 tablespoons chopped tarragon, 2 tablespoons chopped basil, 1 tablespoon chopped cilantro, and 2 tablespoons chopped chives. If you have chervil, that's a fine addition too. (Improvise here—any combination of bright, tender herbs will do, though tarragon is strongly recommended.) Finely chop or pound 3 olive-oil-cured anchovies and add to the mixture, along with a generous amount of fresh ground black pepper. Stir and taste for acid and salt. The tarragon should be slightly more perceptible than the other herbs; add a squeeze of lemon and lime juice if its anise-like flavor is unfocused or unclear. Set aside, refrigerating if necessary.

ONCE THE LOBSTERS ARE COOL, remove the meat in whatever fashion you're most comfortable with. I like to twist the tail and claws off the body. A crab cracker would be ideal, but a mallet or just a pestle can be used to crack open claws. Try to keep the meat as intact as possible. For the tail, a pair of kitchen shears can cut through the underbelly's protective but thin shell. Pry open the tail, using a towel to protect your hands from the shell's sharp edges. If the meat is wet, dab it with a paper towel, and chop the tails and claws into neat ½-inch chunks. Dress the lobster meat with half of the green goddess dressing. Add more dressing if needed, until the meat is coated generously but not overwhelmed. Taste the lobster—the vibrant dressing should highlight the sweetness of the meat. Adjust the seasoning if necessary, adding a few drops of citrus juice or salt.

FOR THE BREAD, find the best hot dog rolls you can and trim off the edges (we use buns from Acme bakery, but something a little richer, such as a brioche roll, would work well too, and a buttered and toasted piece of pain de mie bread works in a pinch). I like to toast the outsides lightly in butter, but untoasted rolls are fine. Fill each with lobster and serve alongside a lightly dressed lettuce salad. You can, of course, forgo the bread altogether if you prefer, and heap a pile of dressed meat on a handful of dressed salad greens.

.   .   .

There are two stores in Bolinas that vend foodstuffs—three if you count the Gospel Flat farm stand belonging to Mickey Murch—one a classic hippie natural foods store called the Bolinas People's Store; the other a local supermarket I've always, perhaps erroneously, referred to as the "General Store." The former is, as you'd expect, a co-op, and is housed in a single-story glorified shanty that sits in a cul-de-sac just off the main drag, directly behind the CommUnity Center. Also in this modest plaza is the Free Box, a small shed brimming with books and shoes and clothes and other miscellany that functions as a community donation center. A hand-painted sign affixed above its door implores you to Expect a Miracle! I have always loved the People's Store, with its vague smell of earthy patchouli and bulk grains and vegan soup bubbling in a Crock-Pot behind the register. And its selection does indeed feel like a pretty on-the-nose reflection of the Bolinas community (comprising lifelong hippies and back-to-the-landers and a newer, gentrifying set of weekenders). On the one hand, you've got your recycled toilet paper, your ineffectual bamboo toothbrushes, your fluoride-free toothpastes, a deep selection of organic granolas, sprouted loaves of whole grain sandwich bread, a respectable diversity of bulk things like flours, dried fruits, and nuts, and of course more soy products and Yogi brand tea flavors than you could ever use. On the other hand, you've got excellent bread from nearby Brickmaiden

Breads, a fancy array of cheeses from Cowgirl Creamery, and things like Bellwether Farm sheep's milk yogurt, as well as beeswax candles, most of the condiments you'd ever require, and a range of organic fruits and vegetables that Mickey either can't or doesn't grow down the road. Still, in the best way possible, this place has managed to fend off the epithet of "artisanal," and feels to me to have retained all of its original character over the last twenty-five or so years that we've been shopping there.

The other store, the "General Store," we less frequently patronize. Located in a structure with an outsize storefront the likes of which you might find in an Old Western frontier town, it contains a sundry and expansive mix of things that were, for the most part, forbidden to me as a child. As a result, I loved going there, even if just to ogle the sweep of boxed Betty Crocker and Duncan Hines cake mixes, the upright boxes of Bisquick, the glut of Jell-O options, Rice-A-Roni-type ready meals, and a proliferation of canned and frozen foods. The display of candy and chips and impressively variegated selection of both jarred and bottled salsas were likewise an actual joy to behold. It's also one of only two places where you could buy beer, wine, and liquor in town, though this wasn't much of a concern for me in my youth. Still, I loved the neon MILLER LITE and BUDWEISER signs hung helter-skelter high up toward the back of the market and, behind those, a mass of loosely organized empty liquor boxes being saved for I knew not what future use. I had spent very little time in what you might call "typical" American supermarkets. I had been to plenty of Safeways or Costcos with friends' families or on my own; I wasn't raised totally isolated from mainstream food culture. But I had never been to the kind of market you might find in a rural town in Southwest Texas or maybe Idaho. And whether I had seen something like the inside of the "General Store" in a film, or just felt it to have an air of theater about it, I can't say, but even a couple recent upgrades to their vegetable display and a touch of remerchandizing haven't diminished its authenticity.

Though we didn't shop there for most of our provisions, we did go for fish and meat, since they had a counter stocked with some of the most local products you could get anywhere: fish from the community's handful of fishermen or meat raised up on a nearby bluff, just beyond the Big Mesa. My mom has Diane, the bespectacled and charmingly garrulous woman behind the meat and fish counter, on speed dial. When we're out in Bolinas in the summer, she'll call Diane nearly every morning to see if there's been a fresh catch that day, and, if the answer is no, whether perchance she might be expecting a delivery just a little later on. If the answer is yes, and especially if the fish in question is a king salmon, my mom will fairly shriek, "Diane, do not do anything to it! Don't cut it up! I'm coming down right now!" And we'll hop in the car—even though it takes only ten minutes to walk there from the cottage—and my mom will stand behind the counter to get a better look at dinner in its virgin state, before even the slightest incision has been made. If the fish is a modest size but still far too large for a family of two, she'll invite everyone she knows in Bolinas to dinner rather than see such a beautiful beast meet a subdivided end. She'll implore Diane to do the bare minimum: a scrape of scales and the removal of guts, but the rest she'll do at home.

There have been a few occasions when the store is dead empty, not a fish delivered for days by the commercial fishermen in town. My mom—rarely willing to accept defeat—has been known to go directly down to the docks on Wharf Road, in the hopes of crossing paths with a recreational fisherman who may have had better luck. Of course, anyone fishing without a commercial license is also unable to engage in a commercial transaction, though it *is* permitted to either gift or barter some, or all, of one's meager personal catch. My mom's usual tactic is to offer three times the value of a given foodstuff in cash (she likes, for example, to pay farmers at the farmers market on average up to twice the asking price because, as she always says, "Eating is a political act! And we must pay the *TRUE COST* of the food!"), but that strategy won't fly here—no one wants to risk his ability to fish for sport. Desperate, she once waved a bunch of Chez Panisse gift certificates—aka "Chez Bucks"—in the air and shouted "Three dinners at Chez Panisse restaurant for just one salmon!" as a handful of fishermen were unloading their small vessels. That night we went home with an exceedingly beautiful fish.

A summer spent in Bolinas has always meant a summer of eating salmon, since some of the best Pacific salmon—also called Chinook or king salmon—is fished out of boats docked right in the Bolinas harbor. "Salmon season"—which is to say, when it's legal to catch the big, beautiful fish that run naturally up the California coast—usually starts in June and stretches through October. By the time August rolls around, we've usually begun to show symptoms of "salmon fatigue," that mild nag of apathy that comes from having been spoiled for abundance. Still, at a moment in which the ecology of our oceans is at its most precarious, it feels like a virtual miracle that there are still salmon in the seas at all and, moreover, that we're lucky enough, not to mention privileged enough, to eat it. There's no better way, to my mind, than to eat it simply: grilled—or baked—wrapped like the gift that it is in a leaf from a fig tree.

Salmon Baked
in a Fig Leaf

I THINK MY MOM STARTED MAKING SALMON THIS WAY in the early nineties, because I remember at one point being offered a taste and bristling ("What was the weird burnt green thing?") and then being forced to at least *try* a bite. It instantly became one of my favorite dishes. And it's been on the Chez Panisse café menu for ages, anthologized in many books, and borrowed by countless other outlets, some of them opened by Chez alums. The best way, I'd imagine, to get a kid to eat fish is to do something to it that makes it taste like coconut—more than a figgy flavor, the leaves impart a sublime tropical essence to the salmon. Which is also why there's really no alternative to using fig leaves to make this dish. You *can* substitute things like grape leaves, but the effect will be different. It's also much easier to find fig trees in urban landscapes than you'd think it might be. There are a number of them growing on the streets of the leafier neighborhoods of New York, London, Los Angeles, San Francisco, and so on, and there's nothing more gratifying than doing a bit of guerrilla foraging. If, however, you have a garden or access to outdoor space, plant a tree! Even if your climate isn't conducive to fruiting, having a direct supply of leaves for baking or grilling fish is reason enough (not to mention you can do other wonderful things with them like grilling halved ripe peaches over a thin layer of leaves, or steeping them in warm milk to make a subtly figgy custard for ice cream).

GATHER AS MANY LARGE FIG LEAVES as ¼-pound portions of fish you plan to serve. Wash them thoroughly in cold water. Lightly coat each fillet with olive oil and season it generously with salt and black pepper. Wrap each one in a large fig leaf, tucking the edges of the leaf beneath the fish, as if it were a gift. I often use toothpicks or the broken-off sharp ends of skewers to securely close the leaves. If the leaf doesn't completely cover the fish, that's okay—it will still impart its flavor. Place the wrapped salmon on a baking sheet and bake in an oven preheated to 400°F until just cooked through, about 6 to 8 minutes. Don't be afraid to pry open a leaf to check for doneness. It's better to undercook fish a little, and return it to the oven if need be, than to overcook it and risk a slightly chalky or rubbery texture. This particular point is something I really learned from my mom; she's never afraid to put something back in the pan or the oven or back onto the grill. It's always preferable to initially undercook something than to overcook it irreversibly.

SERVE THE SALMON ON PLATES with the leaf peeled back to expose the fish. (As a kid, I used to love nibbling on the charred edges of the leaves.) My mom often makes a "compound butter" to daub onto the fish at the very end. A compound butter is just a butter that's been brought to room temperature and mixed with chopped herbs or other aromatics and a bit of sea salt. You can add chopped chives or chopped fines herbes like parsley, basil, chervil, or, for a more colorful, spicy alternative: a mix of chopped nasturtium flowers and leaves, even fresh chilies. I generally prefer to make an olive-oil-based Salsa Verde (page 211) as an accompaniment whenever I make fish, but the flavor of the fig leaves is so special here that it can really be served very simply with just a wedge of lemon, a sprinkling of herbs, or a generous drizzle of a vibrant extra virgin olive oil. If you can cook the salmon on a grill or over a wood fire, you'll get an even more intense flavor, and the fig leaf will conveniently act as a barrier between the fish and the grates of the grill, but both methods yield a lovely, fragrant result.

·　　·　　·

California generally is good at engendering a sense of human small-ness; the scale of its natural environments makes it easy to feel engulfed. I've wondered at times whether my decade-long stretch of English expatriation wasn't perhaps motivated by the need to go somewhere comparatively small and circumscribed. There's no doubt in my mind that geography, native or adopted, has had an effect on the contours of my thinking—nature, as it's doing in these pages, inevitably wheedles its way to the periphery, if not to the fore. And at no time am I so vulnerable to its appearance as when I'm out in Bolinas.

In the late afternoon, driving the final westward stretch around the lagoon or over the ridge to Bolinas can feel like something of a religious experience. The light alone, especially toward the end of summer, takes on a texture something like honeyed muslin. Even as the headland to the west just obscures the sun on its downward trajectory, plenty of brightness remains in the air. You make that critical left turn at the top of the tidal bight, orienting south again, toward Bolinas—by design there's no sign there to mark it—and the spectacle of the blond hills to the east flashes into view, nearly consumed by a dark conifer wood. The whole of the picture is cast in a bluish haze to make it look that much more rendered than real, and for a moment it seems impossible to imagine that you just came from there. Now that I'm back in California, after such a long time away, I often think of the authors who defined my childhood, whose books I read obsessively, looking to have my home in some way explained to me. They were authors like John Steinbeck, Jack London, Mary Hunter Austin—all of whom at times seemed close to ecstasy in their descriptions of the splendor. I feel pretty sure that they'd have lost their minds if they'd visited Bolinas.

Just as you turn away from the shimmering swale, but before you pass through a corridor of farmland that flanks the only road into town, you come across a farm stand belonging to Mickey Murch. Mickey, who's in his thirties now, was born and raised on the land he farms, a swath of marshy lowland called Gospel Flat. About ten years ago he opened a farm stand, an outpost for residents and visitors to buy what must be the most local, carbon-neutral food around. The stand is an unmanned enterprise, relying on an honor system that allows customers to weigh their goods, log their items in the pages of several disheveled legal pads, and pay into a secure custom-welded box. An illuminated sign declares it to be open 24 hours, and indeed it is—I've been there in the fullness of night to buy something for a very late dinner, using just the light of an iPhone to assist in the choice of beautiful chard, beets, and onions.

•   •   •

Every Fourth of July, Bolinas is animated with festivities. It's always struck me as vaguely incongruent: a radical hippie town defined by its opposition to the mainstream—and in every way antiestablishment—commemorating American independence with such bravado. But for as long as I can remember, and even in the darkest hours of American politics, this tiny town has pulled out all the stops on the Fourth. The celebration begins with an intensely competitive game of tug-of-war between the neighboring communities of Bolinas and Stinson Beach, whose beaches are physically separated by nothing but a slim channel measuring no more than a hundred feet, if that. The two towns can access each other only by driving the long stretch of Highway 1 that rims the expanse of the lagoon, which is fed by ocean via this single narrow point of ingress. On the Fourth, a thewy rope is strung by tugboat between the beaches. First the women, and then the men, of both communities face off in the foggy morning, hoping to pull their opposition into the chilly waters. Shortly after the grittier population of Bolinas has pulled off a pair of victories (this happens most years) comes the parade. The parade, though comprising what might reasonably be described as "floats," is where the community sets itself apart from more typical iterations of the genre. Here you have your Psychedelic Seniors, an actually stoned array of over-sixties in head-to-toe tie-dye; the Anti-Plastics Coalition, whose adherents wear outfits festooned with discarded plastic bottles and bags; the Bolinas Community Land Trust, dedicated to maintaining affordable housing in the rapidly gentrifying county; and the best float of all, Mickey Murch and his gaggle of children, riding their tractor through town and showering spectators with freshly dug carrots.

Bolinas is a cool climate agricultural zone and yet most everything seems to grow there in its Edenic soil, not least of all carrots, which in Mickey's hands are some of the sweetest and most flavorful I've ever had. Just about the only thing that *doesn't* exactly thrive in Bolinas are tomatoes, which can't really be dry farmed, what with the daily scrim of coastal fog. Still, I'd take one of Mickey's Early Girl tomatoes over any tomato I ate in England during my ten years there. And anyway, in this warming world, the atmospheric moisture proves ideal for a good many other things: the most tender broccoli (which my mom declares is "the best broccoli I've ever tasted"), huge gorgeous beets, tiny, violet-tinged artichokes, and jeweled heads of lettuce. And, perhaps most important, exceptionally fragrant parsley, cilantro, and basil—the ingredients for the most cherished of sauces: salsa verde.

Salsa Verde

SALSA VERDE, also known among my friends as "manna from the heavens," is one of the cornerstones of my cooking. I rarely go a week without making it. It's also the thing that most routinely results in people telling me that I'm "an amazing cook," even when all they've tasted up to that point is a bite of potato slathered in sauce. In fact, I believe this loose, herby concoction to be disproportionately responsible for any pleasure experienced at my table, which is why I almost always serve it at a dinner party, no matter the menu. If, god forbid, I could eat only one sauce for the rest of my days—and I'm shocked I'm even saying this—I'd choose salsa verde over aioli. Therein lies the depth of my passion for this condiment.

AS SAUCES GO, it's very versatile, and iterations of it exist across many cuisines. Some call it chimichurri, others salmoriglio, schug, or chermoula, and yet others sauce verte, but no matter the language or geography, it's used in similar capacities. This green magic can be ladled over virtually anything: fish, chicken, steak, lamb, potatoes, sliced raw vegetables, beans, or corn, *or* swirled into soups, drizzled over tagines, and spread onto sandwiches. It's also a recipe that can be endlessly adapted. Sometimes, for example, I make it very green and spicy; sometimes I add more exotic spices (fresh curry leaves and grated turmeric root, for instance, were brilliant suggestions from my friend Heather Sperling of Botanica restaurant in Los Angeles), or a tiny touch of honey, to round it out. Once you master the basic recipe, you can decide what herbs and flavors you like most, or you can experiment with different ingredients each time you make it.

AT ITS CORE, though, it's just herbs, alliums, acid, and oil. It can be made very simply with just chopped Italian parsley, minced garlic, lemon juice (and zest), salt, and very good extra virgin olive oil, or you can diversify your selection of herbs and/or add a macerated shallot or slivered green onion on top of, or in lieu of, the garlic. Sometimes I add chopped anchovies or capers, and I almost always throw in a chili. Even if I'm incorporating other herbs, I use at least some parsley as a base—I find this to be an indispensable flavor anchor. Measurements aren't terribly important here, and leftovers are a gift, so don't be afraid of making too much (although a good rule of thumb is that two bunches of herbs and two cloves of garlic will get you 6 very generous servings).

START BY WASHING AND DRYING YOUR HERBS. I default to a mix of parsley and cilantro, but I regularly add other fines herbes like mint, basil, marjoram or oregano, tarragon, chives, or fresh curry leaves, depending on what's freshest and in season. Pluck the leaves from their stems, with the exception of cilantro, which can be chopped stems and all. Finely mince 1 to 2 cloves of garlic. If you're making extra sauce, scale up the amount of garlic, but, as my mother consistently reminds me, while you can always add more, you can't take it out. Put the garlic in a medium bowl and add a big pinch of salt. If using, deseed and mince a small jalapeño, serrano, or Thai chili, and add it to the garlic. Holding a Microplane grater over the bowl, zest a lemon into the garlic, and then squeeze its juice over the top to allow the acid to slightly mellow the bite of garlic and chili. Make a heaping pile of your herbs and use a very sharp knife to chop them—how fine is up to you, but I like mine somewhere in between. I prefer the herbs to be in bigger pieces, if, say, I'm serving a rustic cut of meat, but generally I chop them to medium. If using, chives should be cut separately, since you want them to keep their tubular shape for texture.

ADD YOUR HERBS to the garlic and pour over a few big glugs of extra virgin olive oil, which is at once the binder and also the preservative: it will prevent the cut herbs from oxidizing and turning brown. Mix everything together thoroughly. It should be loose, so make sure to add enough oil. You might need more lemon juice too. The taste should be more acidic than oleaginous, and on the brighter, more verdant end of the spectrum, especially if you're serving it with something meaty and fatty like lamb shank or steak. If I'm using slivered scallions or green onion or diced shallot, I add it at the beginning along with the garlic and will supplement the lemon juice maceration liquid with a glug of white wine or champagne vinegar. Once you've added the oil, taste and adjust the seasoning, making sure you've used enough salt to bring out the flavor of the herbs and acid. The recipe is very forgiving, so fear not if your proportions aren't quite right at first. If you're like me, you'll be making it often enough to dial in a version that's exactly in tune with your palate.

CHAPTER 23

Even the Beans

It will come as no surprise to anyone reading up to this point, or indeed to anyone who is familiar with my mother's public persona, that she is dogmatic, and that her adherence to certain culinary principles can verge on religious fanaticism. One such issue, if we can call it that, is, unsurprisingly, the question of *organic*. By and large, I am of the opinion that her constant interrogation of vegetable shopkeepers, supermarket managers, the poor teenager restocking lettuce, or the waiter setting down a plate of suspiciously out-of-season-looking asparagus is a good thing. Most people should be asked to think of the provenance of the food they vend or serve, but there are instances when it is either (a) the most embarrassing interaction a daughter could endure or (b) completely pointless. I could regale you with stories of the former (see further: stern talking-tos with every grocer I've ever patronized, occasionally to the point where in the wake of her public inquiry I feel I have to withdraw my custom), but an example of the latter came during a Christmas spent in Oaxaca.

Oaxaca is a market town. You can buy some type of snack or raw ingredient every few paces, and there are many, many wonderful covered and uncovered food markets throughout the city and on its outskirts. My mom being my mom, however, made a point of finding the sole self-proclaimed "organic" market in all of Oaxaca (no doubt propped up entirely by visiting gringos like ourselves). It was in this well-intentioned establishment that she purchased a package of black beans destined for our Christmas table. I'm fairly certain that no one else in the entire state of Oaxaca, possibly all of Mexico, had been going to the organic store to buy *beans*. A hundred varieties of bean seemed to be available on virtually every corner: in open baskets, in buckets, laid out in trays like glistening jewels. I will hand it to my mom for sticking to her guns, but soon after we started cooking those organic beans (which we *did* soak for close to twelve hours), it became clear that they had been packaged back in the days of the

Reagan administration and sitting on that shelf for nearly as long. We cooked those beans and *cooked* those beans and kept on cooking those beans, but they refused to soften, or, for that matter, to taste like much, though we'd put practically an entire epazote bush in there to try to infuse the insipid brew. We did eat the beans, semi-crunchy and unredeemed, alongside a delicious pan-fried chicken with warm corn tortillas, but the clear takeaway was that the organic shop was *not* the best place to source beans in Oaxaca.

Still, before my mother inevitably caves to whatever looks best at the market, regardless of farming practices, she always tries— commendably, I might add—to shop according to her doctrine. In a city like Oaxaca, where a lot of the local food production is a priori unindustrialized and small-scale, the quest to buy organic beans was a crazed performance of her incorruptible ideology. There's zero pragmatism in it, of course, but then there's close to zero pragmatism to my mother, generally. And she doesn't care if the exercise proves futile— the value lies in the intention. She takes the idea of "voting with your dollars" very seriously, which is why, even back in California, where one is spoiled for choice when it comes to markets, she insists on doing a lot of her shopping at small outfits like the Berkeley Natural Grocery Company. This is not because the fresh foodstuffs there are better (they emphatically aren't; we argue over this point constantly), but because the store has committed itself to having 100 percent organic produce, whereas other markets continue to offer a mix of organic and conventional, and this, for her, makes them worthy of boycott. Of course she's able to tolerate a bit of fridge-burned frisée from "Berkeley Natch," as it's known in our house, only because most of her produce comes from the farmers market, which is indisputably the best source, or from "Chez shopping" (in which the chefs fill her basket at the end of the day with any little odd bits that might make for a perfect dinner for one). But still, she is inflexible on this point— I will actually hide my grocery bags if I've strayed into a Whole Foods.

Simple Black Beans

COVER A FEW CUPS OF BLACK BEANS with plenty of cold water and allow to soak overnight. If the beans are very small, this step can be skipped, but soaking beans or lentils makes them more digestible and their cooking more uniform. Drain the beans, rinse them, and pick out any obvious split or fractured specimens. Put the beans into a large pot, cover generously with fresh water, and bring to a boil. Turn the flame down to a simmer and add a big glug of extra virgin olive oil, a quartered onion, several peeled cloves of garlic, a coarsely chopped, peeled carrot, a quartered stalk of celery, a handful of cilantro sprigs, a bay leaf, a pinch each of fennel, coriander, and cumin seed, and a teaspoon each of ground coriander, ground cumin, and hot smoked paprika. (You can also skip *all* of the above and just salt generously at the end, but the more aromatics you use, the more layered the flavor of the beans.) Any other chilies, dry or fresh, that you may have around (chipotle and arbol make especially good additions, but a fresh jalapeño is good too) are likewise welcome. Use epazote and/or avocado leaves if you have access to them—they are traditional Mexican bean seasonings that will impart a wonderful depth of flavor. Add more water if necessary during the cooking; the beans should remain hydrated and loose in the pot. Once they've been cooking for a while and are quite soft—this could take up to three hours, or in the case of Oaxaca, more than twenty-four—stir in a tablespoon of sea salt and taste. Err on the side of over- rather than undercooked—you don't want al dente beans (neither does your stomach). Adjust the seasonings, making sure the beans are plenty salted, and fish out any larger, unbroken-down bits of vegetable or herbs. Serve the beans in their liquor in a big bowl or terra-cotta cazuela, and if they're destined for tacos, serve them with a slotted spoon—the bean juice might be delicious but will savage the integrity of a corn tortilla. Otherwise, they are the perfect accompaniment to roasted chicken or chile verde and rice, or can be quickly converted (with the addition of some stock and the use of an immersion blender) to a delicious black bean soup.

CHAPTER 24

Christmas

Christmas was never been much of a "thing" in our house, my father being a virulently atheistic Jew, my mom a Mother Nature–worshiping agnostic. Still, my mom had grown up in a family that celebrated the birth of Christ with a tinsel-covered tree, neatly wrapped presents, and a minor showing of pomp, and she wanted to impart at least a touch of that ceremony to me. I don't know what child is not excited about the prospect of receiving gifts, but I especially loved going down to the tree lot to choose a tree. This was often from whatever impoverished selection remained a mere three days before Christmas (at times we were even the family skulking around the desolate lots on Christmas Eve), so ingrained and yet totally inexplicable was our tardiness when it came to this activity. It may have initially been a tacit expression of respect for my father's repudiation of the holiday, but the failure to acquire a tree in a timely fashion persisted well beyond my parents' separation when I was thirteen. This usually means that our tree is either the runtiest and most hole-filled or the tallest and therefore least salable. If the latter, we'd have to beg the beleaguered tree lot attendant to sever three or four feet of tree so we could get it into our house. One year, we even gathered on Christmas morning around a scavenged bottom quarter of a tree placed on a card table. It could get a bit grim.

Still, whatever we lacked in arboreal splendor, we made up for with decorations. For years my mother has collected antique ornaments, whimsical astral shapes with dangling glass beads, spun-glass twists like braids of colored saltwater taffy, globes whose colors have faded to a beautiful dull silver. And then the strands: gorgeous almond-shaped glass beads strung in strangely abbreviated lengths, which we would link together to make one extra long garland that changed character every three feet. Everything was so ancient and so frangible: we had to spot each other as we affixed ornament to branch, each of us taking turns so that we could step back and carefully plot the next addition or catch a bulb if it looked likely to tumble. Occasion-

ally, a brand-new ornament would enter the house—a gift from an unwitting acquaintance—and before I could ask my mom whether we should hang it, I would know from her withering glare that the answer was no.

There was a "decade" to our Christmas tree—the 1930s. If you were at all in doubt, you needed look no further than the very worn but still very beautiful Depression-era "crazy quilts" that swaddled the foot of the tree. As far as celebrating, we've never engaged in much by way of traditions, at least not beyond the tree-trimming and present-opening. And the latter has grown especially brief now that I'm a good twenty-five years out of childhood. We exchange a few modest gifts, sitting in the small front room that gets used for pretty much only this activity.

In recent years, if I happen to be home for the holidays, things are very mellow come Christmas Day. By the time I emerge from bed, my mom has a fire dancing warmly in the kitchen hearth. Bach's Mass in B minor is set at deafening volumes on the stereo. The air fairly vibrates, the voices in Bach's chorus twining together in ecstatic song. The kitchen takes on a slightly religious cast, the feeling of being much bigger, much grander, perhaps even a touch cathedral-like, as the singers reach higher and higher for notes. Behind the stacks of bowls heaped on the sideboard at the far end of the kitchen, the tall, rect-angular windows admit columns of shimmering white winter light. The enormous arrangement of branches and garden cuttings set per-petually in that corner is blown out in the blaze. We are an audience of two. And we can't even begin to communicate over the beautiful din. Instead, we wordlessly start in on the process of assembling our modest brunch.

For at least a few days, my mom will have been keeping blue farm eggs in an airtight container with a fragrant Italian black truffle, to allow its flavor to deeply infuse them. She scrambles the eggs lightly—almost too lightly, but somehow still enough—and showers them with tissue-thin petals of grated truffle, *just* before serving. I watch them wilt and collapse as they make contact with the warm eggs, expressive, hysterical little wafers. Exceptionally, we eat smoked salmon that's come all the way from Ireland—sent by the Irish cook and revered culinary pedagogue Darina Allen—because it's especially delicious (ahem, *terroir*) and because we are having Irish soda bread and, after all, at least half my mother's ancestors hail from that morsel of land suspended in the Atlantic Ocean. We get out the lovely antique champagne coupes, etched with intricate ribbonlike loops, and share a half bottle of Krug champagne. It's only ten a.m., but this meal is the only one of any significance today. This fairly tempered approach to Christmas Day evolved, more than anything, as a kind of antidote to the previous night, which had been overrun by the boisterous annual Seven Fish Dinner (more on that momentarily).

Darina Allen's Soda Bread

FOR ALL OF MY MOTHER'S CULINARY TALENTS, she is a truly bad baker. The fiddly chemistry of it, the need to be exacting, doesn't suit her temperament. And whatever gene is responsible for burning pies and turning out lopsided loaves is unfortunately something I wholly inherited. Our baking deficiencies notwithstanding, it is on Christmas Day that we attempt the soda bread recipe authored by Darina. This is a very simple recipe and doesn't require rising time or yeast or really anything out of the ordinary. Still, I'd say, we make a genuinely delicious version of it only once in every three attempts (and, I can assure you, there is no flaw in the recipe). I came downstairs once to discover my mother pulling a loaf out of the oven *after several minutes of baking* in order to try to incorporate the measure of salt she had accidentally omitted. This was not one of our finer loaves. But even slices of our lumpy, twice-baked bread tasted delicious spread thickly with butter. That said, when a loaf of this comes out of our oven unblemished, it's just about as perfect a bread as you could hope for: homey, moreish, simple, and the best accompaniment to Christmas smoked salmon and scrambled eggs. (It's also one of the few vehicles that my mom and I agree tastes better with butter than olive oil.) To make a loaf, you won't need much more than an hour, start to finish.

PREHEAT THE OVEN TO 450° F. In a large bowl, mix 1¾ cups of all-purpose flour together with 1¾ cups of whole wheat flour and add a generous teaspoon of baking soda and a teaspoon of salt (passing both through a sieve to eliminate any clumps). Lift the flour up with your fingers to evenly disperse the salt and baking soda. Make a well in the center of the flours and pour in 1⅔ cups of buttermilk. Make sure to have another ½ cup or so of buttermilk on hand in case you need any additional moisture to bring the dough together. Using your fingers, stir in a circular movement from the center to the outside of the bowl in increasing concentric circles. By the time you reach the outside of the bowl, the dough should be ready. Turn it out onto a floured worktop. Sprinkle a little flour on your hands and gently tidy the dough around the edges. Transfer the dough to an oven tray lined with baking parchment. Tuck the edges underneath with your hand and gently pat the dough with your fingers into a loaf about 1½ inches thick. Using a sharp, long chopping knife, cut a deep cross into the bread, extending to its edges. Lastly, prick it in the center of the four sections to, as Darina says, "let the fairies out of the bread." Bake in the preheated oven for 15 minutes. Then turn the oven down to 400°F for another 15 minutes. Remove the baking tray and turn the bread upside down, placing it directly on the oven rack; bake for a further 5 to 10 minutes until cooked (it should be golden brown and the bottom should sound hollow when tapped). Cool on a wire rack.

CHAPTER 25

Seven Fish Dinner

It must have been sometime in the early nineties that we first met Angelo Garro, the Sicilian blacksmith behind San Francisco's Renaissance Forge. Hardly just an artisan, Angelo is an irreducible figure. His appetite for adventure, and for anything foragable from the wild, is insatiable. It was with Angelo that we went olive-picking in the Russian River Valley, salt-cured olives, made olive oil; harvested grapes, made wine, accidentally turned said wine to vinegar; hunted for chanterelles and porcini in West Marin; pulled over on the side of the road to cut heaps of the softest, feathered fennel fronds to make little savory cakes; pursued wild boar in their native habitat; observed ducks and geese being shot out of the sky; and so on. The fact that Angelo's smithy is called the Renaissance Forge is almost too fitting. Not only does the place look like you've stepped into the mise-en-scène of a Caravaggio painting—replete with roaring forge, hundreds of piled or dangling tools, filigreed bits of half-finished forged-iron projects hanging from the ceiling, and drifts of metal shavings like sawdust on the floor—but it is also the actual home of the only person I know who could unironically claim the title of Renaissance man. It's difficult to believe that he bought the place already named. Then again, the previous owner went by *Virgil*. It must have been preordained.

Though Angelo hails from "Siracusa"—or if you ask him, "The Lady of the Mediterranean"—he's been living in North America for at least forty years. I've heard about a stint of blacksmithing in Switzerland as a teenage runaway, a stretch honing his craft in Toronto, but who really knows? The lilt that clings about his speech, his charmingly muddled syntax, his distinctly Italo-jingoist brio—all of these things contribute to his uniquely ambiguous narrative. And anyway, the thing that drew us together more than anything was his full-bodied enthusiasm for cooking and hosting. Anyone with as much hospitality running through his veins was bound to ingratiate himself with my mother. And Angelo's Italianness—so tangible it wafts off him like a potent cologne—was for my mother a kind of pheromonal attractant. This period, after all, marked the beginning of a decades-long process of transferring her culinary fealty from France to Italy.

Our family's relationship with Angelo began modestly enough, with the arrival of his forged iron candlesticks in our dining room (a gift from Bob), occasional bottles of his unpotable homemade grappa, and ultimately the auspicious first prototype of the now-famous Alice's Egg Spoon, commissioned by my mom after an illustration of a late-medieval French implement in a book about hearth cooking. Before long, every one of our formerly sedate Jewish-Protestant Christmases had been transformed into a Seven Fish Dinner.

It was always my understanding that the Seven Fish Dinner held on Christmas Eve was a distinctly Sicilian tradition, Sicily being an island defined as much by its Catholicism as its geographical intimacy with the sea. However, the eating of seafood on Christmas Eve is, I've since learned, a rather more ubiquitous Italian convention, evidently stemming from the age-old Roman Catholic edict that one must abstain from eating meat on the eve of a feast day. As meat or animal fat was disallowed on such days, observant Catholics used the convenient culinary loophole of fish to satisfy their appetites. The Feast of the Seven Fishes was born. To my mind, there's nothing particularly abstinent about eating fish—especially if, unlike my Jewish ancestors, the diners in question are unencumbered by the problem of tref. With all the shellfish and mussels and oysters and clams in sight, this meal more closely resembles a feast Louis XIV would have dreamt up (had he been Italian) than a pious overture to Christmas Day.

Our Seven Fish Dinner was no exception. In fact, *seven* was taken as a loose suggestion rather than a constraint. By the end of the evening, we'd typically clock in at closer to thirteen or fourteen different fish, at once a source of pleasure and ocean-ecosystem-depleting, morning-after guilt. When we first joined Angelo and his fellow revelers for this meal, it was still held at his forge. The forge is at the end of an alley in a part of San Francisco that hasn't changed much in my lifetime: South of Market, a corner that's proven remarkably resistant to gen-

trification. There was always an element of frisson walking down that choked and pitch-dark alleyway in our party clothes, drawn all the more starkly into contrast by the warmth with which we were immediately met inside. We'd shrug off our coats and be pulled by Angelo's welcoming bellow toward the arterial center of the compound—and of course be put instantly to work preparing something. The smithy's burnished interior was lit mainly by candlelight for the occasion, and the aroma of the tinny, well-oiled surroundings mingled with the woodsmoke streaming from his gigantic outdoor grill, creating something more like an atmospheric broth than a fragrance. As Puccini blared in the background from a stereo buried deep beneath sheets of metal, my mom lit branches of rosemary to trail through the room, adding another base note to the brew.

We would eventually sit at a long and serpentine table that ran the length of the forge, but we always congregated first in the kitchen. Angelo's kitchen opens directly onto an inner courtyard; his forge on the other side is accessed by a large wide ramp whose door was perpetually ajar. We'd be standing half indoors, half outdoors, there being essentially no division between the two. When I was younger I used to wonder why all the stray cats of San Francisco hadn't figured out that they could shelter there, especially with the profusion of salami hanging from the rafters. (Maybe they just didn't have a taste for fennel-scented boar sausage?) Angelo is not a precious cook: like my mother, he's prone to inserting his hand into just about any substance to taste, season, or stir it, no matter how bloody or scalding or otherwise uninviting. And his hands have the weathered, worldly look of having been his lifelong servants. He is the only person I have ever witnessed unflinchingly pull the skin off an eel.

The Seven Fish Dinner always kicked off with oysters, which is how—in a world free of budgetary strictures and food poisoning—all things would ideally kick off. Sometimes grilled oysters accompanied raw ones; sometimes someone bravely proffered raw clams. Plates of anchovies draped over toast rubbed briskly with raw garlic and sprinkled with olive oil. Spoonfuls of Santa Barbara uni. Everyone gathered around the fire outside, the light cold and wintery, an urban sky that never deepened beyond a light-polluted, transparent-seeming black.

The frenzy of hors d'oeuvres nibbling would boil over into the dining area and everyone would hastily slip into place, almost instantly beginning to circulate plates heaped with baccalà or shrimp. One of my favorite things was my mom's clam *brodo,* clear and spicy and clean and aromatic—something simple to fortify you in preparation for the next five courses. And you needed fortifying, because two of Angelo's regular dishes, wine-braised octopus and sweet-and-sour eel, were lurking right around the corner. Both these items were sourced in Chinatown, not from my mother's sustainable fishmonger (much to her chagrin), and neither could possibly have been as delectable as the versions Angelo remembered from his youth. I prayed yearly to Neptune, begging him to withhold eels that year. Rarely did he heed my prayers. Sometime after Angelo's rough-and-ready *pasta chi sardî—* which I struggled with immensely, given that my childhood anchovy aversion extended to other similarly putrid small fish—but before my mom's whole grilled sea bass, there was a very welcome intermission. One of the dinner regulars was the rock musician Boz Scaggs, whose nightclub, Slim's, was just across the alley and through a vacant parking lot from the forge. Every Christmas Eve, Slim's hosts the Oakland Interfaith Gospel Choir, and the event, kicked off by Boz in 1988, has since become a Bay Area tradition. As his guests, we were able to sneak in, reeking of fish, just before the singing began, and sneak out, just as swiftly, at its conclusion. This jubilant gospel performance was the closest thing I ever got to church as a child, and this "church" sold booze—that should tell you something about our level of familial piety.

We'd return, flushed in the face from our dash across the lots, and slip through the triangular aperture where the edge of a chain-link fence had been curled back to allow trespass. After an hour or two of song, we'd be *just* hungry enough to fathom eating another course. The fire would have died down and Angelo or my mother—whoever was in charge of the whole fish that year—would have crept out of Slim's early to head back to the forge to put it on the grill. Bundled in a thicket of leafy lemon branches, boughs of bay, and green fennel stalks, the fish itself was almost invisible in its verdant sheath. And as the green branches began to char over the fire, their aroma would fill the forge anew with a smell something like an offering to the gods.

About five or so years ago, my mother managed to wrangle the gathering over to our house in the East Bay. Whether the rationale was to be able to preside more keenly over quality control or merely to avoid the inconvenience of the trans-bay drive, I don't know, because, let me tell you, the fallout, filth and aroma-wise, when you have prepared, eaten, and discarded the remains of seven or more different fish, is *extreme.* It doesn't matter if you think you've scrubbed every square inch of the kitchen, there is always some shrimp juice or octopus ooze or shred of Dungeness crab carcass lurking *somewhere* and it will haunt you for days, perhaps even weeks, a phantom smell like some Ghost of Christmas Very Recently Past. And yet as much as my oversensitive nose flares at the prospect of these fishy remains—indeed, my mother would have to steel herself against my days of complaint— that Christmas Eve feast is one of my favorite nights of the year.

Though both menu and venue have changed over time, certain dishes remain constant: a gigantic platter of cracked and parsley-strewn Dungeness crab; Peggy Knickerbocker's warm baccalà and potato salad; Angelo's garlic shrimp, his wine-braised octopus, and his sardine and homemade farro pasta; my mom's clam broth and, to finish the meal, her whole grilled fish, in its leafy blanket. Some of the recipes are more easily undertaken than others, some I'm happy to leave behind to be prepared just once a year at Christmas. The following are my favorites.

Angelo Garro's Wild Fennel Cakes

I KNOW THESE LITTLE SAVORY CAKES have nothing to do with fish, but they're so synonymous with Angelo's cooking that I can't imagine experiencing a gathering in which they don't feature, or indeed telling a story about Angelo that doesn't include this recipe. My friend Greta and I sometimes refer to them as Angelo's funnel cakes—they're too good to be mistaken for being salubrious. To make them, you will need to scout around the edges of roadsides or trails to look for tall, feathery wild fennel fronds. Consult a local flora guide (or Google) if you require some help with identification, but you'll know you have the right plant if it emits a sweet anisey aroma when you crush a bit of the greenery between your fingers. It's important to harvest fennel when it is very fresh and tender and dark green, which is generally in the springtime rather than the winter. If you find young fennel bulbs at the farmers market with their tender tops still attached, you can use those too.

FINELY CHOP THE LEAVES AND STALKS of enough fennel to yield 4 cups, blanch in salted water for a few minutes, and drain. In a large bowl, mix the fennel, 1 cup of coarse bread crumbs, 5 cloves of minced garlic, and 2 cups of grated Parmesan cheese. Add 2 eggs, freshly ground black pepper, and a big pinch of red pepper flakes and mix together with your hands. Take a rounded tablespoon and form a small cake about ¾ of an inch thick—wet enough to easily mold, but not so wet that it feels loose and comes apart. Fry the cakes in 1 cup of vegetable oil mixed with a few tablespoons of olive oil in a medium cast-iron pan until lightly browned all over (a couple of minutes per side). Allow to drain on a folded paper towel. Sprinkle with flaky salt and serve hot as an appetizer.

Garlic Shrimp

THE SEVEN FISH DINNER is not a meal for the faint of heart; neither is it one for people who have a problem doing things like extracting clams from their shells at the table or slurping oysters or, for that matter, dismantling shrimp heads to get to the sweet meat inside. This shrimp preparation will require some plucky diners (but cooking shrimp with heads and tails intact does give the meat inside so much more flavor—it's worth the extra tableside hassle). Look for the most sustainable shrimp option you can find (since it's very hard to get "clean" shrimp these days) and budget about 4 shrimp per person, so about 2 pounds of whole shrimp for 8 people, depending on their size. I like to use medium-sized shrimp, and in California ours come from Santa Barbara or the Gulf of Mexico. Rinse your shrimp thoroughly in cold water and set aside.

SLIVER 16 CLOVES OF GARLIC (about 1½ or 2 heads' worth) and coarsely chop 2 inches of dried red chili pepper. (You can also use dried red chili pepper flakes or fresh bird's eye chilies; just be careful, as they vary in intensity.) Thinly slice 2 small lemons and coarsely chop a handful of flat-leaf parsley and reserve. Heat a couple of big glugs of extra virgin olive oil in a large, wide sauté pan and add the chili and garlic and 2 bay leaves. When the garlic is just beginning to smell fragrant, but before it begins to color, add the shrimp and a splash of dry white wine and stir vigorously over medium-high heat, until the shrimp are bright orange and cooked through (about 6 minutes, depending on the heat of your pan). In the last minute of cooking add the slivered lemons and parsley, a big pinch of salt, and some cracked black pepper and toss. Serve in a large bowl to pass around family style.

Peggy's Baccalà PEGGY KNICKERBOCKER always brought this beautiful dish, already assembled, to our Seven Fish Dinner. She called it North Beach Baccalà after one of her favorite cooks in North Beach, Joe Delgado, and published it in her wonderful book, *Olive Oil: From Tree to Table,* in 2007. It was inspired by a salad she'd eaten at a restaurant in Granada, but her version omits the oranges and tomatoes and replaces them with warm potatoes, onions, and parsley to make it especially suitable for a Christmas Eve repast.

TO MAKE 4 TO 6 SERVINGS you'll need to obtain about 1 pound of skinless, boneless dried salt cod, which is available in most Italian and Greek specialty stores. Place it in a large bowl of cold water and refrigerate for 24 hours, changing the water at least four times. Drain the cod, put it in a large saucepan, and add water to cover. Bring it to a boil, reduce the heat to medium low, and allow it to simmer until the fish is just tender when you prod it with a small knife (about 10 to 15 minutes). Overcooking will toughen the fish. Use a slotted spoon to remove the cod, but retain the cooking liquid in the pan. Allow the fish to cool and break it up with your fingers in a large bowl, removing any bits of bone or pieces of skin that might have been overlooked. Bring the cooking liquid back to a boil and add 1 pound of peeled russet potatoes cut into large cubes. Cook the potatoes until they are tender, about 10 to 15 minutes, and add the drained potatoes to the bowl with the fish. Add the plucked leaves of a bunch or two of Italian parsley, chopped roughly (about 2 cups), a thinly sliced red onion, freshly ground black pepper, and a couple of glugs of extra virgin olive oil. Toss and serve warm, if possible (though this salad will keep for up to three days in the refrigerator).

My Mom's Spicy Clam Brodo

THIS IS ONE OF THE SIMPLEST SOUPS I know of, scarcely more than clams, a few aromatics, and water. But it is exactly the type of thing to start off a longer, more indulgent meal, or to eat the day after a feast when your appetite is lean. To make this you'll need about 10 smaller clams (like Manila) or 8 medium-sized clams (like littlenecks) per person, so somewhere in the range of 3-plus pounds for 8 people (this is a very easy dish to expand or contract, according to your numbers). Wash and scrub your clams thoroughly in cold water and set aside. Make a mirepoix (that mix of uniformly diced vegetables that forms the basis of many dishes in French, Italian, and Spanish cooking) using a large white onion, a large peeled carrot, and a few stalks of celery. Add to this a large bulb of fennel, also diced. Finely chop a small handful of parsley and sliver 10 cloves of garlic. Heat a couple of glugs of extra virgin olive oil in a large, wide sauté pan and add the diced vegetables (reserving the garlic and parsley), along with a couple of sprigs of thyme, a bay leaf or two, 1 teaspoon of fennel seeds, a big pinch of saffron, and a couple of big pinches of red pepper flakes or a minced bird's eye chili. Cook on medium-low heat, allowing the vegetables to soften. Add more olive oil if necessary to lubricate the mirepoix. Once the onions have become transparent, add the slivered garlic and the parsley and stir until the garlic is fragrant. A few preserved peeled tomatoes (loosely broken apart in your hands) can be a nice addition at this juncture, but they're optional. Pour in 3 cups of water and 1 cup of white wine and bring the liquid to a boil, then turn down to a simmer. The idea is to make a broth out of this mixture that could almost live on its own flavorwise, since the clams will be cooking in it for only a short amount of time, so make sure it tastes good and savory. Add the clams (pouring in additional water/wine if you need it to fully submerge them), cover the pan with a lid, and cook for about 5 minutes, or until all of the clams have opened. Pluck out the bay leaf and thyme sprigs and any unopened clams and discard them. Ladle vegetables, clams, and broth into individual bowls and garnish with a little fresh olive oil and coarsely chopped parsley.

Parsley-Lemon Dungeness Crab

YOU MAY BY NOW have detected a bit of redundancy in some of the flavor combinations here, but honestly, there are few more delicious ways to prepare very good shellfish than with simple ingredients like parsley, garlic, and lemon. If you're lucky enough to live in a part of the world where you can readily get Dungeness crabs, the simplest method is the best. Their flesh is so sweet and delicious, they need very little by way of supplementary seasoning. Other types of fleshy, white-meat crab will work well too for this preparation. Start by submerging your live crabs in rapidly boiling, heavily salted water, budgeting about a third to a half a crab per person, depending on size. (If you struggle with the "live" aspect of this preparation, ask your fishmonger to kill your crabs for you, but this must be done the day you plan to cook them.) When the water comes back to a boil, reduce heat to a simmer. Cook 1½- to 2½-pound crabs for 15 minutes, 3-pound crabs for closer to 20 minutes. Drain the crabs, rinse with cool water, and allow them to come to room temperature.

ONCE THE CRABS CAN BE HANDLED, you'll need to clean them. Turn them on their backs and remove the triangle-shaped flaps called the apron and discard these. Hold the crab vertically and pull the top shell, or carapace, away from the body and discard that too. Likewise, remove and discard the gills/lungs and mandible. There will be a fair amount of oozy gunk (which I wrongly referred to as "crab brains" when I was a kid), so at this point, give the crabs a good rinse under cold water. Use a big sharp knife to cut each crab in half down the center and then again in quarters if they are especially large. Use a mallet to crack the legs without fully breaking them open or off. Place the pieces of crab in a large metal bowl.

ONCE THE CRAB IS READY, sliver the cloves of a head's worth of garlic (using less or more depending on numbers). In a frying pan, warm a big glug of extra virgin olive oil and add the garlic and cook until fragrant and very, very lightly golden in color—do not let it burn. Remove from the heat and pour over the crabs. Add a couple of handfuls of coarsely chopped parsley and the juice of 1 or 2 lemons (Meyer lemons are preferable, if you can find them). Season with a few big pinches of salt and freshly ground pepper and a little more olive oil if necessary to coat. Place in a large serving dish and allow to cool completely before serving family style (this is another course that requires a lot of hands-on eating). One of the beautiful things about this dish is that you can make it well in advance. One less thing to think about when another six to ten fish dishes are vying for your attention! We always have a huge bowl of garlicky aioli (page 69) on the table—it's a multi-use condiment, but it's especially delicious with crab.

CHAPTER 26

The Mystery Nugget

My parents rarely took me to the snow. Even though the Sierra Nevada range is within spitting distance of the Bay Area, neither parent had any particular affinity for cold weather or snow sports. And so most ski seasons would come and go without any effort on behalf of the Waters-Singer clan to foray to the mountains. My mom's well-documented aversion to the snow, coupled with her general apathy toward exercise (the latter did shift when she turned fifty) earned her the sarcastic nickname Alice "Jean-Claude Killy" Waters from my dad. Killy, for those of you who are not familiar with the French giant of 1960s-era winter athletics, was a three-time Olympic medalist in downhill skiing.

Whether or not I had internalized my parents' indifference (forged in the underheated purlieus of their respective non-Californian childhood winters), I was myself no great winter sport enthusiast, either. In fact, I wasn't even that into snow, novel as the substance was for a Golden State native. I was never the first kid out of the lodge to make snow angels or build snowmen or ball up powder for a snowball fight. I found these activities to be, well, *cold*, and, when you added the gear required for skiing, *deeply* uncomfortable. Those boots! Locking you into strained positions of the shin, always a size too small, filled with the odor of the previous renter's foot, etc.

So on the few occasions that I can even remember us all venturing to the mountains together, unsurprisingly we remained indoors and mostly cooked. (The second we hit the geographical snow line, my mom would begin her vexed and repeated observations about the absence of anything edible growing. I think this fact—the passage into a landscape entirely hostile toward the production of food—was at least as responsible for my mom's distaste for ski trips as the idea of skiing itself.) Some people talk about how the après-ski experience is what makes skiing worthwhile; our family treated the whole of a mountain adventure as après-ski. Or, more accurately, *pas-de-ski* at all. Why we even bothered—even if only sporadically—to drive four hours, much of the way on cumbersome tire chains, to largely remain indoors is beyond me, but I do remember one such trip rather vividly, if only for a discovery made while cleaning out my mom's purse.

We were staying at a family friend's cabin at the ski resort Twain Harte and were snowed in (but *actually* snowed in, not just the result of our collective antipathy toward gelid landscapes). I must have been about seven at the time, an age when sorting through one's mother's belongings was good enough entertainment for an afternoon. So to pass the time, I undertook a grand emptying of my mom's perpetually chaotic handbag. My mom is not a slovenly person: our house is tidy; she appreciates order; she infrequently lets a dirty dish dwell in the sink for longer than a few hours. Take one look in her purse, however, and you would believe otherwise. I used to dread the request to locate something—usually her iconic rose-colored sunglasses—from within the bag while she was driving. It typically meant brushing one's fingertips against something shadowy and foreign and often eerily organic (but decidedly not of the USDA-approved variety). There was always a school of loose business cards swimming around its depths, their surfaces bronzed and corners blunted from the absence of a proper sheath. Reliably, an assortment of rumpled receipts had also collected in a corner like a pile of meticulously raked and then abandoned leaves.

There also always seemed to be something gritty and sand-like mixed with a bit of lipstick from an uncapped shade of dark burgundy (my mother's nineties lip hue) that together filmed the inner lining. This grit was *probably* salt—a little waxed paper envelope of the condiment does sometimes travel with my mother for emergency picnics and/or unexpected opportunities for seasoning—but it was always impossible to say for sure while blindly fishing around in the tenebrous abyss for the requested spectacles.

Anyway, on this particular snowy afternoon, I laid out the entire contents of the bag on the dining table and began to sort through its mixture of valuables and jetsam. I grouped receipts in a neat pile, gathered business cards of new acquaintances and sifted out my mother's own, reunited the uncapped lipstick with its chapeau, used my palm to iron out creased bills that had been shoved here and there rather than returned neatly to the billfold, pulled a few francs and a couple of lira from the coin purse. After spending some time organizing the various credit cards and IDs according to a seven-year-old's system of order (i.e., by color rather than function), I found, in the remotest corner of a side pocket, a tiny shriveled dark brown nugget. I plucked it from its nook and, as any child would, smelled it immediately. The top note was, needless to say, dust, cut with a bit of leather, but the bottom note was unmistakably fishy. I inhaled more deeply. Yes, whatever this rubbery shriveled little thing was, it had had a previous life in the ocean. Specimen in hand, I turned to my mom, who was reading on the couch, and said, "Mom, you have fish in your purse!"

Her first distracted response, voice monotone and uninflected, was "What? That's impossible."

She didn't look up from the magazine, so I marched over to her and extended my palm. "It's dried fish. Look."

She glanced at it—I could tell she was still failing to take me seriously—and said, "I have no idea what that is. I'm sure it's nothing."

"Smell it, Mom. I think it's squid."

"Squid?" She leaned forward and sniffed.

Several seconds passed in silence as a wave—more a tsunami—of recognition began to gather force, preparing to sweep through her brain.

"OH MY GOD, YOU'RE RIGHT, FAN! IT'S A PIECE OF OCTOPUS!!!"

You see, my parents had traveled to Japan a year earlier—an *entire* year—and, during that visit in the autumn of 1989, had at times pressed themselves to the very limits of what either was prepared to experience gastronomically. Upon their return I was treated to many stories of the freshest, most beautiful sashimi sprinkled with micro-flowers and green tea salt and the like, but I was also regaled with the more beguiling tales of choking down fish sperm and fish eyeballs and fish bones. I was six and I loved it, especially because the stories echoed the tales of my mother's month-long trip to China with Cecilia Chiang in 1982 during which she consumed everything from snake blood to turtle soup, not to mention a vast quantity of Chinese wine, and huge amounts of chilies in Taipei. She was five months pregnant with me at the time.

One story from the Japan trip that my parents had forgotten to relay, however, was the encounter with a piece of rather texturally challenging raw octopus at a super high-style Japanese restaurant styled by the famous architect and designer Shiro Kuramata. My dad claims it was one of those formidable interiors in which the mere presence of humans (to say nothing of Americans) seemed to disrupt the order of things. Food began to arrive. There was no menu. In fact, there was next to nothing by way of verbal exchange. The chef, my mom remembers, stood so close to them she could feel his breath. When the octopus arrived, there was no escape. The chef glowered. The octopus, so fresh it seemed still to be twitching, lay, unsauced, unaccompanied, on a sand-colored plate like a brazen nudist at a public beach.

Both my parents put the octopus in their mouths and chewed. And chewed. And chewed. And chewed and chewed and chewed. My dad, who is less prone to hyperbole, said he believed they chewed the octopus for close to fifteen minutes. Finally he gave in and just swallowed, flirting briefly with asphyxiation, before a large gulp of sake provided some measure of esophageal relief. My mom began to panic at the thought of the chef's now utterly undivided attention being focused on her own struggle with the rubbery morsel. She made many attempts to swallow it whole. Her body refused. She gagged repeatedly, but as silently and with as little drama as could be mustered. Finally, by the grace of god, she was given a moment, a window: another pair of guests entered the restaurant and the chef looked up briefly. My mom slipped the masticated chunk of cephalopod from her mouth and squirreled it away in her purse. One year later, after another dozen meals in Tokyo, countless other trips in and out of the country, at least a handful of passages through U.S. Customs, and day after day of using this self-same purse, I discovered that even abandonment in the depths of a handbag could not defeat this defiant little squiddy bite.

I would like to say that this was an isolated incident, that the stashing away in a bag of one or more mouthfuls of a given restaurant meal was an unprecedented event, but it would be not only a lie but also a claim that any chef of status would immediately contest. How else are you meant to cope with the delivery of dish after dish of unordered foods (a practice known colloquially in our house as Chef Torture)? Or often worse than profusion: the arrival of the chef's "newest experiment," always "on the house, of course." This could be something like (true story) next-to-raw squab sprinkled with popcorn and burnt—genuinely charred to smithereens—scallions in a sauce of what I'm pretty sure was just blood.

There are many tactics for dealing with the mounting sensation of imminent gout as more dishes arrive and the appetite dwindles, from the ever-popular "move things around on plate" to the more advanced "carve out hole in bread to use as hiding place" to the desperate "put in napkin, take napkin to bathroom" reserved for larger, more conspicuous items. My mom's most trusted method, however, was simply "put in purse." For someone who more or less treated her handbag like a trash receptacle to begin with, stashing the occasional menu item within it was hardly too great a conceptual leap. Very occasionally, some variety of Chef Torture was anticipated far enough in advance for her to remember to stash a plastic bag for the protection of the purse's innards. This almost never happened. Hence incidents such as "The Mystery Nugget."

Grilled Squid
with Yuzu Salt

IT MIGHT SEEM A LITTLE WRONGHEADED to suggest a squid recipe on the heels of a tale of inedible octopus, but squid really is one of life's great culinary pleasures, and something that has been on the menu at Chez Panisse for as long as I can remember. The key, of course, is sourcing very, very fresh squid—I always look for smaller ones and tend to prefer the leggy lower halves over the tubular bodies (which can get a bit tough despite careful cooking).

IN AN IDEAL WORLD, squid would always be cooked on the grill or in a wood oven. Cephalopods—octopus, squid, cuttlefish—are very high in protein and low in fat, which means that they toughen quickly when cooking, making grilling my preferred method for attaining a dish of squid that's both crisp and tender. (The other way to make squid tender is to long-cook it for a half hour or more, but the effect is that of a braise.) I do realize that grilling isn't always a readily available option, so I've included an oven variation as well.

REGARDLESS OF THE METHOD, the squid must first be cleaned (unless your fishmonger has already done so, although squid is one of those ingredients that will taste freshest if this step is undertaken right before cooking). To serve about four people, take 1 pound and trim the tentacles from the bodies, trying to cut as close to the eyes as possible. As you separate the tentacles from the body, gently squeeze them: the squid's mouth, sometimes called a

beak, should pop out. Lay the body of the squid flat, and, using the dull side of a paring knife, skim the body from tail to head, pressing out the squid's guts along with the quill, a translucent bonelike structure shaped like a feather. If the quill breaks while it's still inside the body, I find it easiest to cut the tip off the tail and push it out that way. There's no need to remove the skin, and try to avoid washing the squid—it absorbs too much water if rinsed.

TOSS THE CLEANED SQUID IN OLIVE OIL, adding a scant pinch of salt, freshly ground black pepper, and a pinch of dried chili flakes. If grilling, cook skewers of the bodies and tentacles separately. Thread each body onto the skewer across the opening, which will help it to lie flat. Skewer each tentacle through the thickest part of the ring. Grill the skewers over a hot fire, turning to crisp both sides. They'll take only a few minutes total if they're small, and just a couple more if they're more substantial. Remove from heat and sprinkle with yuzu salt and a squeeze of juice, or a flaky sea salt and a light grating of Meyer lemon zest.

IF COOKING IN AN OVEN, you'll need to preheat the oven to 475°F—nearly as hot as it can get—and place the rack as high in the oven as you can. After seasoning the squid as above, spread the squid out on a sheet pan or two—take care not to crowd the pan. Roast for 5 to 10 minutes, depending on their size. The bodies are cooked through when they are puffed and are starting to crisp.

THIS IS THE SIMPLEST WAY to have squid, but if you have access to fresh late summer shell beans (like cranberry beans or black-eyed peas still in their pods), grilled or roasted squid is a lovely complement to warm stewed beans, drizzled with loose aioli to marry the flavors. Likewise, squid is a delicious addition to a simple salad of rocket and tomatoes, and, cut into slightly smaller pieces, to a quick pasta laced with olive oil, garlic, parsley, and bread crumbs. One of my favorite pizzas at Chez Panisse is made with spicy tomato sauce, squid, tiny capers, aioli, and a dusting of fresh oregano.

CHAPTER 27

Niloufer

There are two people who have had an effect on my palate almost equal to my mother's. And though I ate at the tables of these two far less frequently than I did at Chez or at home, there was something in the alchemy of their abilities that made everything they prepared taste at once foreign and familiar, bright and different and unlike anything I'd had before. One of these cooks is David Tanis, the former long but intermittently tenured chef at Chez Panisse and author of a set of cookbooks I treat as scripture. The other is Niloufer Ichaporia King.

Niloufer is someone I find very difficult to describe. Even when I do so in the most verbose and colorful manner I can muster, I still feel I'm leaving out vast swaths of detail and biography. And the risk always is to produce a poor caricature instead. But I'll start with this: Niloufer is a cook.

Niloufer of course is not just a cook (in my opinion, the best cooks rarely are); she is equally an anthropologist and historian, a collector, a writer, a pianist, an aesthete, a parfumier, a mixologist of bath salts, a style icon, a lover of tropical birds, and many things besides. All of these strands tangibly converge in the home she has shared for upward of thirty years with her husband, David King, and their succession of red-lored Amazon parrots (named Bosco Beets, Ordle, and Five-o, respectively).

The house can only be described as a wunderkammer. Every single surface, vertical or horizontal, has been recruited as a means of display, and there is not an object within it that doesn't feel worthy of careful examination. For a time, when I was little, they also had a house in Stinson Beach, a family home on David's side that had belonged to his mother. It was situated far out on the elongated sickle of sand that extends more than a mile beyond the immediate town, on a street called Seadrift Road that faced not the open ocean but the lagoon. This house was built in the sixties by the Berkeley architect Henrik Bull and consisted of a funky cluster of three linked pentagonal structures. In my memory, however, it was just a single massive open space with a fireplace in the middle—the aesthetic inverse of the warren of book-filled rooms that makes up their San Francisco Victorian. But even that house, whose bones were vastly more Spartan, would accumulate an increasing number of beach curios with every walk along the strand.

David, a very recently retired, career-long scientist at the Howard Hughes Medical Institute at the University of California, Berkeley, is as responsible as Niloufer for the volume of treasure collected in their San Francisco residence. From his days as a shell-amassing boy scientist in the Bahamas, to a very brief hiatus from the scientific community in which he ignited a profound and lasting love for pre-Columbian and Oceanic art, he has assembled a sizable part of the panoply of artifacts, relics, and amusing cultural detritus. Above Niloufer's collection of antique coconut graters and a telephone printed with gigantic numbers for the feebly sighted (inherited from David's mother, and retained for amusement, not out of necessity) hangs a falcon-inspired fertility sculpture whose provenance dates to the era of Captain Cook's voyages to the New World. Likewise, a low table once free for the unburdening of mugs of cardamom-infused black tea, was—last I visited—the pedestal for a canoe-sized African ceremonial bowl. (Niloufer assures me that it's now found a place to the left of the fireplace.) These objects live in unlikely harmony with quirky newspaper clippings and amateur paintings of volcanoes, and other odds and ends. There is no physical catalogue of everything in the house, but I feel certain that David and Niloufer could locate anything, anywhere—a slim volume buried in a bookcase, a rare spice in a corner of a cupboard, a strand of antique jade beads, a family heirloom.

Despite the glut of interesting material to ogle in other parts of the house, Niloufer and David's dinner guests tend to immediately congregate in the small first-floor kitchen. The smells emanating from the stove as Niloufer begins to cook are too intoxicating to ignore. The perfume of chilies scalding in her cast-iron wok or herbs and coconut pestled together for green chutney mixes with that of a tuberose exhausting its tropical odor and the soft, sweet smell of the pure sandalwood oil that Niloufer sometimes dabs onto her wrists and neck. As friends gather, Niloufer (whose "snacks" are famous) might distribute freshly blistered whole wheat chapati and a plate of goat cheese heaped with slivers of ginger and turmeric doused in lime. "Just bundle it all up," she'll say in her subtly raspy, British-inflected accent, indicating that we need to take a bit of initiative at this point in the meal.

Now in her mid-seventies, Niloufer presents a slightly bowed silhouette when she's cooking—as if she's very carefully scrutinizing whatever it is that's bubbling away on her range. When she steps away from the stove, however, it's impossible not to be struck by her features: the thick curly hair, kept short; her prominent, vaguely avian nose; her warm smile. And always a gorgeous pair of earrings, an exquisite necklace of stones. Niloufer was born in Bombay in 1943 to a family of Parsis whose ancestors migrated to Southern India from Persia sometime between 700 and 900 AD. The Parsi tribe brought their native foods and flavors, and of course their recipes, on this months-long journey, and wove them together with the ingredients and conventions of their new home. The cobbling together of culinary traditions is a trademark of Parsi cooking—Niloufer calls it "magpie cuisine" for its tendency to appropriate. A number of Parsi dishes might even include European ingredients or condiments, vestiges of India's colonial heritage, which might account for Niloufer's easy adaptation to the products of the Americas. The culinary innovation that has defined her cooking since her arrival in the United States at the age of nineteen is as much a product of her extraordinary palate and intuition as it is predicated on a childhood cuisine whose recipes were both indigenous and borrowed. The latter includes delights such as Spiced Macaroni and Mayonnaise Sauce (magic), two recipes listed in the pages of *Manpasand Mishtaan*, a Parsi cookbook from 1958 that lived in her mother's collection. Another volume, *Vividh Vani*, dates back even further, to 1915, and is by Niloufer's account even more eclectic. At one point in Niloufer's childhood, a friend of her mother gave her a recipe for Italian Eggs. Niloufer describes it as "compellingly delicious but like nothing that had ever touched or left the shores of Italy."

The fusion of these disparate food traditions emerges with perhaps the greatest clarity at the spring equinox for the celebration of Navroz, or Parsi New Year, which typically falls on or around the twentieth of March. For nearly two decades now, Niloufer has come to Chez Panisse on this auspicious night to serve as head chef. As the menu takes shape, she and the cooks navigate the middle ground between the restaurant's culinary aesthetic and her repertoire of flavors and recipes, with the added responsibility of needing to create a culturally appropriate festive meal. On the night of the dinner, the front stairs and entryway of the restaurant are decorated with chalk stencils of fish; fragrant strings of marigold, tuberose, and gardenia garland the entrance and downstairs dining room. David, who contributed pen-and-ink illustrations to Niloufer's wonderful cookbook, *My Bombay Kitchen*, might embellish the cover of each menu, perhaps with the imprint of a bisected gourd rendered in a bright yellow dye of pure turmeric.

The kitchen is transformed with Niloufer at the helm: little-used spices bloom in her dishes, chilies are abundant, and the fragrance of cilantro prevails (one of the more recent Parsi New Year menus included a salad of lobster with a cilantro mousse). At the end of the meal, the deceptively simple falooda arrives—one of my favorite desserts—made of ice milk, single cream, rose syrup, and plumped holy basil seeds. This drink commemorates the moment in Parsi history when the head priest of the Zoroastrians led his people to the west coast of India to settle. There they encountered a Hindu ruler who showed the priest a vessel full of milk to indicate that his lands were already brimming to capacity. In response, the Parsi leader dropped a pinch of sugar into the milk without displacing any liquid, demonstrating that his people would only enrich the native culture without disturbing it. The version of falooda that Niloufer makes at Chez Panisse combines most of the traditional ingredients, but is sometimes enhanced with just a hint of mulberry syrup, a drop of California fruit to intensify the flavor.

Though I love these Parsi celebrations at Chez Panisse—there is something epic about the occasion, given the sheer anticipation felt by guests, many of whom book their reservations a full year in advance—I most of all love eating a casual weeknight meal at Niloufer and David's. Even though I would describe Niloufer as one of the most sophisticated cooks I've ever met, she prepares food in a disarmingly unfussy manner. She is a cook who—like my mother and some of the others who populate the pages of this book—is neither fiddly nor maddeningly precise. She uses her hands to feel out a volume, and always tastes, adjusts, and tweaks as she goes along. She's also the person from whom I first learned I could just chop up the stems of cilantro along with the leaves, that the latter needn't be preciously plucked from the stalks as one might with parsley or chervil.

Likewise, a casual hand-torn pile of Vietnamese basil leaves might be showered onto a dish only as it lands on the table, and almost without looking, an afterthought that nonetheless delivers the perfect final note of flavor. Her way of navigating ingredients makes you feel that she and the ingredients are old friends. Her trick for cooking rice, for example, relies on the measurement of her knuckles. She places her finger to the surface of the uncooked rice in a pot and pours water over it only until it comes up to the first knuckle of her pointer finger. This trick has never worked as brilliantly for me, but then again, rice and I are not old friends, and my fingers are surely inferior measuring devices.

The falooda, in both its symbolism and its flavor, are for me more broadly emblematic of Niloufer's cooking, and of my experience as one of the children who grew up, at least in part, at her table. Like that Zoroastrian priest, who did in fact defy the laws of physics to make his point, Niloufer constantly subverts expectations in her approach to cooking. How else to explain how she got a twelve-year-old to eat pig's feet? And to count those pig's feet as one of the most memorable dishes of her life? It was not just that the feet were cooked in such a way as to minimize their gelatinous texture, nor that they were served with a delicious bright salsa of diced green mango, red onion, cucumber, Mexican cucamelon, and cilantro stems. It was because I trusted that whatever actions Niloufer performed in the arc of her cooking would transform the ingredient. The names of things, freighted with associations, in her kitchen become subservient to taste, to smell—to all the senses. And this is true even if her interventions prove shockingly minimal. And yet she is also driven by I know not what inner force to try new combinations of things. It's this unflagging curiosity that makes her unique. Often I've thought of her and David both as scientists—each doing the work of experimentation, inquiry, and discovery that a life devoted to a certain passion doesn't just require, but indeed demands.

Falooda

THIS "DISH," if you can call it that (I gather, from Niloufer, that in India it's really more a street food milk shake), is one of my favorite desserts. My affection for it stems mainly from its distinct texture, which comes from the half-frozen plumped holy basil seeds—themselves a bit like tiny tapioca pearls—but I also love that you can closely control the flavor and sweetness. I prefer it with as little syrup as possible, and with homemade ice milk instead of vanilla ice cream, so that the effect is more refreshing than rich or cloying. Start by soaking 2 tablespoons of basil seeds in 3 cups of water for 1 to 3 hours, or until the hydrophilic seeds swell many times beyond their original size. Select 6 clear glasses that are more or less equal in size. When the basil seeds are plumped, divide them equally among the glasses so that the bottom is lined with a seeded layer. If the glasses are small, limit the amount of basil seeds to 2 teaspoons per glass; if taller, 1 to 2 tablespoons in the bottom of each glass will do. To create a layered effect of basil seeds, rose syrup, and then milk, you counterintuitively add milk (or half-and-half if you are feeling decadent) before adding the rose syrup. Pour in enough well-chilled milk until it comes within an inch of the top of the glass. Add about 2 teaspoons of high-quality rose syrup to each glass, the amount depending upon your preferred level of sweetness and the amount of basil seeds and milk in each glass. The rose syrup will eventually settle in a thin pink line between the basil seeds and the alabaster milk. When it does, finish the falooda with one small scoop of vanilla ice cream (or ice milk or gelato) in each glass, serve, and tell your guests, as Niloufer always does, to "Stir it first!"

Niloufer's Summer Fritters   FOR A BIRTHDAY OF MINE ONE YEAR, Niloufer made a whole array of fried delights, which tasted something like a hybrid of Indian pakoras and ethereal Japanese tempura. The batter was a mix of chickpea and rice flours, spices, sparkling mineral water, and salt. She laid a few sheets of brown kraft paper over a butcher block and started frying, using a massive cast-iron wok filled with blistering hot vegetable oil, seething with fine bubbles. She fried some of the more expected vegetables, like eggplant sliced into purple-rimmed moons and whole spring onions cut in half lengthwise, but also things I'd never tried before: tender little branches of fresh curry leaves, squash blossoms plumped with paneer cheese filling. The whole while, her movements were easy; she remained unflappable, which is not the mien of most people attempting to deep fry. I can manage it, but am plagued throughout by anxieties relating to scorching the oil or foods therein, or just generally burning down the house, or, most likely, ruining whatever I am wearing regardless of whether I have donned an apron. Everyone at the party that year gathered around the table where Niloufer had laid down the paper, as if pulled in by some gravitational field, and plucked the golden bits directly from the now oil-streaked surface, which resembled a monochromatic Pollock canvas more and more with each batch.

ESSENTIAL TO A GOOD FRY is that the objects for frying be completely dry. If any of your selections need washing, do this well in advance of cooking. Perhaps even wrap them in an absorbent dish towel so that they have a chance to amply dehydrate. Before mixing the batter, prepare your vegetables—include about 5 or 6 different choices with about 6 to 8 pieces of each vegetable. Leafy greens like spinach or amaranth or herbs like curry leaves or oregano are less commonly fried, but the interplay of crispiness and the tender leaf inside is delicious. Vegetables to consider are Japanese eggplants cut into ¼-inch thick ovals; onion rings (or trimmed scallions or spring onions); slices of potatoes or sweet potatoes; summer squash, lotus root, cauliflower, or broccoli. Size matters when frying—you want the vegetable to cook in the time it takes to get the coating perfectly browned and crisp. When slicing something like sweet potatoes, summer squash, or cauliflower, be sure each slice is no thicker than ¼ inch.

WHEN EVERYTHING IS CUT AND DRY, combine 1 cup each of rice flour and chickpea flour in a large bowl. Add ¼ teaspoon of baking soda and ½ teaspoon of salt. Stir in 1 to 2 cups of fizzy mineral water or club soda to make a batter the consistency of heavy cream (if unsure, err on the side of slightly too thick). If the batter is too viscous, however, add enough soda water to make it coat but not glob onto the vegetables. Into a wok or deep saucepan, pour a vegetable oil with a high smoking point, such as rice bran oil or peanut oil, until it reaches a depth of 3 inches. Heat until it is hot, but not smoking, usually in the range of 360 to 370°F. You can check whether the oil is hot enough by dropping in a little dollop of batter—if it floats and sizzles immediately, the oil is ready. Dip a vegetable into the batter, shake off the excess, and drop it into the hot oil. Fry in batches without crowding the pan until each vegetable is beautifully golden. I like to do as Niloufer does and lay out opened brown paper bags on a table, creating a surface for the just-fried vegetables to drain any excess oil. Serve immediately with a generous sprinkling of flaky sea salt.

Semolina Birthday Breakfast Pudding   THE DESSERT I REQUESTED from Niloufer at every birthday (even if I knew I was going to have a cake too) was essentially a gussied-up Indian-spiced Cream of Wheat–like pudding she'd make for special occasions. It was coarse semolina cooked as you would a porridge, but with slivered almonds and cardamom pods too, both of which would grow tender in the cooking. The texture was exceptionally rich and silken. Once cool, the semolina would be folded through with whipped cream, then poured into a bowl and coated with diaphanous sheets of silver leaf, pink rose petals, and another sprinkling of toasted slivered almonds. I was a lover of Cream of Wheat as a child, with its mild, soothing consistency, its rim of milk hovering around its edge like a planetary ring. It was delicious stuff and I ate it for hundreds of breakfasts. Needless to say, however, it paled in comparison to its glitzy, exotic cousin. But I never wanted Niloufer's birthday pudding more often. I loved the wait, secure in the knowledge that another birthday would indeed come, and with it, her irresistibly delicious gift.

THE SEMOLINA used in this pudding (which falls somewhere between a loose polenta and the most luxurious rice pudding) is scant, but it thickens with cooking. First melt 2 tablespoons of ghee or unsalted butter in a heavy-bottomed saucepan over medium heat. Stir in 2 tablespoons of semolina (known as rava or suji in an Indian grocery store). Whisking constantly, add 1 pint (or 2 cups) of whole milk, along with a pinch of salt, bringing the mixture to a boil. Immediately reduce the heat and continue whisking until the pudding thickens. Stir in 3 tablespoons of sugar and another pinch of salt and ½ teaspoon of crushed cardamom seeds. Continue cooking the pudding until it thickens to a consistency that you like. Taste for sweetness; I prefer mine less sweet than is traditional. To embellish this simple comforting pudding, you can add what you have on hand: a splash of rosewater and/ or vanilla extract, a handful of toasted sliced almonds, or raisins plumped in grappa or in melted butter or ghee. Grated nutmeg is warming and fragrant, as is a pinch of powdered cinnamon. You can serve it as is as a breakfast porridge, but my preference is to save it for a special occasion and make Niloufer's "birthday version" instead. For this, use an immersion blender or food processor to puree the thickened pudding with ½ cup whole almonds until it is creamy smooth and the nuts are chopped. Turn the semolina pudding into a bowl and let cool. Whip ½ cup cream until it has soft peaks and fold it into the cooled pudding. If you haven't already, stir in crushed cardamom, rosewater, or vanilla, and then pour it into a beautiful bowl. Decorate the top of the pudding lavishly with sliced almonds or chopped pistachios, or add edible gold or silver leaf as Niloufer does. Refrigerate until you're ready to serve, as far as one day ahead. Just before serving, scatter the surface with fresh edible flowers like just-picked violets or the petals of a brightly colored rose.

CHAPTER 28

Everything Tastes Better with Lime

I think my mom and I started to write a "cookbook" in 1994, or at least some time after the blockbuster film *Forrest Gump* swept the nation. Anyway, that's my best guess given that our as-of-yet-unpublished book, *Everything Tastes Better with Lime,* more or less adopts the style of Bubba Blue (one of the film's central characters) and his litany of shrimp-related preparations. In other words, our cookbook wasn't so much a *cookbook* as it was a spoken word concatenation of foods improved by the addition of lime juice. Progress on our book project has been slow—it is wholly dependent on our being stuck in standstill traffic and at a loss for higher quality entertainment—yet the work is ongoing. Let me tell you, though, that should this book ever be published, it will be a veritable tome, because one thing we coauthors did discover is that almost everything does in fact taste better with lime. Here are some (of the *exceptionally complicated*) examples:

- papaya with lime
- mango with lime and chili
- margaritas (limeade for the young lass aged eleven)
- roasted squash with lime and slivered kaffir lime leaves
- zesty lime "gelée"

- lime blossom syrup
- vanilla yogurt with lime juice
- lime-infused fruit macédoine
- lime meringue pie
- lime granita
- guacamole with *extra lime*
- flank steak marinated in lime, olive oil, cilantro, and pounded garlic
- chimichurri with lime juice and zest
- lime-zest-infused butter

Etc.

Thinking back on that mid-nineties moment, when my mother's repertoire really didn't dabble in flavors much more exotic than cumin, I think we probably also owe Niloufer some credit for the genesis of our lime-centric cookbook. It was in Niloufer's kitchen that lime reigned over lemon, and that all manner of less familiar ingredients might be expected to appear over the course of a meal. And limes were not just limes at Niloufer's. They came in all shapes and sizes and even colors, and a range of varieties (rangpur, kaffir, sweet, key, and Persian). Teeny-tiny super-juicy limes whose skin was a pale yellow and flesh a pale green were often served alongside whatever it was we were eating. Especially fish, which most cooks understand to be complemented by citrus, but also any variety of meat, be it pig's feet or chicken legs—sections of lime were an indispensable condiment.

Niloufer's Sweet Potatoes with Lime and Cilantro

THERE IS NO EASIER PREPARATION for sweet potatoes or yams, but if you've been eating them with the usual seasonings (butter, sage, etc.) this will come as a very welcome surprise. Preheat the oven to 425°F. Scrub your potatoes and trim off any gnarly bits, but leave the skin on. If your potatoes are especially large, cut them in half lengthwise first. Otherwise, proceed with slicing them into pieces about ½ inch thick. Toss these in a bit of olive oil, sprinkle with a big pinch of salt and some black pepper, and distribute evenly across a baking tray. When the oven is hot, roast the potatoes until tender (about 30 to 45 minutes depending on size). Use a wooden spoon or spatula to turn them every so often to help them brown uniformly. Remove from the oven and scatter them on a platter. Shower them with the juice of a lime and sprinkle with plucked cilantro leaves. Niloufer makes a variation of this with winter squash too, in which the squash is peeled, deseeded, and cut into half-moons, then baked with finely cut kaffir lime leaves. Right before serving, it too gets a douse of lime. Both are delicious, simple ways of taking a slightly different approach to preparing a familiar ingredient. After we first tried this method at Niloufer's house, it became a staple of ours.

I'll never forget a trip we took to Troncones in Mexico with Niloufer and David when I was about twelve. One night we went to a tiny village fairground to ride the rickety small-scale amusement park rides, whose lights streaked through the darkness like neon contrails. One of the stands at the fair was selling the thinnest potato chips I'd ever seen, fried on the spot in a vast cauldron of vegetable oil, which would hiss menacingly with the entry of each fresh batch. Niloufer bought a white paper bag brimming with golden discs for us to share. She used a pepper shaker filled with ground dried red chili to sprinkle spice over the lot and then—somehow—materialized a lime to juice over them too. The freshest, whisper-thin chips, the salt, chili, and lime—it was a perfect combination. The heat of the chilies made the edges of my lips hum, the salt and acid puckered my tongue. It became a feeling more than a taste, a reverberation through the body, amplified by the rattling and jangling of the little train cars that whipped us around in vertiginous ellipses. The taste ruined me for regular potato chips for all time. I still never feel compelled to eat them. But if you can summon the wherewithal to make homemade potato chips, be sure to have a wedge of lime and a pinch of ground chili at the ready.

Potato Chips   A LITTLE-KNOWN FACT ABOUT MY MOTHER is that she absolutely *loves* potato chips. I'm not sure when this love was ignited exactly, but I'm sure it's a vestige of childhood road trips or suburban summer barbecues. Still, while some of the nostalgic foods she loved as a kid have found updated, healthier, more upscale analogs, her beloved potato chips have never been replaced with something qualitatively "better." You'd think a beautiful plate piled high with *pommes frites* would scratch the same itch, and she does like such things, but they've never unseated the humble chip in her heart. In fact, the basic garden-variety bagged chips available at airports and gas stations and, well, virtually every grocery store on earth still prove irresistible to her (though she exercises restraint, allowing herself the indulgence only in liminal scenarios, which tend to dovetail with those that permit the consumption of hot dogs—i.e., airports or other places associated with transit). Antithetical as potato chips may seem to the whole of what Chez Panisse stands for, my mother's love of them means that they do crop up from time to time on the menu in the upstairs café—but often made with a more visually arresting variety, a Pink Fir Apple potato, say, that yields a gorgeous blushy chip.

MY VERSION isn't even the Chez Panisse approach, since I don't have a deep-fat fryer at home, and I find getting enough peanut oil (which I never keep on hand in any quantity anyway) to the right temperature to be a fiddly undertaking. Instead, I roast them. Start by preheating the oven to 400°F. Thoroughly clean, dry, and then peel a couple of medium-sized starchy potatoes like Yukon Gold or Idaho before cutting them into ⅛-inch slices on a mandoline. (It is virtually impossible to do this uniformly with a knife, but mandolines—especially the plastic versions available in Japantowns and of course online—are cheap, last forever, and are a very worthwhile investment.) Immediately toss the slices with a liberal coating of a light olive oil and season generously with fine sea salt before arranging them on a baking sheet in a single layer with plenty of room around each slice. Bake in the oven until the chips turn golden brown, about 15 minutes. Right as you remove them, season with some cayenne pepper, then transfer them to a rack to cool for a moment so that you get the best crispy texture. Before they're completely cool, douse in fresh lime juice and serve immediately.

CHAPTER 29

Thanksgiving

My mother and father met at a housewarming party at my dad's Berkeley loft in 1981. My mother was thirty-eight years old, my father twenty-six. A pair of mutual friends, the artists Patty Curtan and Stephen Thomas, had invited my mom to come along, reportedly having said to her, "We don't know if you'll be good for Stephen, but we think he might be good for you." My mom went to the party and never left, or at least not for two entire weeks—my parents were inseparable from the very instant they met. A mere eight months later, my mom was pregnant, having discovered that my father, despite his youth, was willing to give parenthood a whirl. On a mid-August day, seven and a half months into her pregnancy, I was born, weighing just over four pounds.

Just a few days beforehand, my pregnant mom had been in New York for the wedding of the restaurateur (and former Chez Panisse cook) Anne Isaak to the legendary Random House editor Joe Fox. Just over a month into her third trimester, she'd stood before a grill on a beach in Sagaponack, Long Island, turning Maine lobsters over an open fire for the celebratory dinner. New York in August is not exactly known for its temperate climate, and the heat cast off by the grills couldn't have been making the conditions any more bearable. There is no doubt in my mind, however, that my love of lobster was forged in those inhospitable conditions, for in response to the heat and perhaps also to the delectable smells wafting off the grill, I violently lurched in utero as if to say, "Let me out! I'm hungry!" Worried by this unusually gymnastic movement, my mom returned to Berkeley the next day and immediately paid a visit to her doctor. The unambiguous recommendation was that she remain on bed rest for the balance of her pregnancy. As my dad remembers it, she was devastated and cried through the whole of the night. She was concerned for my well-being, yes, but moreover was made miserable by the thought of confinement, so contrary to her nature. I was born at 4:44 a.m. the next morning.

Among the first people to drop by the hospital—after I'd been discharged from the incubator and cleared for visitations—was a baby not ten days my senior, the son of my mom's best friend, Sharon Jones. Nicolas Monday, or Nico, had been rather less keen to enter the world; he arrived two weeks late, at a healthy nine pounds. Despite our discrepancy in size and general well-being (I had colic, jaundice, and rosacea; he, a proclivity for unbroken slumber), we did, naturally, become something approximating brother and sister. My mother was his godmother, Sharon was like a second mother, and we grew up in houses just a few blocks apart. Even before jointly entering the gentle crèche of Duck's Nest Preschool, Nico and I were thrown together with a third child named Joel in a makeshift day care presided over by the angelic and exceptionally long-tressed Trudy. Trudy was the girlfriend of my mother's former gardener, Marc Mathieu, who himself at times doubled as a babysitter and was responsible for my first longer word being *lawn mower* and for my early introduction to *Star Trek*.

I remember Nico being present at most of the important moments in my life, and I at his, from the celebration of our joint August birthdays to the annual excitement of watching Fourth of July fireworks down at the Berkeley Marina to graduations and marriages and the

now-regular reunions at Thanksgiving. We haven't lived in the same country for the better part of the last decade, and before that, we'd carved out pretty separate lives on opposite coasts. Still, as children and later as teenagers, we'd often find ourselves at the same largely adult-saturated events and would invariably slink off together—sometimes in the company of a bottle of purloined wine, sometimes just to talk. Of all of the many moments of confidence fostered between us—in times more or less emotionally clement—there is still one image in particular that stands out to me.

While we were between the ages of four and sixteen, give or take, our families would head up to the Sacramento–San Joaquin River Delta together to visit Rainer "Bumps" Baldauf and his wife, Bea, at a poplar-shaded marina called Grindstone Joe's. They had a big beautiful sailboat that they'd dock there, and we were invited up most summers to take advantage of the stark inland heat, multitude of water sports, and—most important, as far as my mom was concerned—expansive outdoor kitchen. Bumps was a charismatic Teutonic figure who had managed the popular San Francisco spot Trader Vic's in the 1960s and installed the first pizza oven at Chez Panisse in the 1980s, after transitioning into restaurant kitchen design. I knew him, however, as a great master of the art of water-skiing and the genius behind a Dutch-oven-baked loaf of bread he'd produce whenever we visited. His wife, Bea, was his counterpoint. She was possessed of a strong but pacific character that made her seem transplanted from another era, an impression enhanced by the tidy cotton bandanna she always wore tucked over her hair. The two of them radiated a kind of old-fashioned good nature that is today in short supply. On these long day trips up to the delta (we'd arrive in the morning and leave late at night), an intensive period of aquatic sport was followed by many hours of cooking in the communal outdoor kitchen, multiple episodes of swimming, and maybe some feeding of the local school of bloated, lugubrious carp.

Late in the afternoon, as the sun was beginning its mellow descent, the kids would head out to wander along the edges of the labyrinthine waterways, tracing smaller rills to their points of evaporation. On the bank most immediately across from the kitchen and outdoor dining commons—though an indirect, lengthy walk by land—lived a triad of resplendent mature fig trees, as big as buildings. Nico and I would head over there, the two of us, leaving behind his little brother Oliver, or sometimes letting him tag along, and climb into the branches of the trees. Ostensibly, we were there to collect ripe fruit for dessert, but we'd dally in our perches, each tree a kind of cathedral, its architecture no less impressive. Of course the smell too was intoxicating, as we sat in the trees surrounded by fruit at all stages of ripeness. There was the tang of the green sap, a thin and irritating milky lacquer on our arms and shins, the sharp odor of the fallen, overripe fruit fermenting in the dry grass beneath us, and then the leaves warming in the delta sun, a shield of foliage whose scent was tropical, reminiscent of toasted coconut. It was in these arboreal confessionals that we discussed some of our most acute troubles, and in which Nico allowed himself—even as adolescence encroached—to drop his guard from time to time. We'd sometimes come back hours later, smelling of grass and itching with sap, but carrying perfect specimens of green Adriatic and black Mission figs in our T-shirt hammocks. Warmed so thoroughly by the sun, the figs had practically been turned to jam, their sanguine interiors as exquisite as jewels. If we'd taken long enough with our excursion, dinner would be ready and Bumps would just be pulling his famous loaf of bread out of the coals. He'd have made his rosemary-flecked dough and let it rise while we were out on a ramble, and, at the beginning of dinner preparations, when the coals in the barbecue pit had grown amenable, would have placed his bread in a preheated cast-iron Dutch oven coated in cornmeal and nestled it back into the embers.

THIS IS BUMPS'S RECIPE almost exactly as it was published in the softcover spiral-bound booklet *Grindstone Joe's Cookbook,* put together by all the members of the marina association probably close to twenty years ago, and shared with me by his son, Hans. Bumps's introduction to "Iron Pot Baking" is priceless:

There must be a million different sizes and shapes to these fantastic cooking devices—some are oval, some are round, some domed, some flat topped; legs—no legs! All bake well. We prefer an indented top, 6-quart round pot with legs. Legs are important—aren't they always? Well, these are important because they keep the pot off the hot barbecue hearth. If a pot has no legs—3 small (1½-inch) stones under the pot will do. Be sure pot is clean and "seasoned" with safflower oil. Be sure the lid fits tightly.

THE SPONGE:
3 cups lukewarm water
1 tablespoon honey
1 package dry yeast (granulated)
3 cups organic unbleached bread flour
Oil (for pot)

THE DOUGH:
2½ teaspoons salt
½ cup olive oil
2 tablespoons finely chopped fresh rosemary leaves
3 cups organic unbleached bread flour
½ to ¾ cup polenta or cornmeal

THE SPONGE: In a mixing bowl pour in lukewarm water; add honey. Pour in yeast. Stir with a wooden spoon until yeast is dissolved and a foam starts to come to the surface. Add flour, cup by cup, working out the lumps. When the milky batter is smooth, cover the bowl with a cloth and set in a draft-free space. Let rise 45 minutes "quietly."

MAKING THE BREAD DOUGH: After the sponge has risen and fermented, it is ready to be made into dough. To the sponge, add salt, oil, and chopped rosemary leaves. Stir thoroughly. Slowly add the flour, cup by cup, stirring with a wooden spoon. Soon the dough will stick to the spoon. Remove the spoon and start kneading with the right hand and adding flour with the left hand. When the dough starts to work well in the hand it is ready for the "first rising." Place the dough on a table or platter that has been "floured"—clean the bowl—add a touch of oil to the bowl and coat the inside. Place the dough in the bowl. Pat the top and sides with oil and cover with a cloth. Place the bowl and dough in a draft-free place; let rise 1 hour.

PREPARE THE IRON "DUTCH OVEN" POT for baking by coating the inside (of the pot and lid) with oil, wiping excess oil out with a towel. Pour polenta (or cornmeal) into the pot—coat the inside completely. When the dough has risen, "punch" it down and knead it for 10 minutes. Fold it upon itself into a round loaf. Place into the polenta-coated pot. Pat oil onto the dough and let rise for 1 hour. As soon as you have placed the dough in a draft-free space and covered it again, prepare the charcoal fire.

PLACE 1 BAG OF CHARCOAL IN THE PIT—ignited and timed, 45 minutes to 1 hour is required to get good coals—the same amount of time it takes for the last rising. When the coals are ready, take the iron pot up to the barbecue, but do it gently; set it near the barbecue. Arrange the coals in a circle just two inches larger than the pot, with no coals under the pot. Place the pot into the "ring," making sure no coals directly touch it. Place the lid securely on the pot and, using tongs, place 6 charcoal embers on top of the lid. Let bake 1 hour. Lift the lid to check for brownness and give it a little tap. If done, remove from the fire. Remove the bread and let cool before cutting into slices.

Nico now lives in Gloucester, Massachusetts, with his wife, Amelia, their four-year-old, Charlie, and their infant son, Henry. Amelia grew up in nearby Annisquam, and so, when an old diner came up for rental on a pier on Lobster Cove, the two of them decided to experiment with running a seasonal restaurant there. In 2010, The Market Restaurant was born. I suppose between the two of us (Nico and me, that is), at least one was going to have to pick up the "family trade." Though it didn't exactly seem obvious when we were teenagers, it was Nico who went on to train as a cook, first in France, then in Italy, and eventually at Chez Panisse. And it was Nico who has the right kind of temperament and set of instincts for the craft—his physical, frill-free approach has made him a confident, gifted chef. Before heading permanently to Massachusetts, where he and Amelia also run a second year-round, wood-fired pizza joint called Short & Main, he spent years on the line both in the upstairs and downstairs kitchens of Chez. It was, in fact, at the restaurant that Nico met Amelia, who started out as garde-manger before joining the line upstairs. They cooked there together for six years before picking up and moving east. Nico is gutsy and instinctual, a generous, warm, almost fatherly figure in the kitchen. Amelia too is a fabulous cook, and has a palate so close to mine I almost worry there's a kind of narcissism in loving her food. She and I even briefly joked, in our twenties, about starting a cooking show together. But it's really all about the two of them—they're a perfect team.

There are few people I like to cook with more than Nico and Amelia. It's such a pleasure, now that I'm back in California, to reunite in Berkeley for the Thanksgiving holiday. Thanksgiving has always been my mother's holiday, the one meal a year for which she managed to ditch some of her anxieties over excessive provisioning. She's someone who, left to her own devices, would keep an exceptionally Spartan fridge. A necessary sidebar here to say that I find this, generally, to be sort of remarkable, given that my reflexes are so completely opposite. Where she shops in a quotidian Continental capacity—picking up only what she needs for a given meal, and rarely for more, per person, than what she can imagine eating herself—I tend to buy enough food for each guest to eat at least seconds. She's also famous around the restaurant for ordering a "child's portion" of whatever main course she's selected, or a "child's menu" if she's eating downstairs. She absolutely loves food, of course, but never eats that much of it. Whether this is a result of Martine's rubbing off on her (my mom always marveled at how Martine could stretch a single chicken to feed eight) or simply the remnants of a cook's rigorous approach to portioning and food waste avoidance, or whether she just really does have a modest appetite, it's hard to say. But it did tax the family dynamic when I was a teenage athlete, in some seasons playing nearly twenty-four hours of soccer a week. I was so ravenous, even after our dinners together, which were delicious but characteristically abstemious, that I'd sometimes make pasta with olive oil for myself or have a bowl of cereal after she'd gone to bed. Anyway, on Thanksgiving she relaxes this particular set of quantity-related anxieties and we really do make nothing short of a feast.

Over the years, and without anything by way of a formal passing of the torch, Nico has assumed the onus of preparing the meal, though the venue has remained the same. (I don't know of another house in Berkeley, besides my mom's, that has an indoor hearth equipped with a rotisserie big enough for a Thanksgiving bird.) It's been funny to watch my mom sit back more and more as we take over the kitchen. She lets Nico minister to the proceedings, especially if that means his bringing an extra goose and making foie gras gooseneck sausage or some other considerably more daring preparation. She always has a few pots of homemade chicken or duck stock waiting—knowing we'll need it for various recipes—but largely busies herself with the table, laying down the festive linens and etched wineglasses and dispersing the brass candlesticks along the table, installing an arrangement of autumnal branches cut from the back garden. In the context of working alongside Nico and Amelia, I also take a bit of a back seat, happily chiming in when necessary, but performing the actions of a sous-chef. They're the professionals, after all—I'm just a lover of good food.

During the time that I lived in England, I was more often than not unable to return to California for Thanksgiving. When I was still in graduate school and trying to adhere to something resembling an academic schedule, and especially once I began teaching, leaving for a completely unrecognized holiday over a long weekend in November was folly. Still, for a family of atheists, this culinary tradition was tantamount to a high holiday. Even if I lived abroad, I could not just *not* worship. Though I did celebrate Thanksgiving in my first year at Cambridge, it was only after I moved to London the following year and met a former Chez Panisse pastry cook, Claire Ptak, that things really began to amplify in intensity and devotion.

Claire had moved to London a few years beforehand and immediately set up a bakery called Violet, whose American-style baked goods she sold at the popular Broadway Market in Hackney, and eventually at a shop and café right across London Fields. Her cakes have such a cult following now that she was recently selected to be the official baker of the wedding cake for Prince Harry and Meghan Markle's royal nuptials. Anyway, we became friends not during her time at Chez, but rather in Vienna in 2006, on the occasion of a series of dinners my mother had been commissioned by the opera director Peter Sellars to produce there. From time to time, whenever my mom is asked to play a culinary role in some type of cultural event held outside the United States (a festival to commemorate the 250th anniversary of Mozart's birth, say, helmed by Peter), she'll call on a trusted team of expatriated former Chez chefs. These cooks form a kind of international "special forces" unit (or Foreign Legion?). Over the years, its ranks have counted, among others, David Lindsay, David Tanis, Sally Clarke, Seen Lippert, David Lebovitz, and of course Claire.

Claire and I took it upon ourselves to make a "proper Thanksgiving dinner" in London. She, naturally, would be in charge of all things sweet; I, for the most part, would oversee savory. We quickly learned that England is not set up to accommodate this American festive occasion, which comes a month before most families expect to provision with a turkey for Christmas. We had to call poultry farms directly and beg them to fatten at least one bird just a touch more expediently, make pleas to specialty butchers around town, try to bribe chefs. We had to scour London for things like fresh cranberries, super-ripe persimmons, and American-style baking pumpkins. We invited any Americans we knew, but always had a disproportionate number of baffled Brits present, who, though accustomed to large feasts at Christmas, had never experienced anything on the scale of Thanksgiving. ("Oh my! But there are so *many* different dishes! Marshmallows?! *With* sweet potatoes?!") This part of the dinner population was also inordinately aggrieved by our "sing for your supper" tradition, in which—being native Californians—Claire and I would insist that each person at the table tap into their inner gratitude practice and say aloud one thing they were especially thankful for.

Over the years that Claire and I "produced" Thanksgiving in England—for it truly is a production—dinners were held in a diverse array of settings, including two different flats in London, a funky shared house in Cambridge, and a couple of different rental cottages in Cornwall, but always with a healthy group of adherents, friends who'd come to recognize the superiority of the holiday. What remained constant, aside from Claire's assiduous menu-planning and ingredient lists (god bless that Chez Panisse training), was our dedication to brining the turkey after my mother's trusted method. Because refrigerators, and in general any appliances requiring electricity, are often comically small in Europe, there was no way to get an immense turkey, inside an even more immense liquid-filled bucket, into the fridge. Most years it was cold enough to leave the turkey outside for a few days in its seasoned bath. To accomplish this, a new plastic trash can would be purchased from a local hardware store to serve as a brining receptacle. (My mom would have died.) One year, however—the year we were in Cambridge—the weather was unseasonably mild—not exactly hot, but definitely not *cold*. Claire and I considered alternatives, but the turkey had already been purchased and no one we knew, short of professional chefs back in London, was in possession of an adequately commodious refrigerator. So we added a bit of extra salt to the brine recipe, swore we'd cook the hell out of the turkey, crossed our fingers, and left it outside. Come Thanksgiving morning, I went to retrieve the bird, only to discover that in the non-frigid temperatures it had discharged some variety of gelatinous substance, transforming the liquid into an exceptionally viscous alien goo. I did what every great chef would do: I took that bird out, rinsed it right off, and popped it in the oven, then lugged that goo-filled trash can down the street to pour its contents down a municipal drain. The turkey was delicious, and—gratefully—no one fell ill.

Despite the changing venues, the struggles to find suitable ingredients in England, the rotating cast of characters, and the physical absence, for several years, of any of my blood relatives, Thanksgiving has nonetheless always managed to feel like Thanksgiving. There is a quality of "homecoming" that transcends location, and not just because I reach deep into the repertoire of my mother's recipes to animate her table through mine, but also because she is somehow present even when she's not. It's her voice I hear insisting I consider everything about the experience of arriving at the table—not just the food, then, but the lighting and the smell of the room, the flowers, of course, but also the napkins, the cutlery, and *definitely* the wine. Recently, I was speaking with Claire about her experience of working at Chez Panisse, and we ended up instead talking about how the time she spent there (which amounts to just a third of the time she's spent so far in London) changed so many aspects of her life. You can pick out another Chez Panisse alum, she said, because they are imprinted with the same set of values. They will be infinitely more likely to organize a meal around priorities like beauty and purity and taste, things that often get sidelined in favor of ingenuity and flourish. It is a cliché to say it, but Chez Panisse is really not so much a job as a way of living.

I am often reminded of a story my mom has told many times before, a story she relays to illustrate her own naiveté but also to highlight her commitment to a certain kind of obsessive impulse. It involves an episode, in the late 1970s, in which she was invited to cook among a number of famous international *male* chefs at a dinner hosted by Playboy at New York's Tavern on the Green. Instead of executing an elaborate preparation, she brought dozens of flats of perfect organic lettuce plants *still in their soil* to the catering kitchens so that she could pick the leaves freshly just before serving them in a French-style *salade mesclun*. At a time when iceberg was still the dominant lettuce in most supermarkets and homes, and upscale chefs would never deign to prepare something as simple and lowly as salad, this was her contribution. And of course no one remembers anything else about the meal, because the salad was so radical in its simplicity . . . but also so delicious.

Anyway, when it comes to Thanksgiving, it's a matter of finding balance. Even though the Thanksgiving feast is a meal *filled* with flourish and excess, it is nonetheless often defined by the simplest dishes. And if you're looking to make a dinner that in any way resembles my mother's, insist on serving a salad at the end—an uncomplicated one, just winter greens like chicories, endives, and frisée with a handful of parsley leaves—even if everyone around the table groans and protests and claims they can't eat another bite. Remind them, as she does, that there's no better digestif, and pass a big bowl of it around regardless. Not only is it always a bright and refreshing way to finish the savory courses, but, as you survey the room, you'll see a look of pleasure and relief on the faces of your guests. If there's one lesson I've learned from my mother, it's that salad is *never* unwelcome.

My Mom's
Brined Turkey

UNLESS YOU LIVE IN A POLAR CLIMATE, do not use the preceding method of outdoor natural refrigeration. Still, I do recommend this brine, despite the fact that liquid brines have become increasingly contentious in recent years. The jury's out on whether it's better to dry-rub a bird, steep it in liquid brine, or, as Claire and I attempted one year, inject brine directly into the turkey using a giant hypodermic syringe. That said, I have—syringe experiment excepted—only ever made a turkey using this method and it has always yielded beautiful results. The best-tasting bird will also be the one that's been raised on the cleanest organic feed and in humane free-range circumstances. Thanksgiving is a time, if ever there was one, to be especially intentional about sourcing a sustainably reared, heritage breed animal.

START BY BRINGING A GALLON OF WATER to a boil in a large nonreactive pot that will hold your turkey and, critically, fit comfortably in your refrigerator. Stir in 1½ cups sugar and 1 cup kosher salt until completely dissolved. Turn off the heat and add your chopped vegetables: 3 carrots, 2 big onions, 3 leeks, 2 stalks of celery, and your aromatics: 4 bay leaves, a small handful of black peppercorns, a small handful of coriander seeds, 4 star anise, several sprigs of thyme and sage, and a big pinch each of crushed red pepper flakes and fennel seeds. Add another 2 gallons of water. When the liquid has cooled completely, place your turkey in the brine. Weight it with a plate or a pan, if necessary, to prevent it from bobbing up to the surface. Refrigerate for 72 hours.

PREHEAT THE OVEN TO 425°F. Remove the turkey from the brine and let stand at room temperature for 30 minutes (discard the brine). Use paper towels to pat off any moisture and fill the internal cavity with Bread and Wild Mushroom Stuffing (page 275). Tuck the wing tips under the turkey and tie the legs together with butcher's string. Place the turkey on a roasting rack set in a large roasting pan and roast until the skin starts to brown, about 40 minutes. Use a long rosemary sprig or pastry brush to baste the turkey with melted butter. Reduce the oven temperature to 350°F and continue to roast the bird, periodically basting it with more butter (and any juices being cast off into the pan), about every 30 minutes, until a thermometer inserted into the lower part of the thigh flesh registers 165°F. Keep the turkey roasting in the oven for another 1 to 1½ hours, depending on its size. If the skin begins to darken too much or starts to burn, cover it loosely with aluminum foil. When the turkey is ready, transfer it to a large, clean cutting board and allow it to rest, loosely covered with foil, for 20 minutes. Remove the string, spoon the stuffing onto its own dish, and carve the bird with a sharp knife. If, like me, you are not amazingly skilled at this task, have a friend hold up a YouTube video of someone carving a turkey, or call your mother and get her to verbally walk you through the steps.

Bread and Wild Mushroom Stuffing THIS RECIPE STARTED as my mom's bread and mushroom stuffing, but has really become something altogether more my own. My mom's preparation is a touch more minimalistic; I favor a maximalist version—it's for a feast, after all, and in general I bend toward a "more is more" approach to flavor and seasoning. Start with a couple of loaves of day-old rustic bread and carefully cut off the crusts with a serrated knife. Preheat the oven to 350°F, tear the bread into roughly 2-inch square pieces, and spread it out on baking sheets. (When you buy the bread, consider that you'll you need about a cup of bread per guest.) Place the pans in the oven and allow the bread to dehydrate until very lightly toasted. Set aside to cool.

CLEAN AND TRIM a diverse selection of fungi. For this recipe I prefer a mix of yellow and black chanterelles; porcini, hedgehog, and lobster mushrooms; and morels (though you can use just one type, or whatever you can find that looks good). Cut the mushrooms into smaller uniform pieces and set aside. Prepare your chestnuts: turn the oven up to 400°F. Using a sharp knife, cut an X-shape into the flat side of each chestnut, and place them X side up on a baking sheet. Sprinkle a little water over the chestnuts to help them steam, and roast for 15 to 20 minutes, stirring occasionally, until they're tender and the skins yield easily. Remove them to a clean towel and gently crush them, leaving them swaddled in the towel for another five minutes to steam. Peel the nuts while they are still warm, break them up into chunky pieces, and set them aside in a bowl. I have made chestnuts this way for this recipe, but I have also bought high quality vacuum-packed or jarred chestnuts to save time and effort. There's really very little difference in taste, so it's up to you whether you'd like to engage in this slightly more hands-on process.

MAKE A MIREPOIX: Dice a few stalks of celery (with leaves removed), a few peeled carrots (different colors are nice, if you can find them), and a large yellow onion and place in a pan with a sprig of thyme, a bay leaf, and a glug of good extra virgin olive oil. Sauté over medium-low heat until the vegetables have softened, then add a bit more olive oil and 4 or 5 minced cloves of garlic. A minute later, add your mushrooms. Sauté until everything is fragrant and beginning to soften. When the mushrooms are cooked, season with a bit of sea salt, stir to incorporate, and set aside to cool.

IN A LARGE BOWL, add your torn bread; your mushroom-mirepoix mix; 1 cup of dried currants; the prepared chestnuts; 1 cup of roughly chopped, toasted pecans; a bunch of scallions or green onions, green parts and all, slivered diagonally on the bias; and a big handful of roughly chopped Italian parsley. Stir. Start by adding ½ cup of heavy cream, ½ cup of homemade chicken stock (page 57) or vegetable stock, and a splash of good-quality Armagnac, Cognac, or Calvados. Sprinkle with a hefty pinch of fine sea salt and some ground black pepper, and use your hands to toss everything together. Hands are really the best implement here, because they allow you to monitor the amount of moisture in the mixture. You want it to be moist but not at all soggy, so, while you'll no doubt need to add a bit more stock and cream (though more stock than cream), do it slowly, continuing to toss the ingredients, taste, and adjust the liquids and salt. It should be tasty at this stage, because all it's doing is going in the oven to warm up and marry— most of the cooking has already happened. Loosely pack the stuffing into a gratin dish or two, depending on quantity, reserving a couple handfuls to fill the cavity of your bird. Then cover tightly with aluminum foil and bake in a 375°F oven for 30 minutes. Remove the foil and return to the oven for an additional 10–15 minutes, until the top is lightly browned.

Roasted Cranberry Sauce THIS HAS GOT TO BE one of the easiest ways to make cranberry sauce, but it's also my favorite. I think roasting the berries does something to intensify the flavor that a stove-top preparation doesn't. Start by placing one of the racks in the upper third of the oven, so that it's closer to the element at the top. Preheat the oven to 350°F. In a large bowl, toss 6 to 8 cups of fresh cranberries with 1½ cups packed light brown sugar, the finely grated zest of a lemon and an orange, ½ cup fresh orange juice, a couple of whole cloves, 2 sticks of cinnamon, a couple of cardamom pods, and a pinch of sea salt. Spread out the berries in a large glass or ceramic baking dish and roast, stirring occasionally, until the cranberries have softened and the juices they're casting off are starting to thicken, about 45 minutes. If it seems a bit loose, don't fret— cranberries are rich in pectin, so as the sauce cools, it will firm up even more. Give it a taste and adjust with a little more sugar or acid if necessary.

Brussels Sprouts with Salsa Verde I LOVE BRUSSELS SPROUTS, so I'm not someone who needs to have them particularly disguised to eat and enjoy them, but this is one of my favorite ways of preparing them, not least of all because there's a nice kick of spice and herbs that comes through from the addition of salsa verde. This is not your typical Thanksgiving vegetable side dish, but it's sure to win over even the most hardened Brussels sprouts haters. Start by peeling back and trimming your sprouts; then halve them lengthwise through the stem and set aside. Bring a pot of water to a boil, salt it generously, and blanch your sprouts for a couple minutes to parboil. Strain the spouts and lay them out in a single layer on a large dry cloth. Allow them to cool and dry completely.

Shortly before you're ready to sit down for dinner, heat one or two large cast-iron pans and glaze with a thin film of olive oil. When the pan is very hot, lay the halved sprouts facedown in the pan. You want them to get a lot of color, even blacken—flip them to brown the backs. Do this in stages if your pans can't very comfortably accommodate the total number of sprouts. Transfer the blackened sprouts to a large bowl and toss with several tablespoons of Salsa Verde (page 211). Taste and adjust seasoning: they might want a bit more salt or lemon juice.

Winter Squash Gratin

I MAKE SOME VERSION OF THIS GRATIN every year. A beautiful dish to serve directly from the pan at the table, it's very simple to make. Use a large cast-iron pan if you have one (though a casserole dish works just as well). Many types of squash are good for this recipe, but you want one that's big enough so that when you slice it, it'll yield sizable pieces to nicely layer in the pan. My favorite is a variety I got to know well in England called Crown Prince, a big round squash with burnished, ghostly gray-blue skin and bright orange flesh and loads of flavor. It's also nice to see the variegation of color in the pan; the green of the skin and orange flesh make a beautiful combination. Still, a large butternut squash is also a good option and easy to find in most grocery stores (resist smaller varieties like kuri or delicata; they'll be a pain to cut up and arrange). One of the revelations of more recent years is that you can just leave the skin on with most squash varieties when you roast them. I wouldn't do this if I was cubing it, but if you're thinly slicing the squash, there's little enough skin on each piece that it becomes more of a pleasing texture than an impenetrable rind. That said, if—once you bisect your squash—you notice the skin is particularly thick, use a peeler to remove it. There's no need to be insanely thorough about the process; just take off the toughest outer layer.

PREHEAT THE OVEN TO 400°F. Start by chopping a large onion into a medium dice. Add this to a heavy-bottomed pan, add a big glug of olive oil, and cook on medium-low heat, stirring frequently, until softened and caramelized. Turn off the heat and allow the onion to come to room temperature. Meanwhile, peel and sliver the cloves of half a head of garlic and set aside. Halve your squash, use a spoon to scrape any seeds and fibrous innards from the cavity, and, placing the squash cut face down, use a large sharp knife to slice ⅛-inch-thick vaguely crescent-moon-shaped pieces. Cut as uniformly as you can, as this will help the gratin cook evenly. You can use a mandoline instead if you have one on hand and it fits your squash easily. If using a round cast-iron pan, arrange your squash slices overlapping radially, as if making a rosette. If using a square or rectangular dish, lay them out, slightly overlapping, like the scales of a fish. Oil your pan lightly and lay down a bottom layer of squash. Spread a bit of your caramelized onion around over the top, a scattering of garlic slivers, a few knobs of butter, a dusting of fresh

thyme leaves, a healthy grating of Parmesan cheese, a drizzle of heavy cream, and ample salt and black pepper between (you'll repeat this with each layer, as if making a lasagna). When the layers reach the top of the pan, pour about 1 cup of chicken stock and another glug of cream over the whole thing—this will keep it hydrated while baking. Sprinkle some more Parmesan over the top, as well as a few thyme leaves and some black pepper and salt. Place in the middle of the oven to cook for about 45 minutes to an hour, or until a small paring knife easily pierces through to the bottom of the pan. If at any point the top is looking too brown, cover loosely with a sheet of parchment paper or tin foil. When done, allow to rest for 10 minutes before cutting it into portions.

Persimmon Pudding

THIS IS A DISH that Chez Panisse makes in the autumn when persimmons first begin to arrive from the farms, but the version I like to make is adapted from a recipe our friend Sue Moore always prepares a little later in the season for our annual Christmas Eve Seven Fish Dinner. One of the beautiful things about this recipe is how unbelievably forgiving it is. And I don't say this lightly. I'm a terrible baker and even the cake genius, Claire Ptak, trusts me to execute this without failure.

SET THE OVEN TO 375°F. Butter an oval gratin dish of about 14 inches lengthwise (although any shape of pan or even cake tin of roughly these dimensions will work). Sift together in a medium bowl 1½ cups of flour, 1 teaspoon of baking soda, 1 teaspoon of baking powder, 1 teaspoon of ground cinnamon, and a big pinch of each of the following: fine sea salt, ground clove, ground allspice, ground ginger, ground black pepper, and grated nutmeg. Stir the dry ingredients to incorporate. Scoop out the flesh of three large, *very ripe*, almost translucent Hachiya variety persimmons. (Sometimes you need to buy them a week or two in advance if they're on the less ripe side so that they're ready for this recipe.) Place the flesh into a blender and process until smooth. In another bowl, beat 3 eggs together with 1 cup of light brown sugar (darker sugar or white sugar work fine too) until fluffy. Stir in 8 tablespoons (1 stick) of melted butter, 1 teaspoon of vanilla extract, and a couple of tablespoons of freshly grated ginger (I like mine on the fiery side, so you can reduce this measurement according to your preferences). Stir the dry ingredients into the butter-egg mixture. Then slowly pour in two cups of half-and-half. Follow with the persimmon purée and stir until just integrated. Fill your pan up to the three-fourths mark (it will rise, significantly). If you have more batter, do not overfill; just grease and use another smaller pan too. Bake for 45 minutes to an hour, until the top is set but still glossy in the center. Remove from the oven and allow it to cool before serving. It will be very moist, and though you'll be able to cut it easily like a cake because of the high pectin content of the persimmons, it will have a texture more like a steamed pudding. Serve with vanilla-scented, Calvados-spiked whipped cream.

Claire's Quince Meringue Ice Cream

THIS ICE CREAM is something that Claire Ptak made one Thanksgiving sort of on a whim, and it's since become a Thanksgiving fixture (at least whenever I'm cooking with Claire). I can't remember the exact circumstances, but the ice cream was born of at least one or two of the ingredients being left over from something else she'd been baking earlier—some quince purée? some Greek yogurt? a bowl of egg whites? Anyway, it was one of the few times that my back-seat driving resulted in the improvement—rather than the ruination—of a new dessert creation (my tendency to play it fast and loose with quantities and ingredients is not an asset in baking). This ice cream, which folds a soft meringue into the quince purée, is one of the best ice creams I've ever tasted. I'll never forget the look on our faces as we spooned the freshly frozen custard into our mouths, standing in Claire's London kitchen while our guests polished off the last of the Thanksgiving meal. We knew this stuff was sensational—we were giddy.

CLAIRE, LIKE MY MOTHER, keeps a big bowl of quince in her house throughout the autumn. They exhaust a beautiful, enveloping perfume and look humbly beautiful with all their fuzzy, irregular protuberances. Claire recommends poaching a large batch at the beginning of the season to use in a variety of recipes, as they keep in their syrup in the fridge. To poach the fruit, quarter, peel, and core about 2 pounds of quince (4 medium-sized fruits) and slice the quarters into ¼-inch-thick wedges. Combine 2 cups of sugar and 6 cups of water in a 4-quart pot, bring to a boil, and simmer slowly until the sugar is completely dissolved. Split a vanilla bean and scrape the seeds into the sugar syrup. To the syrup, add the bean pod, a sliced half of a lemon, a stick of cinnamon, 1 teaspoon of fennel seeds, and the quince. Keep the fruit submerged as it cooks by covering the surface with a round of parchment paper weighted with a plate or a smaller pan. Simmer slowly until the quince is tender, about 45 minutes. In a tightly sealed container, it will keep, refrigerated, for 2 weeks or more. Claire's ice cream is, so far, the best thing I've ever tasted that uses quince. This is her recipe.

MAKES ABOUT 1 PINT OF ICE CREAM

5 ounces poached quince

3 tablespoons quince poaching liquid

2 large egg whites

½ cup superfine sugar

1 teaspoon golden syrup (recipe follows)

Pinch salt

¾ cup heavy cream, cold

1 heaped tablespoon plain yogurt

USING A STICK BLENDER or food processor, blitz the poached quince with half of the poaching liquid until smooth. Add the remaining liquid and blitz once more. Set aside.

PLACE THE EGG WHITES, sugar, golden syrup, and salt in a heatproof bowl. Balance the bowl over a small pot of boiling water, whisking continuously until the sugar has dissolved and the mixture starts to become frothy and opaque. If you have a candy thermometer, use it, bringing the mixture up to 167°F. Remove from the heat and use an electric mixer with a whisk attachment to make stiff peaks of meringue.

IN A LARGE, CLEAN BOWL, whip the cold heavy cream and yogurt to very soft peaks. Fold in the meringue just to combine. Then fold in the quince purée.

A note from Claire: "Decide if the ice cream mixture tastes balanced. Remember that it is going to be frozen and freezing dulls flavor. Therefore it should taste a little sweeter than you want the finished ice cream to taste. If not sweet enough, start with adding ½ teaspoon sugar, stir, and taste again. If too sweet, add 1 teaspoon of heavy cream. Is there enough acid? Because quince is not acidic, it may want a squeeze of lemon juice to cut the warm sweet flavors. Lastly check for the salt. There is a pinch of salt in the meringue, but another pinch might just make the flavor of the quince pop and come to life. Remember, these are tiny adjustments that can make a big difference. Go slowly and add only a little at a time because you can't take it back out. Pour the mixture into your ice-cream maker and follow its instructions. I tend to under-churn a little so as not to make the ice cream too icy."

Golden Syrup GOLDEN SYRUP is just a caramel-colored viscous syrup made from cane sugar, but it's not readily available in the United States, where corn syrup is king. In Britain, Tate & Lyle's Golden Syrup is ubiquitous; in the States you'll have to buy it online, or at a grocer with a diverse range of imported goods. It is, however, pretty simple to make, and requires very few ingredients. The recipe below will yield 16 ounces of syrup, which can be stored in a sterilized jar in a cool, dry place.

START BY POURING 3 tablespoons water and ½ cup sugar into a heavy-bottomed saucepan. Swirl the saucepan a couple times to combine the water and sugar. Heat to a simmer over medium-low heat. Watch it carefully as it simmers as the change in color will occur rather suddenly after about 10 or 15 minutes. When it has turned a nice caramel color, slowly add 1¼ cups of boiling water (do this with caution as the liquid will splutter and steam). Add another 2½ cups of sugar and bring it back to a simmer—the sugar will dissolve as it cooks. Add a slice of lemon to prevent the syrup from crystallizing, then turn the heat down and allow it to simmer for about 45 minutes. Remove the lemon slice and allow to cool completely before using.

CHAPTER 30

David

I have eaten food prepared by David Tanis on more occasions than I can count, and yet there are a handful of memories that linger most in my mind, or perhaps, more to the point, on my palate. But before I can speak to some of those flavors (namely lemongrass tea and ginger scones in New Mexico, Korean scallion pancakes in Berkeley, turkey biryani in Paris), I have to say something about the man himself. David, who has led the kitchen at Chez Panisse variously—and

intermittently—throughout his career, is exactly the opposite of that stereotypical macho domineering type A chef associated with most world-class kitchens. I have never seen him particularly flummoxed, perspiring, ranting, or stressed. He seems almost to float, or perhaps shuffle, in a state of serenity, whether cooking at home or in a commercial kitchen. I suspect that this is largely owing to the fact that he has, beyond a shade of doubt, "the gift," that preternatural ease that stems from just *knowing* (in the marrow) that whatever you cook will be delicious, but also from the fact that the knowledge of *how* to cook a particular dish a priori precedes even the thought of *what* to cook.

I make David sound like an ethereal creature. He is not. In fact, he cuts a rather earthy figure—a stolid diminutive but sturdy bespectacled form, possessed of a Samson-worthy salt-and-pepper mane and the kind of physical strength truly fearless cooking requires. And the hands—the hands are hands out of time. They are the hands of August Sander's pastry cook from 1928, the hands of a French turn-of-the-century cabbage farmer, the hands of someone who will grab a whole scarcely deceased fish, make a quick longitudinal incision along its belly, and unflinchingly reach inside to pull out a fistful of bloody entrails. I love to cook, I have been doing it since childhood, I have been surrounded by culinary greats my whole life, but you will *never* see me do this. They are also hands I have watched gently rearrange tiny sprigs of chervil—that frilly, most dainty of herbs—until the appearance of a plate is just right, or artfully drizzle a spoonful of spiced oil into a bowl of vibrantly bicolored soup. To say that David is deliberate is an understatement. But rather than suggesting a preponderance of planning, his deliberateness very directly, I feel, expresses his unique circadian rhythm (an internal clock that has made him a bit ill suited, at times, to the bustle of a restaurant kitchen, but the best person ever to go to a farmers market with). When you arrive at his house for a meal, you might find someone having a real-time experience of working through all the ingredients and possibilities, but food will always materialize soon and it will always be delicious. The process is a bit like watching an act of prestidigitation. By the time the plate is served, you've witnessed the inner workings of the illusion, but you could never hope to replicate the trick. Therein lies the magic.

When I was younger—and maybe still, although now I think my mother would wholeheartedly agree—I'd tell her (just to be irksome) that David was my favorite cook, that he stood head and shoulders above her in my esteem. I don't actually believe in such rankings, but if I did, David would be more than deserving of the title. I am biased, of course, by a native palate that thrills to the mix of flavors he brings to a dish: base notes of deep comfort, with a trill of bright citrus and fresh herbs and chilies. He has an intrepid tongue. In fact, he is the only chef in the history of my life, but also, I think, in the history of the restaurant, that my mom has trusted to cleave from the tried repertoire of distinctly Chez Panisse flavors and dishes. The restaurant was of course founded as an homage to traditional French cooking, and over the years its menus have not traveled much farther than the immediate Mediterranean. Italian ingredients and preparations are mainstays, and Moroccan flavors are warmly admitted, but the ingredient list never strays too far east—or south or north, for that matter. I should say that I think this consistency is a great strength, and partially responsible for the restaurant's enduring appeal, but when you have a David Tanis at the helm, you sort of *will* him to rebel. During David's various tenures, some of my favorite menus would crop up, menus that somehow managed to stay within the Chez vernacular while introducing the unexpected flavors of, say, a Chinese banquet (steamed pork buns!) or a South Indian chaat house or a Korean barbecue joint. If this is sounding hagiographic, so be it. David's a goddamn treasure and I hope he lives and cooks forever.

The year was 2004. I'd gone to France to meet my mom for the seventieth birthday of the legendary *New York Times* editor and bureau chief and truly first-rate gourmand R. W. "Johnny" Apple, which fell

just five days before Thanksgiving. Johnny had elected to celebrate, with all of his dearest friends, in the vaunted dining room of L'Ami Louis, the least fussy, yet perhaps most decadent, restaurant in Paris. The story of that party (cue towering Jenga-like stacks of toasted baguettes and bricks of foie gras to spread upon them like butter) is perhaps better left for another time or, best of all, allowed to settle into a dim and mythic history, undisrupted. But the party coincided with the period when David and his partner, Randal Breski, were living half the time in Paris and half the time in Berkeley. The downstairs restaurant at Chez has had two rotating chefs for decades; the kitchens up and down are both run by pairs, with four chefs total. This meant that while one chef would lead the week, the other would tie it up: three days on, three days off. I'm not sure how, but my mother was convinced to dismantle the well-oiled system to permit David and the other longtime chef at Chez, Jean-Pierre Moullé, to each spend half a year in France: six months on, six months off—a year's worth of pay. This, to me, is a testament both to my mother's unorthodoxy, but also to her love of David's cooking. She'd bend whatever rules necessary to keep him on the line.

In any event, this was during the period when David and Randal were living in a seventeenth-century apartment near the Panthéon, out of which they ran a wildly popular supper club—progenitor of the genre, I'm inclined to suggest—that they called Au Chien Lunatique in honor of their beloved terrier, Arturo. Theirs was not a lavishly spacious home, but it had exceptionally high ceilings and those dark wooden beams that look most magisterial and correct when they feature in the architecture of the Old World, and a perfect, if minimal, array of used and antique furniture and "objets" sourced by Randal. I've always thought of the two as "front of the house" and "back of the house" respectively, and indeed they've often operated professionally in that capacity. I remember Thanksgiving itself only *vaguely*—owing, I'm sure, to the overindulgence in libations characterized by a person not quite yet allowed to legally consume alcohol. There were enough people at the table to snake, in a loose L-shape, through both dining and living rooms. I have no idea where they found enough chairs. Dinner was delicious, convivial, and drawn out across the afternoon and evening hours as all the best meals are. David prepared everything in a galley kitchen the size of a modest walk-in closet.

They next day, though, that's the meal I really remember. I'm not sure why, but I ventured back to their apartment on my own. Maybe simply to spend a bit more time with the two of them. It was just the three of us, all a bit bleary, and yet by some miracle we eventually discovered that our hunger had returned. No one wanted to go out in search of provisions. It's very unlikely to have been the case, but in my memory everything in Paris was shuttered that day anyhow; we'd have to make do with what we had on hand. I say *we*, but really we were leaning on David—whose appetite for cooking never seems to wane—to receive some divine inspiration. He rummaged a bit in the pantry and pulled out a few things. First some basmati rice to simmer on the stove, infusing it with spices, saffron, cardamom, some sea salt, a nob of butter. Next he picked over the gaping turkey carcass for the last delectable bits of meat. Some yogurt and a small cucumber were located in the depths of the tiny under-the-counter fridge. Before long, David was serving us a warm, spiced pile of fluffy rice layered with dark turkey meat and flecked with herbs. Alongside it, a pale pink raita, studded with cranberries from last night's sauce and little bits of onion and cucumber. It was exactly what you want to eat after Thanksgiving dinner: something so completely other, and yet somehow also recycled. After all, what's Thanksgiving without leftovers? I remember marveling at the ingenuity it took to make this meal on the spot. But also, that he had revealed that one thing that is most essential to good cooking, that matters more than the aesthetics of the plate or the innovation of the concept or the presentation: it was absolutely *delicious*.

Leftover Turkey Biryani

THIS IS NOT SO MUCH A RECIPE as it is an assembly, nor so much a biryani as it is a suggestion of one. David published a wonderful version of this recipe a few years ago in *The New York Times*; this is an adaptation of that one that omits the oven step. Because you'll be using leftover meat that's already been fully cooked, the traditional process of steaming the rice together with the meat in a tightly sealed vessel is a step you can skip (although this'll make the outcome that much more impressionistic and untraditional). Start by picking all the good bits of turkey, dark and light, off your bird, shredding any larger pieces, and set aside.

MAKE YOUR RICE: Wash 2 cups of basmati rice until the water runs almost clear. Put it in a large saucepan, add enough water to cover, and soak it for 1 to 2 hours. While the rice is soaking, toast 1 teaspoon of saffron threads very lightly in a small skillet over a low flame. After the rice has soaked, pour in enough additional water (or chicken stock, page 57) to reach the first joint of your index finger lightly placed on top of the rice (this is Niloufer's method; it's usually about ½ inch of water above the rice). Add 1 teaspoon of salt, ½ teaspoon of ghee, a couple of whole cloves and cardamom pods, a cinnamon stick, the toasted saffron, and a few black peppercorns. Bring to a boil, stir once, lower the heat to a scant simmer, cover the pan, and cook for 15 to 20 minutes (older rice will take a touch longer). Let the rice sit, covered, for at least another 10 minutes.

WHILE YOUR RICE IS COOKING, heat a heavy-bottomed pan with 2 cups of vegetable oil, and in batches fry a small handful of raisins, until plump; a small handful of slivered almonds, until lightly browned; and a thinly sliced medium onion, until lightly browned. Drain these on paper towels, lightly dust with fine sea salt, and reserve for garnish.

PEEL AND QUARTER a few medium-small potatoes, parboil them in salted water, and drain. Finely chop a large onion. In a dry skillet, toast a big pinch each of dried coriander seeds, cumin seeds, poppy seeds, dried chili flakes, and black peppercorns, and the seeds from two whole cardamom pods. Once they begin to brown slightly and grow fragrant, remove from heat and grind together in a suribachi or mortar and pestle, until you have a coarse powder. Add to that a pinch of ground cinnamon. Heat a big spoonful of ghee in a medium-sized pan and add the potatoes, lightly browning them over medium heat, then add the onion, ½ cup of broken raw cashews, 2 grated cloves of garlic, and a grated nob of ginger (a Microplane grater works best). Stir in your powdered spice mixture. Sauté until the onions are translucent and the potatoes softened and browned. Add 1 tablespoon of tomato paste and 1 cup of chicken stock. Add your picked turkey bits to the pan and stir them together with the potato mixture, warming the meat through and allowing the flavors to marry for several minutes. Add ½ cup of thick plain yogurt and a big pinch of salt, and cook for another minute, stirring. Taste and tweak the seasoning if necessary. Remove from the heat.

TO SERVE, fluff your rice with a fork and spoon a cupful onto each plate. Ladle the meat and potato mixture over the rice, then layer with another cupful of rice. Scatter with the deep-fried garnish and a handful of coarsely chopped cilantro. Serve with cranberry raita, halved hard-boiled eggs, and any nice chutneys you may have lurking in the back of your refrigerator.

Cranberry Raita   THIS LITTLE SAUCE is a version of David's genius repurposing of leftover cranberry sauce (page 277), which transforms the more standard yogurt-based Indian relish into a beautiful rose-colored condiment. Start by peeling and deseeding a large cucumber. Grate it on the largest setting of a box grater or slice it into thin crescents and sprinkle with salt, allowing it to sit for 20 minutes. Place it into a colander and squeeze out the water. Stir the cucumber into 2 cups of lightly whisked plain unsweetened yogurt. Add a diced small red onion and a finely chopped Thai chili. Toast a scant ½ teaspoon of both cumin and mustard seeds and add to the yogurt. Stir in a pinch of chiffonaded cilantro and mint leaves and a few spoonfuls of cranberry sauce to incorporate. Taste for salt, and adjust if necessary.

CHAPTER 31

The College Garden

At my eighteenth birthday, amid an ocean of family friends, my parents and Bob presented me with a handmade book called *Fanny's Exclusive College Survival Cookbook*. This book, eclectically art-designed by Bob, is a collection of more than fifty-five recipes and related visual ephemera from virtually every dear family friend in my life, from Marion Cunningham to Sally Clarke, Lulu Peyraud to Angelo Garro, my aunt Laura and uncle Jim to Margaret Grade of Manka's Inverness Lodge. Though the remit may have been "something quick and easy enough for a college student," the submitted recipes ranged from Susie and Mark's Oak Mesa Whiskey Sours to Cecilia Chiang's Steamed Rock Cod. My favorites, for the comedy, if not for the edible contents, were Calvin Trillin's Scrambled Eggs That Stick to the Pan Every Time, Sue Murphy's recipe for A Perfect Back Scratch and David King's "wake-up snack," perhaps the only "recipe" that acknowledged the extent to which I would shortly be pulling all-nighters to get my freshman-year papers done on time. The recipe is as follows: "Take 3 or 4 large tablespoons of full-caffeine instant coffee—put it in a glass. Add an equal amount of warm or hot tap water. Mix it to a paste. Make sure there is no dry instant coffee left. Now eat it. You can have a 'chaser'—like some more hot tap water. This should keep you awake for hours. You don't even need a kitchen—you can do this all in the bathroom." The recipes I used the most, however, were Samantha Greenwood's carrot cake, penne and cheese, and chocolate cake—the things you want to make when you're eighteen and newly culinarily emancipated from your sugar-phobic mother. I also made Sharon Jones's pancakes, revelatory for their simplicity, so often that that page, more than any other, is warped and splattered and almost illegible. That book remains one of the best gifts I've received in my life.

Anyway, a month after my birthday, my parents took me back east to start my freshman year of college at Yale. I had, at this point, spent time in places where good ingredients were scarce (soccer tournaments, summer camp), but this was the first time I was looking at an extended shortage of provisions, and furthermore, absolutely nowhere to cook. As important to my mother as furnishing my fourth-floor dorm room with an oscillating fan to combat the oppressive weather was equipping it with some semblance of a kitchen. While my dad sat at my desk with the fan placed in front of him, purring in the direction of his face, my mom took off alone for several hours. I chatted with my roommate, Julia Frederick—who would become my closest friend—and her parents about the coincidence of our unintentionally matching bedsheets and blue Adidas sneakers and yet apparently divergent tastes in music (I was a West Coast rap devotee, she a lover of Led Zeppelin). Finally my mom returned, lugging, with heroic strength, a small refrigerator up the stairs. She was also carrying a bag brimming with other useful appliances: a teakettle, an (illegal) hot plate, a few pots, a cutting board, a wooden spoon, and a set of decent knives. These things she arranged in a serviceable configuration on "my" side of the shared quarters. Julia's parents had no clue who this crazy Berkeley lady was—they looked on bemused as she rearranged the dorm furniture.

Next came the foraging: a dispiriting drive around New Haven in search of good produce. Things have changed a bit since—especially with the arrival of a farmers market—but in 2001 it was not a promising culinary landscape. The best thing we could find—because "organic" still took precedence over the nice-looking array at the Italian grocers—was the sort of hippie health food store my mom had wrongly thought she'd left behind in the seventies. Called Edge of the Woods, this market was a good place to stock up on whole grains and things like applesauce, pasta, and other dry goods, but I don't remember it boasting much by way of a produce aisle. And it was miles away from campus; if I wanted to go there, I had to hitch a ride with a friend or take a taxi. Once we had some staples in hand (olive oil, red wine vinegar, sea salt, a pepper grinder), we returned to my dorm room to find a somewhat cooler but now very hungry father. Fortunately, this coincided with the "Welcome Lunch" for new students and parents at Commons, the largest and most central dining hall on campus.

We proceeded over there, across Elm and Wall Streets, down to the entry on Church, and into the cavernous cafeteria. Parents were milling around confusedly with their spawn and lining up at long tables fitted with stainless steel chafing pans designed to keep the contents of the buffet passably warm. The second we stepped foot inside, my mom started to shake her head. "It does *not* smell good in here." The statement was unnecessary; our family was for once united in our distrust of the smell of a place. "It doesn't even really smell like *food*," my dad constructively added. It smelled terrible, of course, but I felt quite smug about my having held out until not just one, but both, parents had registered complaints, having been the butt of so much olfactory persecution throughout my life. Still, we filed toward the half-open trays so my mom could perform a closer analysis. She was met with portions of waxen corn on the cob, anemic burgers, geriatric hot dogs, iceberg lettuce—the theme evidently was "1950s American barbecue." "We're not staying!" my mom announced. We left without eating, and eventually located a decent sandwich shop a few blocks away.

Later that afternoon, the university president, a man named Rick Levin, hosted the same group of two thousand students and their parents at his mansion on a leafy stretch of Hillhouse Avenue. The idea was for students and parents to enter a reception line and, one by one, shake the hand of the man who would preside over their education for the next four years. These "greetings" necessarily took place in extremely abbreviated fashion—no one had more than four to six seconds with the president. When my mother reached the head of the line, however, she clamped Rick's hand in a steely handshake,

refusing to let go until he had acknowledged her message: "You and I, we're going to change the food here. I'm coming to see you very soon." He looked bewildered—there wasn't an aide handy to explain that my mother was impassioned, yes, but not a lunatic, and in fact was a rather famous chef from Berkeley, California. Little did he know that she intended to make good on this vow. Within a couple of months she was sitting in his office, describing her vision for Yale's agrarian future. It included a sustainable dining program, a college farm, university-wide composting and recycling, a teaching program for kitchen staff, and the implementation of courses dedicated to food and agriculture.

In the meantime, I had discovered Froyo, that addictively textured sweet frozen substance discharged by machines in every dining hall campus-wide. I had also discovered a small student activist group that went by the name Food from the Earth. I joined their ranks more or less immediately, though I lacked conviction that our small numbers would garner much attention from the university's administration. Nonetheless, I was committed to advocating for organic food in dining halls (though in truth I rarely ate in them—I had my own "kitchen"), writing petitions, and attending meetings with students who looked like the kids born to the hippie parents I'd grown up with in Berkeley. My nascent activism was, however, rendered somewhat redundant by my mother's swift and forceful intervention. With her at the helm, a steering committee of students, faculty, and staff was convened by the university to start immediately tackling the dining program. A pilot was inaugurated at the appositely named Berkeley College, a residential college possessed of a master more favorably disposed to my mom's vision than the one governing the college with which I was affiliated. Berkeley was to begin serving exclusively local, seasonal, and sustainable food in their dining hall. This food was also to be prepared by staff who'd signed up for professional training in the culinary arts; most of the "cooks" working in the Yale cafeterias belonged to the janitorial union and were offered little by way of specialized instruction. It didn't take much, anyway, to figure out how to microwave trays of frozen food. Needless to say, when it opened, the new dining hall was a hit. Faced with the prospect of consuming *real food*—freshly prepared salads, roasted seasonal vegetables, Chez Panisse–style pizzas—students began forging IDs and sneaking in through back entrances at mealtimes.

It wasn't long before a project director was nominated, a man named Josh Viertel. I'd met Josh at the Mountain School, a semester program in Vermont for high school juniors that we'd both attended. He was installed there for the year teaching the environmental studies course. Back at Yale, I called my mom to tell her I thought Josh would make a compelling leader for this as-of-then-unnamed initiative. During the summer after my sophomore year—by which time I had consumed a lot of frozen yogurt . . . things were dire—Josh was leading a set of interns in breaking ground at the Yale Farm on Edwards Street. When I returned at the start of my junior year, the garden was already productive. Fledgling, yes, but full of beautiful vibrant produce. Volunteers were working there daily. Students had begun to sell modest amounts at the farmers market. There were plans for a wood-fired pizza oven.

I did occasionally volunteer in the garden, which grew more resplendent and fruitful with each passing semester, but I was more proficient in the act of "harvesting." My mom had not just planted the figurative—and to some extent literal—seeds for this project, she had also fundraised the initial monies required to build it and then showed up time and again to defend it. She did all of this without taking a cent by way of compensation. If you consider, for a moment, the fact that she and my father were at the time paying my tuition, you could even say that *she* was paying *Yale* to improve its reputation as a leader in the food and sustainability movement. Since the inception of the Yale Sustainable Food Program, many of the university's competitors have sprung to action, setting up copycat dining and farm projects across their campuses. And, as of a few years ago, the program at Yale was finally endowed. All this to say that I didn't exactly feel loads of remorse whenever I'd swoop by the garden for an early evening dinner-picking graze. This usually occurred just after nightfall—I was not so bold or entitled that I presumed I could pick without recrimination in broad daylight amid student volunteers—and I was often accompanied by my mom's cousin, Cathy Waters. Cathy, a talented graphic designer who had donated her time to create the project's visual identity, lived in New Haven with her husband, Dennis Danaher, and the three of us were often the beneficiaries of my mother's extended largess.

My mom reaped great pleasure from the project. The extent to which the students showed their enthusiasm for farming and for the table was a huge inspiration to her, and the program gave her a template to implement at other institutions of higher learning (the Rome Sustainable Food Project being another example). But really the reason my mother got involved was that she had a hard time thinking of me across the country without access to the type of food I'd grown up on, food that still had chi, or life force, as we like to say in our house, food that had been grown by people taking care of the land. Of course, this story could be read as an example of my extraordinary privilege—not only was I a student at a prestigious university, but I also had a doting mother who would go to any length to secure a perfect tomato for her daughter. That's true, of course—I *was* richly spoiled. But the more remarkable thing, really, is that my mother had the tools to effect change and *used them*. It may initially have been to supply me from afar with something of a feeling of home, but it also secured better food and more sustainable environmental practices for thousands of other students, and for generations to come.

When asked one time, by one of the many reporters who visited the Yale Sustainable Food Program, if the farm struggled with the local population of deer coming in uninvited to eat the produce, Josh replied, "We don't have deer, we just have Fanny."

Garden Salad
Tacos

THIS IS ONE of the most frequently prepared meals in our house, and something I made all the time in college. Secretly, my mom has a thing for mild, meltable cheeses like Monterey Jack. She never eats them on their own, but there's reliably a block in her fridge to use for a grilled cheese sandwich or for a preparation she calls Garden Salad Tacos. These very adaptable, very quick-to-assemble tacos are possibly the best recipe in these pages, if only because they combine a degree of deliciousness and ease that makes them perfect when you need to make something tasty and fast. That said, I've also made them for plenty of breakfasts and countless lunches, even when I've had more than enough time to make something more elaborate. The contents of the tacos are, as the name would suggest, basically just a dressed green salad.

TAKE A COUPLE OF HANDFULS of washed salad leaves, coarsely chop them, and put them in a mixing bowl. Use a mandoline to sliver a few radishes and add them to the leaves. Add a chopped small tomato and a handful of cilantro leaves. Heat two corn tortillas over the open flame of a gas stove top until lightly blackened (you can skip this step if your stove is electric). Place the tortillas on a small baking tray and, using a box grater, blanket the tortillas with grated cheese. Put the tray into a toaster oven—the only electronic appliance permitted in my mom's kitchen, though she has used a Sharpie to crudely blacken any of the offensive chrome fittings—or under the broiler in the oven, to melt the cheese. Meanwhile, dress the salad with a splash of red wine vinegar, a splash of olive oil, and a pinch of salt. Taste and adjust for seasoning. Because of the fat in the cheese, it's nice to have the salad be a touch more acidic than you would normally make it. When the cheese is bubbling, remove the tortillas from the oven, fill with the dressed salad, and serve immediately. There are many variations, depending on what other ingredients you like or have on hand. Sometimes I sprinkle a bit of diced hot chili (like jalapeño or serrano) and some slivered green onion over the cheese before putting the tortillas in the oven; sometimes I add avocado or cucumber to the salad.

CHAPTER 32

On the Road

My mom has been a regular at the Telluride Film Festival since its inception. In fact, I don't think she's missed a single year in the festival's forty-six-year history. This devotion speaks not just to her love of film—after food, and of course Edible Education, it's been a significant strand in her life—but also to her enduring adoration of Tom Luddy, the festival's founding director and my mother's romantic partner in the late sixties and early seventies. Despite my mom's commitment to attending this hard-to-reach film industry idyll, I have myself been able to join her there on only a couple of occasions. It falls on Labor Day weekend, a persistent conflict with the first few weeks of school and an impossible moment to steal away for a jaunt to Colorado. And once I moved to England, attendance became an even remoter possibility. Still, there were two years back to back, right after I graduated from college but before I headed to the UK for graduate school, in which the opportunity did arise. All I had to do was coordinate the latter third of a cross-country road trip with the storied weekend of cinematic immersion.

The second of these consecutive trips to Telluride took place in 2006, on the heels of a drive from New York to California with my college boyfriend, Tom Schmidt. We were in our early twenties and shortly about to embark for Cambridge, so we took a long and circuitous route through the American Southwest, stopping in at places like Marfa and camping in a psychedelic landscape of colored sands and bits of wood turned to stone in the Petrified Forest National Park. At the culmination of the festival weekend, Tom had to fly back home to New York. I planned to navigate the last seventeen hours of road to Berkeley solo. My mom is not someone who enjoys long, uninterrupted stretches of road or any type of driving that doesn't yield immediate rewards. It's virtually impossible to imagine her as a young woman motoring for desolate stretches across Turkey (and yet there *is* photographic proof that she did so). Still, as I began to pack up my car for the westward journey, my mom took a look at me and impulsively offered to ride along. She had already booked a return flight to California, but—in a moment of spontaneity I could tell she was gearing up to immediately regret—canceled her plans so that she could copilot her daughter out of Telluride, across Utah, and through the Sierras. We had never gone on a real road trip—that most American of rites of passage, full of unbroken road, slow-moving RVs, and fast-food chains—just the two of us. This would be a first.

I can't remember why, but for a short period, I left my car unattended with my mother. When I returned, she had squirreled away a large, newly acquired cooler and camp stove in the trunk of my VW station wagon. "You don't really need this enormous spare tire, do you?" I could see she was searching for somewhere to lodge two precariously open bottles of olive oil and vinegar, and watched with horror as she seized my down pillow and wedged it between them. But there was nothing to do but yield to her will: I helped make way for these bottles, as well as a few more, including a greater quantity of rosé than seemed prudent given the brevity of the expedition. I leaned in to see the other "essentials": a wooden spoon, a package of paper plates, disposable silverware, a pocketknife, a colander, and the most critical of camping appliances—an egg poaching pan. Scenes of my mom performing camp-style cooking, in real-food-starved locales, flitted to mind. I'd seen her cook a pot of beans on a Bunsen burner in a Salina, Kansas, motel room; grill corn on the side of a Florida highway; make fennel cakes for a hundred in a hotel kitchenette in Berlin; and turn kebabs over a fire fashioned of broken hotel furniture in Hawaii (I may have dreamt that last scene). Now I pictured her poaching eggs on the hood of my car. In my momentary absence, she had not just acquired all the basics for an outdoor kitchen from the local hardware store, but had also stopped in at the farmers market to acquire enough fresh produce—hence the cooler—to see us through at least a week on the road. I peeked into the densely packed coffer to discover tomatoes, cucumbers, peaches, plums, onions, garlic, a dozen farm eggs, lettuce, peppers, berries, assorted herbs, Parmesan cheese—all sitting on ice. She was clearly intent on us eating "locally" for the next four states. Our drive, however, at most would take two days.

Because we only barely managed to get out of Telluride well into the afternoon, our first day's drive was necessarily unambitious. We started out heading north along the meandering roads that flow into the flatlands, then through Montrose, the gateway to Black Canyon to the east. Skimming the northeastern edge of the Uncompahgre National Forest, we hooked westward through Grand Junction— nicknamed "River City" for its perch at the confluence of the Colorado and Gunnison Rivers—and an hour and a half later pulled into the small, 900-person town of Green River, Utah, just before sundown. In the first half of the nineteenth century, the settlement of Green River was positioned on a river crossing for merchants traveling the Old Spanish Trail trade route; eventually it became a critical throughway for the U.S. mail service. Incorporated in 1906, the town retains vestiges of a Victorian approach to city planning: a modest grid, a central green, a scattering of churches. During our brief stay, we also discovered that it was home to the World's Largest Watermelon, an outsize sculpture of a watermelon slice, which sits under a comically perfunctory shade structure in a barren parking lot. The massive, slightly

dilapidated crescent of painted wood dates, I've since learned, from the 1950s and is a mainstay of Green River's annual Melon Days Festival.

We surveyed the modest surroundings for a motel, and found something adequate: a Budget Inn, I think, if memory serves. We were certain, based on pure speculation, that we would find a Mexican cantina of sorts, a purveyor of a decent taco for dinner. Mexican food is the saving grace of the American culinary landscape. Even in some of the most desolate environments, you can usually sniff out a taco. Unfortunately, we had no such luck in this little outpost. And since it was Labor Day, nothing was open aside from the gas station, where we bought a flimsy book of matches from a man perched in a glassed-in island between pumps. But we were not defeated by the absence of eateries. After all, we were driving a car brimming with provisions, the freshest of which were certainly not going to get any fresher the longer they remained in the vehicle.

After checking into the motel, we scuttled over the road to the park, lugging our cooler and other vital libations. First things first: My mom opened a bottle of rosé, despite my daughterly reprisals and unresearched insistence that Utah had laws against open containers in public parks. She decanted some wine into a paper cup, and then from nowhere materialized a beeswax candle. She shoved it into the open bottle and struck a match to light it. "See, it's not open anymore, it's just a *candlestick*." I could not argue with this rationale, especially in light of the ingenuity, not to mention the genuinely appealing atmospheric glow it cast over the picnic table.

"How about green eggs, Fan? I'm sure the bottom part of that poaching pan would work for frying." *Green eggs* referred to a frequent household preparation in which sunny-side eggs would be showered, almost to the point of rendering the eggs themselves invisible, with a handful of chopped herbs while they were sizzling away in the pan.

Using a paper plate as a cutting board, I executed my best pocket-knife chiffonade of a handful of herbs. Meanwhile, my mom was busy contriving a sense of ambience. She pulled a large linen napkin (she seems to have an unlimited supply) from some nook in the car and spread it over the splintered tabletop. She set out another two paper plates and some cutlery. She propped the stove on the table and heated some olive oil in the frying pan, then poured in the eggs and covered them with herbs. I laid a few quartered lemon cucumbers and some tomato slices over a plate piled with lettuces and drizzled them with an improvised dressing. Lacking her beloved mortar and pestle, my mom made a vinaigrette instead by vigorously mashing a garlic clove in a paper bowl with the pocketknife. We called the concoction "Vinaigrette au goût de paper plate"—not as delicious as our standard preparation, but still serviceable. From time to time, throughout dinner, she'd remove the burning candle-cork, top up her glass from the "candlestick," and replace it again. The sun disappeared wearily beyond the flat western horizon, and for a time we sat there silently opposite each other, faces glowing in the candlelight, before turning in for the night.

The next morning I awoke to the sound of muted rapping. I groaned from my twin bed, where I lay twisted in a brightly patterned bedspread. "Oh! I didn't want to wake you!" my mom said as she emerged from the bathroom with a summer fruit macédoine macerating in two plastic motel cups. I wandered into the bathroom, where she'd been cutting fruit, to discover a pool of orange juice beneath the hair dryer and a sink flecked with bits of peach flesh and raspberry seeds. We hit the road early, fruit cups in hand, hoping to make it to someplace picturesque where we might, some hours later, pull off the road to have lunch. The midday heat, even in September, was ferocious as we careened westward. My mom wore one map as a sun hat as she searched another for an adequate lunch spot—these were the days before iPhones.

"I think there's a park coming up any second now. It looks like it should be off to the right." My mom, a self-proclaimed "excellent *navi-*

gatrice," was living up to her title. Momentarily, a sign for Cave Lake State Park flashed into focus. "Ohh, a lake! That sounds refreshing! Pull over!" I turned off onto the loose gravel road, and a haze of fine dry earth rose in our wake. The loamy scent of parched sagebrush and resinous creosote rushed into the car as I negotiated us deeper into the wilderness and farther from the highway that would take us to the edge of California that night. We were beginning to worry that this Cave Lake might still be a considerable distance when my mom spotted a coppiced stand of dark green willow trees and a ribbon of lush grass.

"I think that's a river, Fan! Pull over!" She pawed around for the more detailed Nevada map and, with a look of incredible satisfaction, announced that we had arrived at Steptoe Creek.

I guided the car astride a thicket of yellow flowering sage and purple thistle that towered over my tiny mother when she got out. We unloaded the car and settled into the long grass in the shade of the willow canopy, spreading out the ever-present linen *torchon* as a stand-in for a picnic blanket. My mom very quickly decided on pasta—which is usually what she decides on if left to her own devices. I waded into the rushing stream and filled the poaching pan with water to cook the noodles. My mom chopped tomatoes and garlic and tore the remaining unwilted basil leaves for a garnish. I'm not sure if it was just the pristine creek water—which I nonetheless insisted on boiling for a water-sterilizing eternity—but it remains one of the most delicious tomato pastas I've ever eaten.

River Water Tomato Pasta

THIS IS A PASTA TO MAKE when the season's tomatoes are at their peak, when they won't need peeling or reduction to concentrate their flavor. Of course, you don't need river water, but if you ever find yourself near a swiftly running body of water and have a burner and a pan at the ready, why not give it a try? We used a dried egg fettuccine for this, which is a nice choice as it cooks in about the time you'll need to warm the garlic and tomatoes to make the sauce. While the water is coming to a boil, mince a couple of cloves of garlic. Chop your tomatoes, cutting out the little cores at the stem. You can use a selection of tomatoes of different sizes and varieties, but make sure to cut them into fairly uniform pieces. Especially sweet varieties like dry-farmed Early Girls or halved Sungold cherry tomatoes work best. In a large sauté pan, heat the garlic in a big glug of extra virgin olive oil until just fragrant and add the tomatoes, a big pinch of salt, and a scant pinch of red chili flakes. Throw the noodles into a pot of generously salted water and simmer until just cooked, then use tongs or a spider to remove the pasta to the tomato pan. Toss, taste, and adjust the seasoning, if necessary. It might want more salt, a little splash of vinegar, or more oil. Shower with torn basil leaves and grated Parmesan cheese and serve immediately.

•　　•　　•

We spent the next six hours barreling west through silver deserts on Route 50, which bears the melancholic moniker of "The Loneliest Road in America." My mom read me stories from Raymond Carver's collection *Cathedral*, pausing only to reprimand me for speeding or to complain about the sciatica afflicting her leg, neither of which we did anything to remedy. We argued the merits of leather seats versus fabric. We worked on our forthcoming fictional cookbook, adding at least a dozen new recipes to *Everything Tastes Better with Lime*. We explored a hypothetical scenario in which a mother and daughter were stranded with nothing to eat but an infinite supply of eggs, which was more or less a reflection of how we felt in the moment. Finally we caught a glimpse of Lake Tahoe, an immense, glittering basin that sits on the border of California.

When we reached the southern shore, we searched urgently for a picnic site. Only an hour or so of daylight remained before sundown, and the winds off the lake were a startling contrast to the placid aridity of the desert. We managed to keep the stove lit by huddling around it, using a towering Ponderosa pine as a windbreak. First my mom sautéed a mixture of sliced peppers and onions and slivered garlic over the endangered flame. Meanwhile, I used the pocketknife to gnaw through what remained of a stale loaf of bread, yielding a few rugged slices. She fried these in the pan in a pool of spluttering oil until they were crispy and golden. Then we finally—finally!—used the poaching pan for its intended purpose. When the eggs were done, she loosened them from the pan onto the bread and spooned the softened vegetables over the top. We ate this egg bruschetta alongside a salad of the last tomatoes splashed in vinegar and oil and watched as a final slip of sun dipped behind the western ridge of the mountains. The lake was ablaze.

We drove the rest of the way to Berkeley in contented silence. Just before midnight, we pulled into our driveway and inhaled deeply, absorbing the herbaceous smell of our garden. We'd made it, despite my mother's initial misgivings. We were home.

Coming Home Pasta

There are a few things, or, I should say, a few *dishes*, that I associate with coming home after a long period away. The main one, of course, is Coming Home Pasta. Whenever my family left for a stretch of weeks— what to a child resembled an eternity—we would come home to our strange-feeling house and immediately set about orienting ourselves through food. To be fair, we oriented ourselves through food whatever the place or the time or the country or the continent, but the fact that such an orientation felt necessary even at *home* I think does speak to our family's particular brand of devotion.

I can very distinctly remember the feeling of coming home to the Berkeley house after a long trip. As we spilled through the front door, the house would creak under our luggage, as if in our absence it had grown unaccustomed to the weight both of us and of our cargo. The house smelled a bit stale and of dust, always, a scent amplified by the ancient floor heaters as they were switched on and began to roast the particles accumulated after so many weeks of disuse. We always seemed to be returning after nightfall, and so these memories of nostos (a bit of Homerian vocabulary feels warranted here) are tinged with the inky hue of night, or rather have since taken on a fuzzy, wine-dark haze, much like the color Homer paints of the Odyssean seas. And indeed it was always a moment for opening a bottle of wine, usually red, because that meant that no one had to have remembered to chill it before leaving. Plucked from the cellar, it could be counted on to immediately slake parental thirst. One or the other guardian (or Bob) would descend through the trapdoor in the kitchen floor—an architectural feature I am so used to as to be inured to its eccentricity, though this detail is never lost on new visitors to the house—and proceed to the musty-smelling cellar below where, during my father's tenure at least, a very considerable wine inventory was stored.

No one unpacked. Rather a wordless series of actions was set into motion: the putting on of a pot of water to boil, the burning of a parched rosemary branch left out in the basket on the table (our family's incense), the lighting of a candle, the rustling in the pantry drawers for a bag of pasta, opened or unopened—it didn't matter. I was usually dispatched to the garden with a flashlight to pick a few handfuls of herbs. This generally meant parsley, sometimes a bit of oregano—only the herbs that could withstand a good stretch of neglect and whose flavor didn't change too much if they'd mostly gone to seed. Sending me out into the dark of the back garden had the added benefit of giving my mom a brief window in which to quickly extract a few anchovies from under salt in their container in the fridge and add them to the sauce (if you could even call the frugal dressing characteristic of Coming Home Pasta a *sauce*). I would have balked at their inclusion; once anchovies were incorporated into a dish and decently disguised, however, I would eat them contentedly. Other things were rummaged for: some still-firm cloves of garlic to mince and fry in oil in the gleaming blue-black lap of my mother's favorite cast-iron pan; some chili flakes to join the garlic there in its hot oil shimmy. The smell of the house would begin to transform.

There was reliably a nubbin of ancient Parmesan in the fridge, blooming with pale age spots but unspoiled. It would taste fine, even good, grated and married with the other heady flavors of garlic and chili and herbs and anchovy and sometimes a handful of coarsely chopped salt-packed capers, whose flavor was pleasantly abrupt and tangy. Sea salt, black pepper, and a good, voluptuous pour of olive oil at the end. This was Coming Home Pasta. We ate this concoction in relative silence. The darkness made it seem frivolous to switch on music; conversation felt redundant after so many hours trapped together in transit. So we twirled our next-to-naked noodles and ate to know that we had made it—made it back home again to the table.

Making Coming Home Pasta scarcely requires more articulation of method than I've already given it—it is very open to interpretation and should be adapted to whatever you have on hand. Alice Trillin, the very beloved wife of Calvin "Bud" Trillin—the man I think of as my Jewish godfather, though I realize that's a contradiction in terms— wrote me a not-dissimilar recipe called Lonely Girl Pasta for *Fanny's Exclusive College Survival Cookbook*, the book my parents and Bob presented to me as a high school graduation gift. Alice submitted her recipe the year she passed away, and I've always felt more than a pang of sadness reading over its gentle and pragmatic instructions and economical ingredients. Still, I believe her recipe presumed the presence of at least a bell pepper or broccoli floret in the refrigerator, still fresh enough to merit inclusion. Such was not the case in our house, both because bell peppers and broccoli were generally frowned upon (I think my mom associated them with the insipid canned vegetables of her youth) and because her obsession with voiding the icebox of its contents prior to our departure bordered on compulsion. Her close friends and I tease her that one of her biggest pet peeves is an abundantly stocked fridge.

But despite the spareness of the ingredients and the unfussiness of the preparation, this is in fact a delicious pasta recipe. The Italians—progenitors of time-tested dishes whose names are nice-sounding translations of things as uncomplicated as "cheese and pepper" (*cacio e pepe*), "garlic, oil, and chili" (*aglio, olio, e peperoncino*), and "tomato" (*al pomodoro*)—can be trusted on this subject: often the best-tasting dishes are the simplest.

The second you walk through the door, put the water on to boil. Even if it comes to a boil before you've gathered your wits or prepared the other components, there's something about the way a pot of simmering water immediately lends atmosphere to a room and imparts a sense of homeliness. Salt the water abundantly. Locate whatever leftover, desultory dry pasta you may have in your pantry. If you are feeding more than one person and have a little bit of three kinds and not enough of any one, boil three separate pots of water. (Do not be tempted, as I often have, to boil different shapes or types of pasta in the same pot; it's a guaranteed disaster of under- and overdoneness.) I don't mind combining the varieties afterward so long as they're all more or less the same species, although this admission no doubt amounts to some form of sacrilege—just try not to mix a fusilli with a linguine, etc.

Garlic—garlic is the next most important ingredient. Yes, this pasta can be made with an onion instead—that lesser allium—diced and softened in olive oil in a pan, but garlic is the flavor that I think most brings you back into yourself, most provokes that necessary feeling of reembodiment after a period of travel. Still, use the garlic only if its cloves are very firm and shiny once unsheathed, and the smell, when sliced open, is peppery and fresh and not at all dusty or stale. Mince the garlic (the more cloves the merrier) and fry in a heavy-bottomed pan in a good glug of olive oil. Once the garlic starts to smell fragrant, add a few pinches of chili, if you like spice, and then a couple of chopped anchovy fillets (the best I've ever tasted—and this from a former skeptic—are the high-quality Spanish varieties packed in olive oil). A few chopped capers are also welcome at this stage, but be sure to rinse them if they've been kept in salt. Be careful that the garlic never begins to brown or burn while your attention is elsewhere. Turn off the flame immediately if it starts to migrate in that direction.

Your pasta should be al dente, both because the toothiness of the noodles in some way compensates for the slightness of other ingredients, but also because you will be coming home hungry from a trip and will want to remove the noodles at the first possible moment. Heed this impulse. Use a spider or tongs to transfer the pasta directly into your frying pan, adding a bit of the salted cooking water if you feel it needs lubrication. Grate a generous amount of Parmesan into the pan and add a handful of chopped parsley if you have fresh herbs in your garden or in a window box. Correct with extra olive oil, a squeeze of lemon, a pinch of salt, or some ground pepper, if necessary. When it tastes just right, yell out *"À table!"* as my mother did before every single meal, as if calling not just her child, but the whole neighborhood, to the table. There's always enough food for one more.

Acknowledgments

I could not have written this book without the support and guidance of many people very dear to me. I am indebted, first and foremost, to Brigitte Lacombe, for agreeing to undertake this unorthodox project with me and for making pictures that I will treasure for the rest of my life. For all the work and love and reading and editing and hosting and invaluable feedback, I am so grateful to Cristina Mueller; Samantha Greenwood; Jessica Washburn; Peter Gethers; Stephen Singer; Bob Carrau; Tony Oltranti; Sue Murphy; Lulu Peyraud and Laurence Peyraud; Martine, Claude, and Camille Labro; Susie and Mark Buell; Bud Trillin; Andrew Owen; Fritz Haeg; Hilton Als; Claire Ptak; Sarah Fielding; Greta Caruso; Molly Altenburg; Niloufer Ichaporia King; Nico Monday; David Tanis; Randal Breski; Mary Jo Thoresen; Peggy Arent; Mariah Nielson; Lauren Ardis; Tom Schmidt; Kari Stuart; and of course, La Famille Panisse.

Fanny Singer is a writer, an editor, and a co-founder of the design brand Permanent Collection. In 2013, she received a PhD from the University of Cambridge on the subject of the British pop artist Richard Hamilton's late work. In 2015, she and her mother, Alice Waters, published *My Pantry*, which she also illustrated. Having spent more than a decade living in the United Kingdom, Fanny recently moved back to her native California. Based in San Francisco, she travels widely, contributing art criticism and culture writing to a range of publications.

A NOTE ABOUT THE TYPE

The text in this book was set in Miller, a transitional-style typeface designed by Matthew Carter (b. 1937) with assistance from Tobias Frere-Jones and Cyrus Highsmith of the Font Bureau. Modeled on the roman family of fonts popularized by Scottish type foundries in the nineteenth century, Miller is named for William Miller, founder of the Miller & Richard foundry of Edinburgh.

The Miller family of fonts has a large number of variants for use as text and display, as well as Greek characters based on the renowned handwriting of British classicist Richard Porson.

COMPOSED BY NORTH MARKET STREET GRAPHICS, LANCASTER, PENNSYLVANIA

PRINTED AND BOUND BY MOHN MEDIA, GÜTERSLOH, GERMANY

DESIGNED BY MAGGIE HINDERS